I0810617

IMAGES
of America

Mount Pleasant Borough Westmoreland County

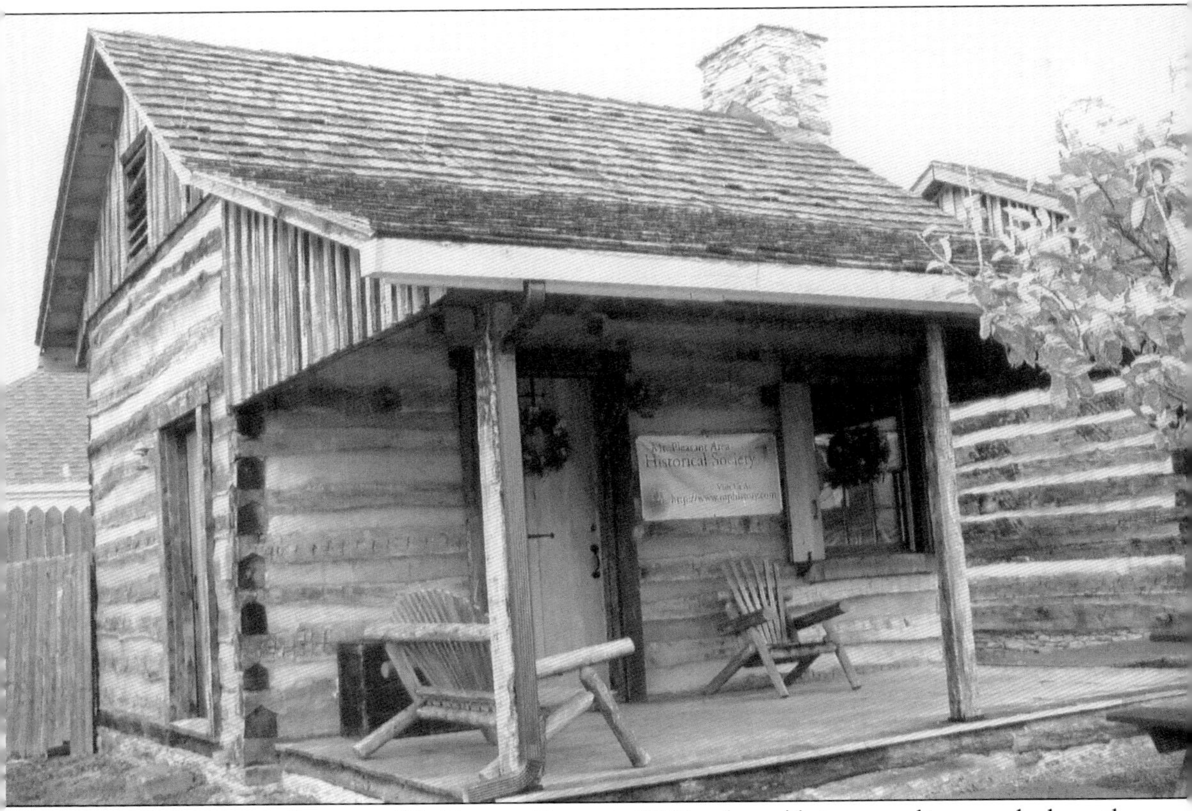

While razing a house on Washington Street in 2004, a log addition was discovered where the kitchen had been located. This dates back to about 1820, and in 2006 it was dismantled and rebuilt. It has been named the Chestnut Log House. The house is maintained by the Mount Pleasant Area Historical Society and is showcased during the Glass & Ethnic Festival held annually in September. (Courtesy of the Mount Pleasant Area Historical Society.)

On the Cover: Mount Pleasant Public Swimming Pool was located in the general vicinity of today's Ramsay Terrace. In this c. 1910–1920 photograph, parasols and picture hats are visible. This was a great place to gather on sunny days. (Courtesy of Steve Billey and Brian Billey.)

IMAGES
of America

MOUNT PLEASANT BOROUGH WESTMORELAND COUNTY

Friends of the Mount Pleasant Public Library

ARCADIA
PUBLISHING

ISBN 978-1-4671-2219-1

Published by Arcadia Publishing
Charleston, South Carolina

Printed in the United States of America

Library of Congress Control Number: 2014931054

For all general information, please contact Arcadia Publishing:
Telephone 843-853-2070
Fax 843-853-0044
E-mail sales@arcadiapublishing.com
For customer service and orders:
Toll-Free 1-888-313-2665

Visit us on the Internet at www.arcadiapublishing.com

Dedicated to the memory of Bernadette Kattera, school librarian, member of the Friends, and loved by all who knew her. She passed away while this book was in process (April 21, 2014).

Contents

Acknowledgments

The Friends of the Mount Pleasant Public Library have collected and prepared a pictorial history of Mount Pleasant. We are indebted to many people in the community for their assistance in providing photographs and anecdotes of the times and places in and around our town. Our hope is that the book evokes as many memories for the readers as it did for the authors.

Special gratitude is extended to the writers who compiled the images and prepared the introduction and captions: Theresa Benedict, Dr. Kathleen Ceroni, Kathleen Clark, Rose Eckman, Theresa Gerson, Bernadette Kattera, Nancy Sebek, Karen Stefl, Mary Lou Shick, Dr. Gerri Spinella (Walden and Concordia Portland University), Bonnie Wilson, and Friends of the Mount Pleasant Public Library.

Many thanks to the following, who provided us with photographs and information for the book: John Barber, John Doncaster, Nancy Barnhart, Donald Baumann, Theresa Benedict, Steve Billey, Brian Billey, Debbie Brehun, Dr. Kathleen Ceroni, Kathleen Clark, Sandy Potoka Coppula, Vincent Coppula, Margaret Detling, William Dolan, Veronica Echard, Rose Eckman, the family of Anthony Gaudiano, Jean Gaudiano, Theresa Gerson, Anna Marie Grzywinski, Laura Hooper, Ruth Kauffman, Margaret Krystyniak, James Lozier, Richard Meason, Jerry Miele, Barbara Miller, Donald Miller, Margaret Milliron, The Mount Pleasant Area Historical Society, the *Mount Pleasant Journal*, the Mount Pleasant Public Library Archives, Charlotte Mowry, James Myers, William Potoka Jr., Merl Pritts, Fay Pritts, Louis Rega, Cheryl Rega, Michael Rega, Nancy Sebek, Mary Lou Shick, Dr. Gerri Spinella, Mary Agnes Spinella, Kathy Stanislaw, Karen Stefl, Kenneth Trice, James Vaughn, Bonnie Wilson, LaRoyal Wilson, Ida Wiltrout, and Joseph "Coke" Yancosky.

Images of America: *Mount Pleasant Borough, Westmoreland County* is designed to provide historical information for the reader's appreciation. Every effort has been made to ensure that the information is as accurate as possible. Therefore, this book should serve only as a general guide and not as the ultimate source of subject information.

INTRODUCTION

Mount Pleasant is a picturesque community and the oldest borough in Westmoreland County, Pennsylvania. This area has an abundant history dating back to the Revolutionary War. The country surrounding Mount Pleasant was settled around 1770, and in 1755 Gen. Edward Braddock's expedition through here opened the area for settlers. Until this time, the Eastern Woodland Indians inhabited the countryside.

In 1793, Michael Smith erected the first house. On June 9, 1798, he obtained a license to sell spirits and opened the first tavern. Located on Glades Road, one of the bustling routes between east and west, this frontier tavern was a notorious place. The town became known for its whiskey production and distribution. Lawlessness abounded, and this quiet community became known as "Helltown." It maintained this name until two travelers from Cumberland, Maryland, stopped at the log tavern. They asked the landlord the name of the town and were surprised to hear "Helltown." They suggested it should be called Mount Pleasant because of the pleasant location and the view of the mountains. This is one of the many theories concerning the town's name. In the spring of 2011, a small group of home brewers opened a microbrewery on the outskirts of Mount Pleasant and called it Helltown Brewery, reminiscent of the early days of rebellion.

Before 1810, there were only 34 houses in Mount Pleasant, all of which were built of logs. In 1812, the first brick house was built. While razing a house on Washington Street in 2004, a log addition was discovered where the kitchen had been located. This structure dates back to about 1820. It was dismantled and rebuilt in 2006 and has been named the Chestnut Log House. The house is maintained by the Mount Pleasant Area Historical Society and is showcased during the Glass Festival held annually in September.

Mount Pleasant was incorporated as a borough in 1828. At the time of its incorporation, the population was 300, and there were 29 lots on 34 acres. In the 1850s, the main lines of the railroads bypassed the community, but in 1871, the Mount Pleasant & Broadford Railroad opened, and the community was no longer isolated. This railroad became part of the Baltimore & Ohio Railroad. An interurban trolley served Mount Pleasant and facilitated transportation to other communities from 1906 to 1952.

The basis of its economy was glassmaking. Bryce Brothers Glass began operation in 1896 and produced apothecary wares, lamps, and bottles. Their pressed-glass Roman Rosette and Ribbon Candy patterns were well known. Lenox, Inc. bought Bryce Brothers in 1965 and continued to manufacture glass. Lenox was identified with elegant tableware, and its glassware has been used in the White House since 1920. L.E. Smith Glass opened in 1907. This company manufactured the first glass headlights for the Model T Ford car, and four of these are displayed at the local glass museum, which opened in 2013.

Another economic factor was the development of the coal and coke industry. H.C. Frick, who was born in nearby West Overton, formed the H.C. Frick Coke Company in 1874. This enterprise came about because Mount Pleasant sits on a nine-foot coal vein, which is part of the Pittsburgh coal seam. This lucrative undertaking used the beehive-oven technique to turn coal into coke, which was used in manufacturing steel. Bituminous coal mining brought many immigrants from southern and eastern Europe. Labor problems would result from unfair working conditions and safety factors. On January 27, 1891, an explosion six miles northeast of Mount Pleasant at the Mammoth Shaft Mine killed 109 laborers, and another mine disaster occurred on April 2, 1891. The men working at the Morewood Mines, which were located west of Mount Pleasant, went on strike. Deputized men of the 10th Regiment of the National Guard were sent in to put an end to this uprising. Mass chaos ensued, and the deputies fired two rounds into the crowd. This action resulted in six miners being killed outright and three fatally wounded. Of the 109 men killed at Mammoth, 79 are buried in a common grave at St. John's Catholic Cemetery in Scottdale, Pennsylvania. Also, after the Morewood Massacre, there were seven more men added to this common grave. A total of 118 men were killed in these two incidents. The Morewood Massacre proved that H.C. Frick was known for his heavy-handed dealings with the workers and the unions.

At the present time, Mount Pleasant is the first municipality outside of Washington, DC, that has a veterans video wall. The participation at the annual Memorial Day celebration shows the patriotism of the people, and the many functions sponsored by the borough are well attended and show that this is still an active and thriving community. The town was the first in the state to establish a community rain-garden retrofit. This project helps eliminate storm-water issues. It was the first municipality to form a business district authority. All of these accomplishments show that Mount Pleasant is a progressing community.

The census of 2010 estimates the population of Mount Pleasant Borough to be 4,454, including 1,994 residents over the age of 50. Although the numbers indicate that the residents living here are older, the town continues to attract people to tour the glass museum, dine at the many fine restaurants, and enjoy the beautiful mountains. A bike trail established at the east end of town has attracted bike enthusiasts from many areas. To the people who were raised here and departed for various opportunities, Mount Pleasant is still considered home. This is being proven by events like the June 2014 reunion held for the 1930–1969 classes of Ramsay High School—1,700 invitations were mailed, and the response has been overwhelming. One graduate attending was 102 years old and very excited about the reunion.

The Mount Pleasant Area Historical Society was formed in 1995. It continues to promote the town's heritage and to preserve its history, which is vital to this unique community.

One

Honoring Our History

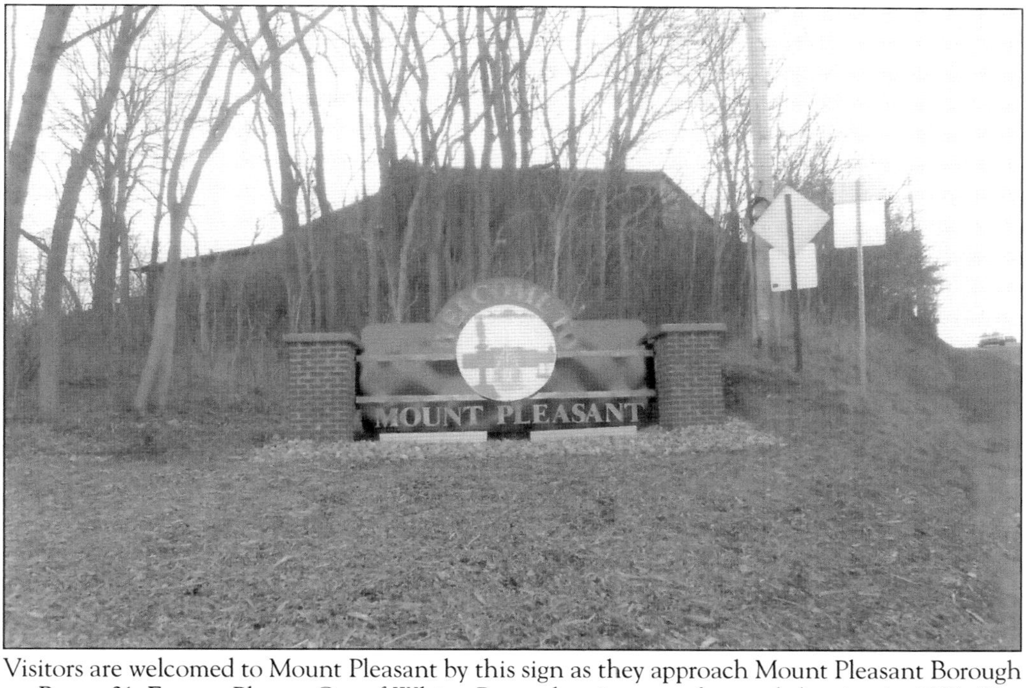

Visitors are welcomed to Mount Pleasant by this sign as they approach Mount Pleasant Borough on Route 31. Fayette Plasma Cut of White, Pennsylvania, manufactured the sign in 2013. The street department of Mount Pleasant laid the foundation for the sign, and there are plans to add lights to it. (Courtesy of Nancy Sebek.)

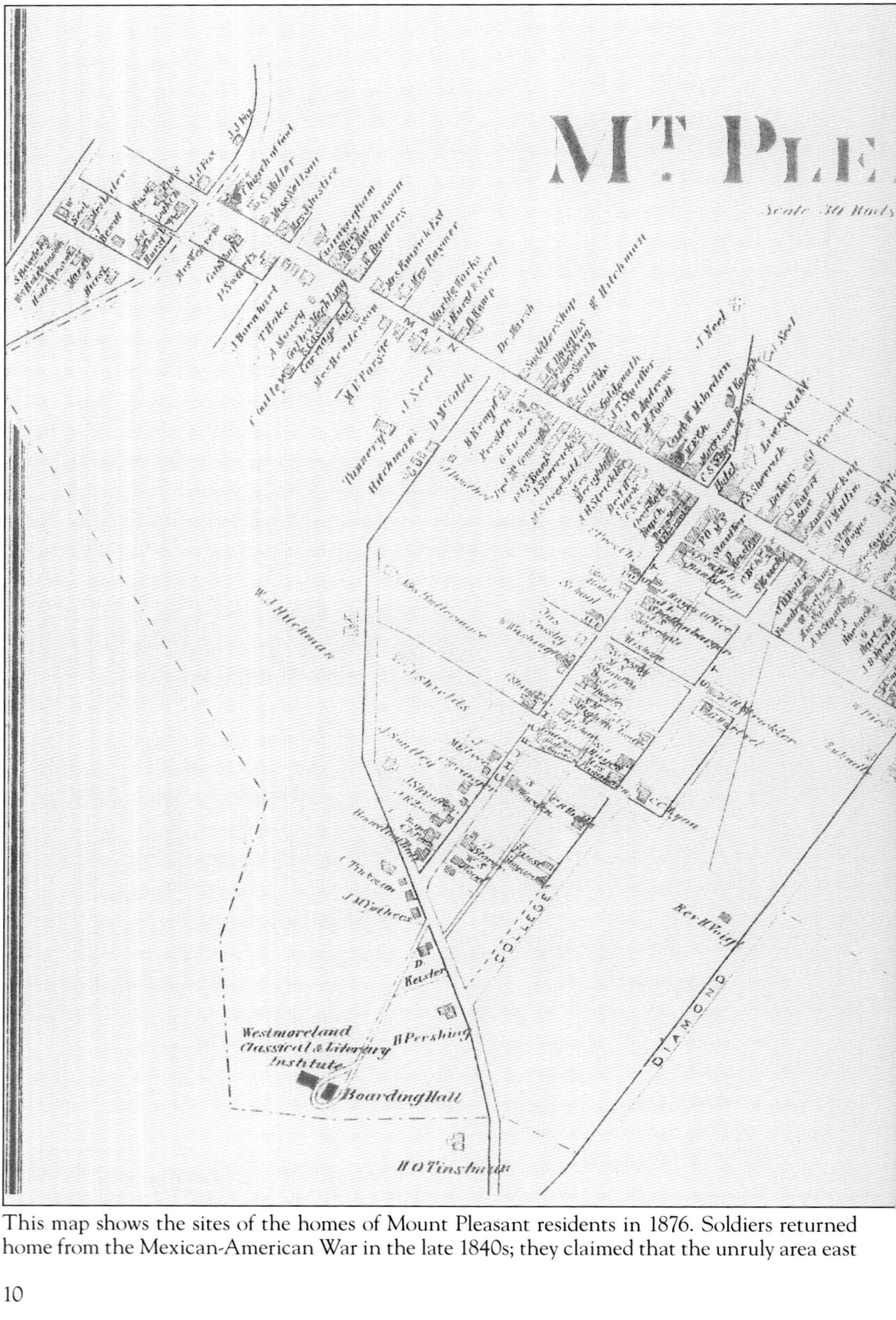

This map shows the sites of the homes of Mount Pleasant residents in 1876. Soldiers returned home from the Mexican-American War in the late 1840s; they claimed that the unruly area east

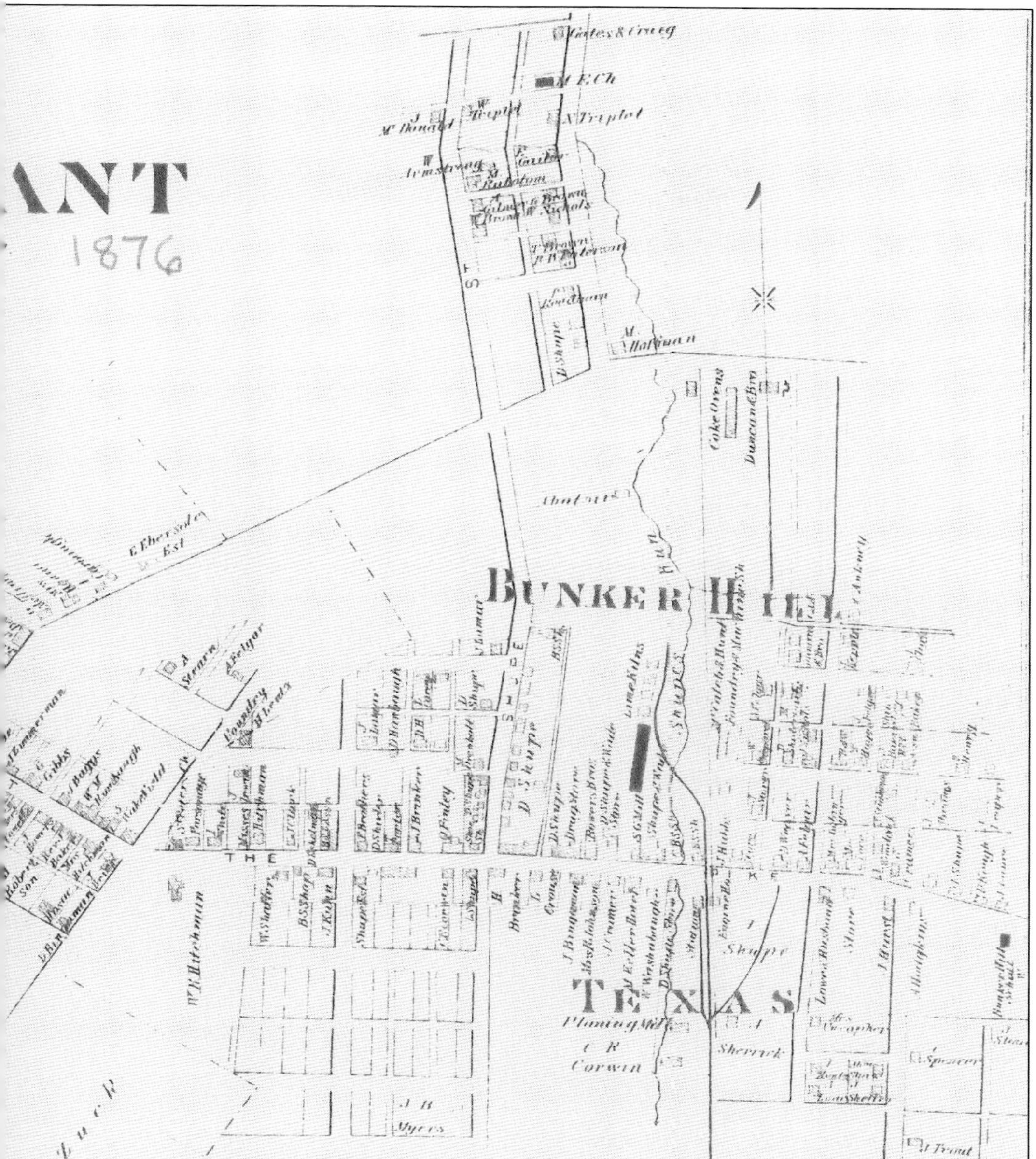

of town reminded them of the Republic of Texas. The name Texas endured, which is why it is included on this map. (Courtesy of the Mount Pleasant Area Historical Society.)

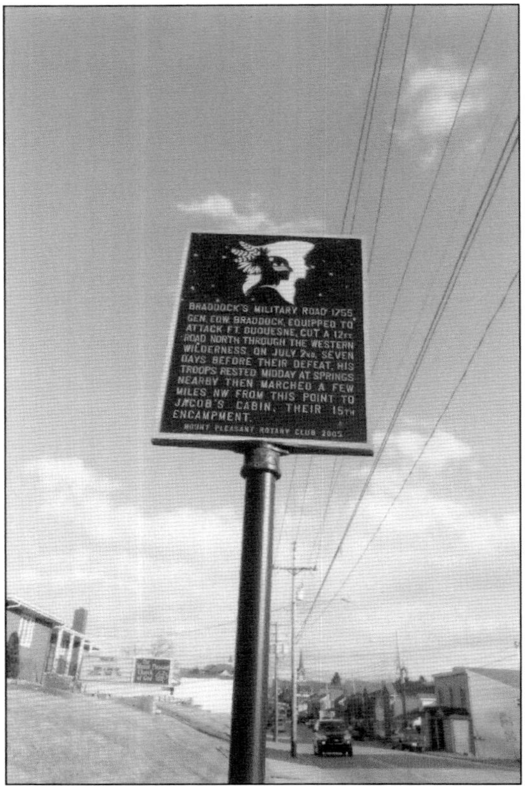

Located at West Main Street, this marker signifies Gen. Edward Braddock's military trail through Mount Pleasant in 1755. En-route to Fort Duquesne, he traveled along Route 819. The entourage turned right up a grade to the present site of St. Pius Cemetery and on to what is now Braddock Street. Bearing left toward the western end of town, he forged a trail known now as Braddock Road Avenue. (Courtesy of Nancy Sebek.)

Born in Mount Pleasant in 1852, Henry W.B. Mechling brought honor to the community when he was awarded the Congressional Medal of Honor for bravery during the Battle of Little Big Horn in 1876. Later in his life, he opened a blacksmith shop on the present site of Veterans Park. A granite memorial honoring Mechling is situated at Veterans Park on Diamond Street. (Courtesy of Nancy Sebek.)

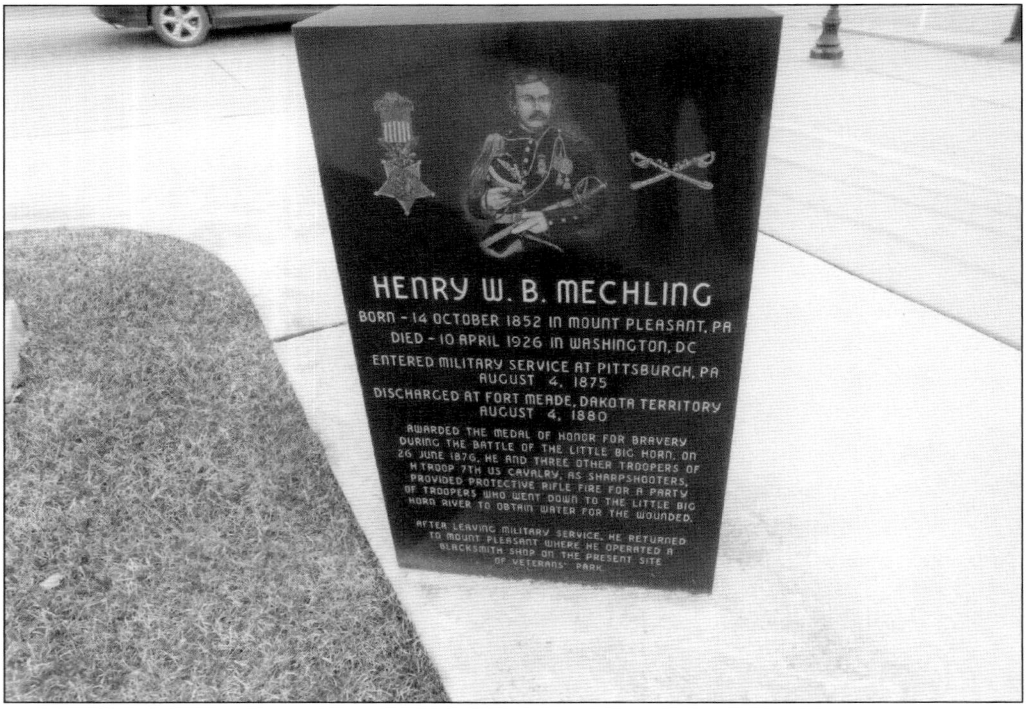

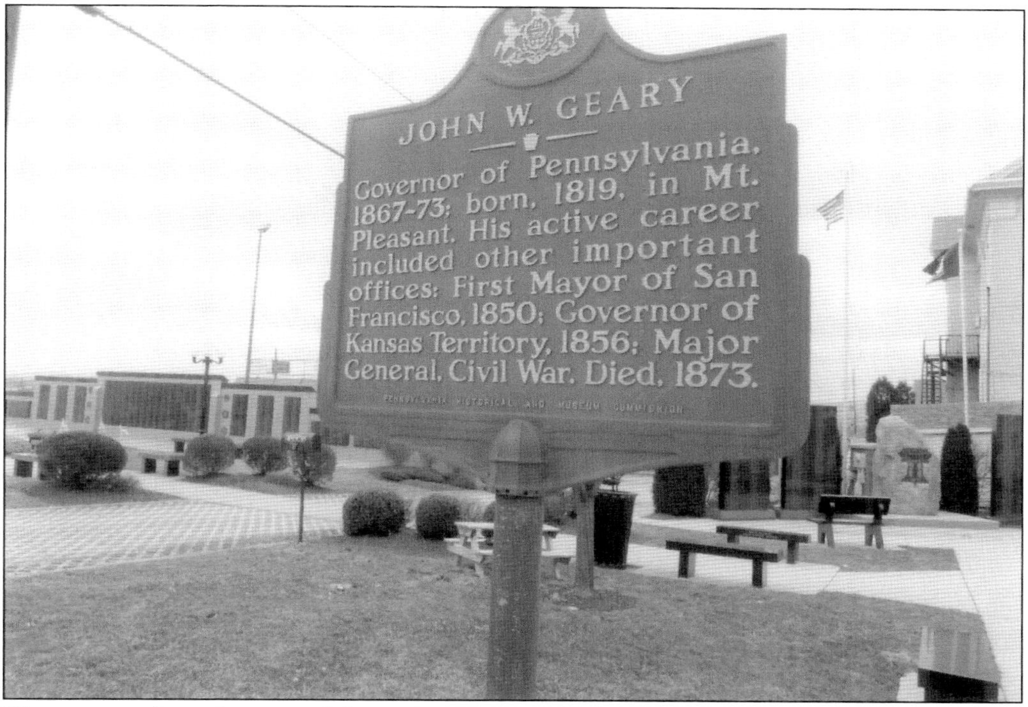

This memorial sign honoring John White Geary is displayed at Veterans Park. Geary was a prominent figure as a Civil War colonel of the 28th Pennsylvania Infantry. This simple highway marker, obtained through the Pennsylvania Historical and Museum Commission, initially was situated along Route 31 and was relocated to Veterans Park. (Courtesy of Nancy Sebek.)

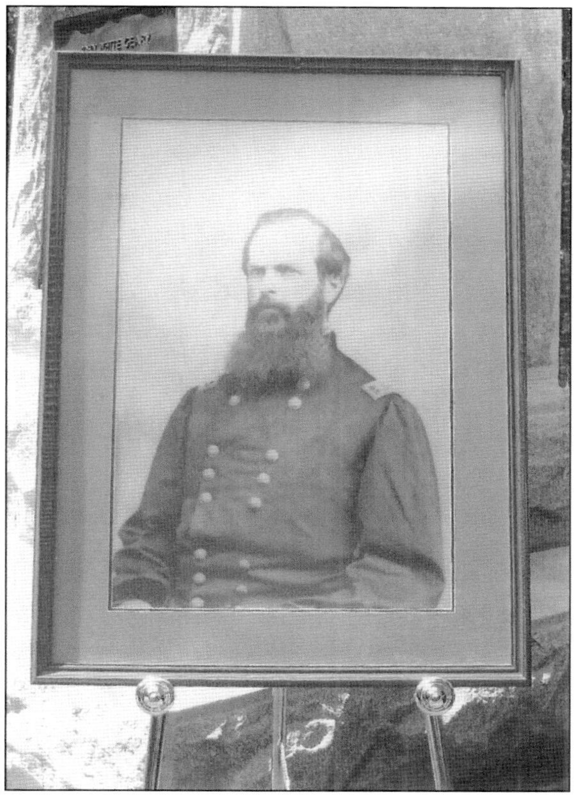

John White Geary was born in 1819 in Mount Pleasant, Pennsylvania. His illustrious career took him to San Francisco, California, where he became their first mayor in 1850. He was governor of the Kansas Territory in 1856 and was commissioned a colonel of the Civil War by Pres. Abraham Lincoln. After serving two terms as the governor of Pennsylvania, he died at the age of 54. (Courtesy of the Mount Pleasant Area Historical Society.)

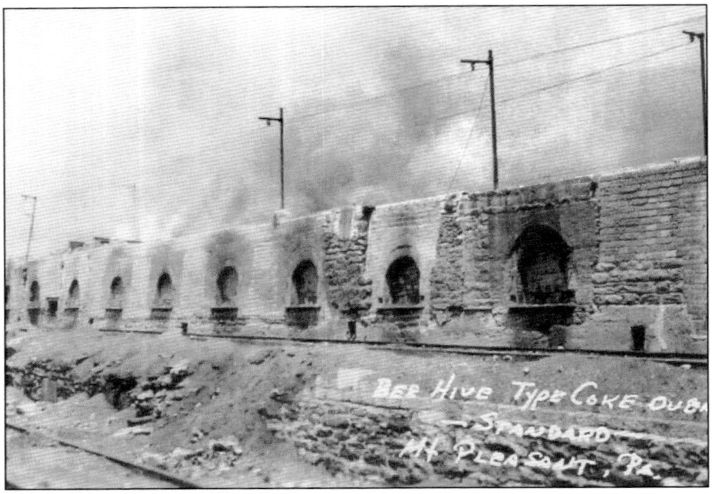

The beehive coke ovens were located in Standard Shaft in 1878. This oven was so named because its dome shape resembled an old-fashioned beekeeper's hive. They were used for turning coal into coke. This type of oven originated in Europe during the Middle Ages. One can view hundreds of ovens in a row, which was referred to as a battery. (Courtesy of the Mount Pleasant Public Library Archives.)

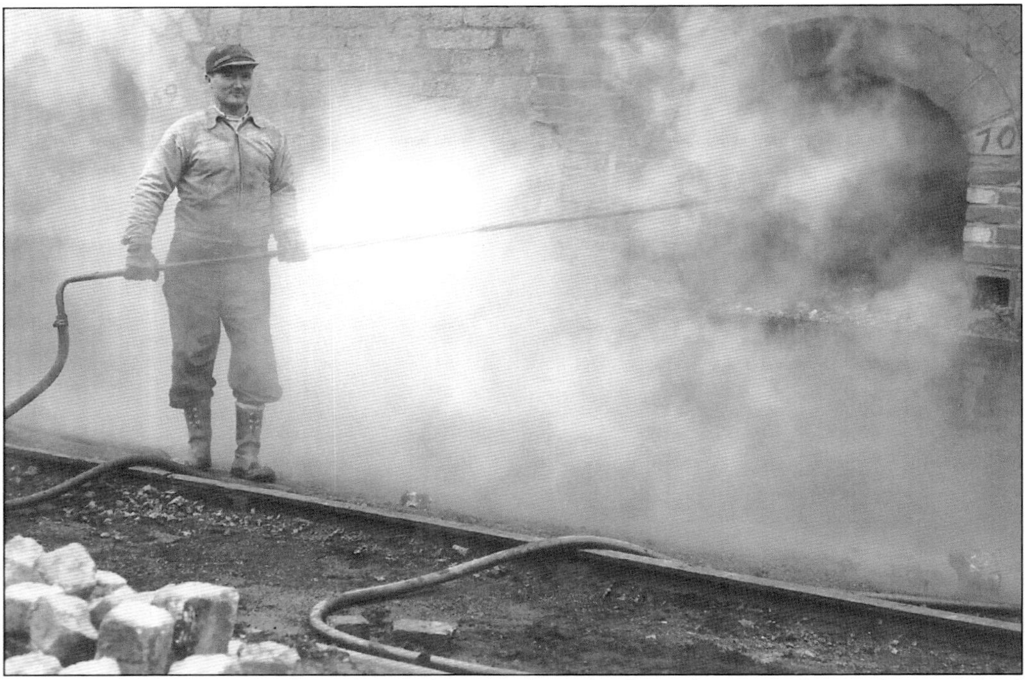

Many employees spent arduous hours drawing the coke from the ovens for production. Coal was put into the top by a larry car to produce even layers. Air was added to ignite the coal, and carbonization was completed in two to three days. Water was used to cool the hot coke, and it was manually extracted through the side door. (Courtesy of the Mount Pleasant Public Library Archives.)

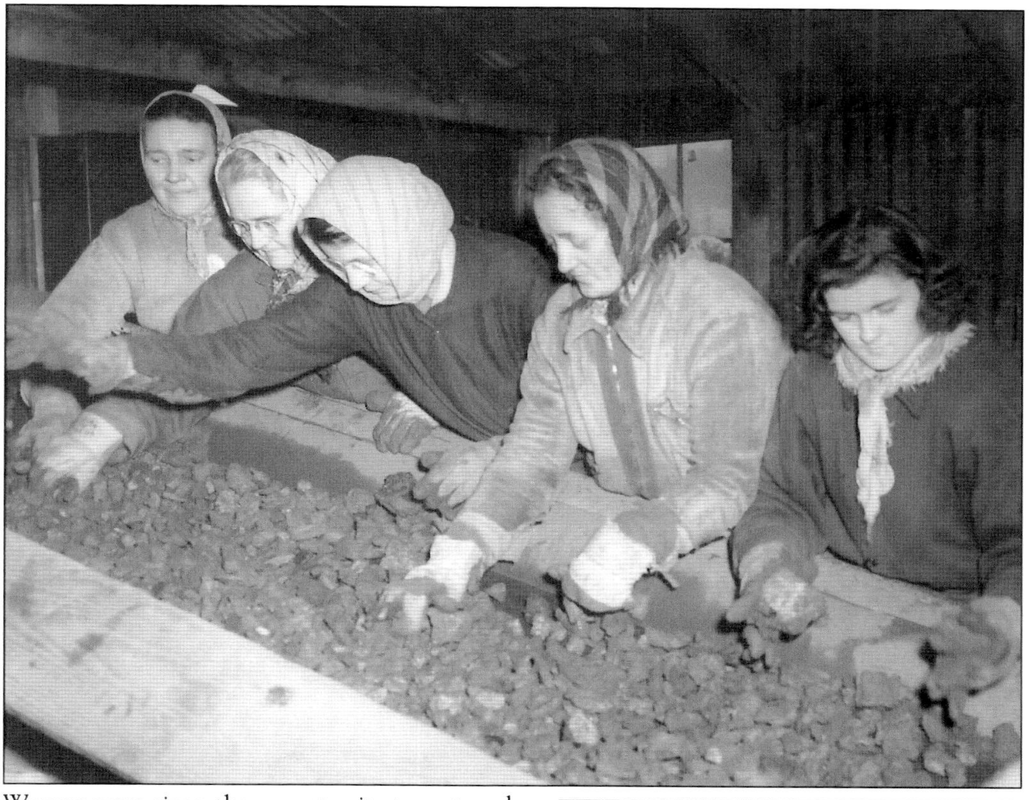

Women were given the opportunity to sort coal by hand and thus make extra wages for mining families. Prior to sorting coal, the women were employed deep in the mines, but the Mines Act of 1842 forbade them from continuing this dangerous work. The working conditions were deplorable. (Courtesy of the Mount Pleasant Public Library Archives.)

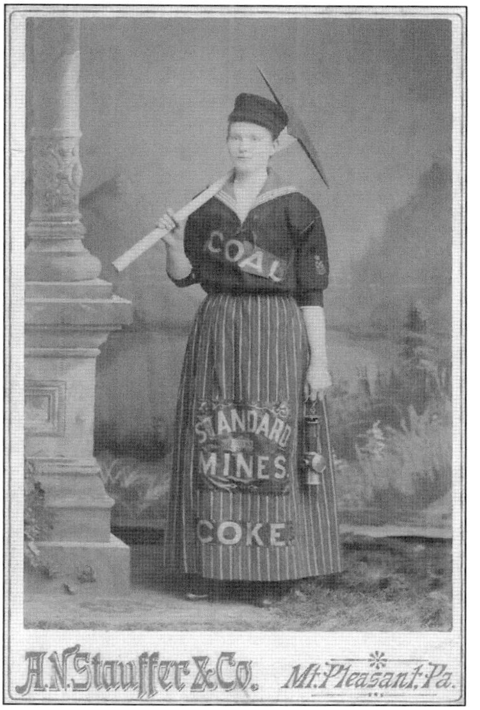

In 1870, Charlotte Goodman depicted a romanticized icon of women in the coal and coke industry. Married to a local miner, she was a representative of Standard Mines. She is shown holding a coal pick and lantern, which were symbolic tools of the coal miner. (Courtesy of Donald Baumann.)

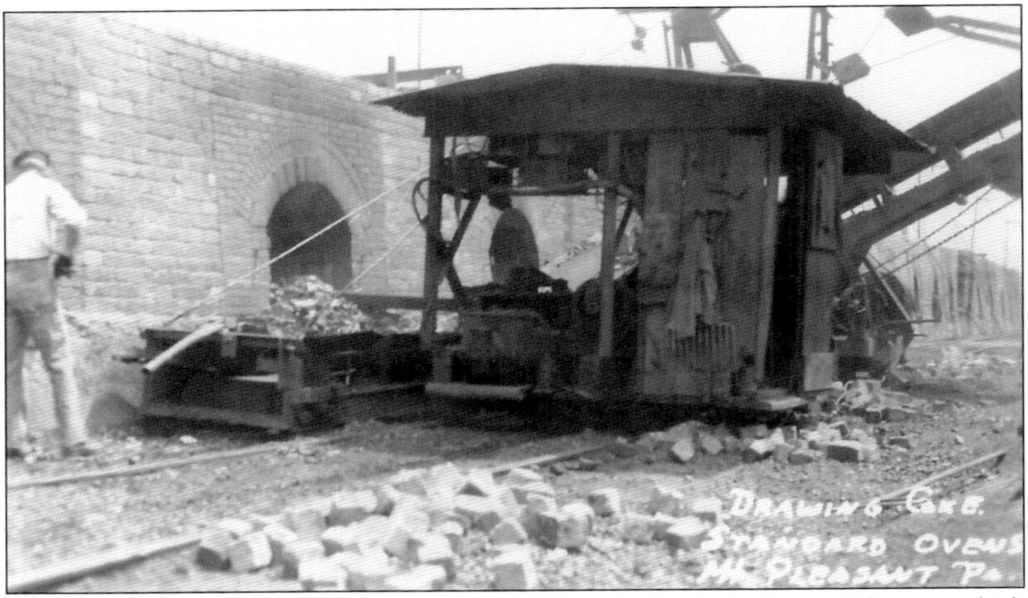

In the 1900s, this coke-drawing machine was used to draw the finished coke out of the oven, which was then fed into a waiting railroad car. Water was applied to quench or cool the coke. The machine pictured was at the Standard ovens in Mount Pleasant. (Courtesy of Kathy Stanislaw.)

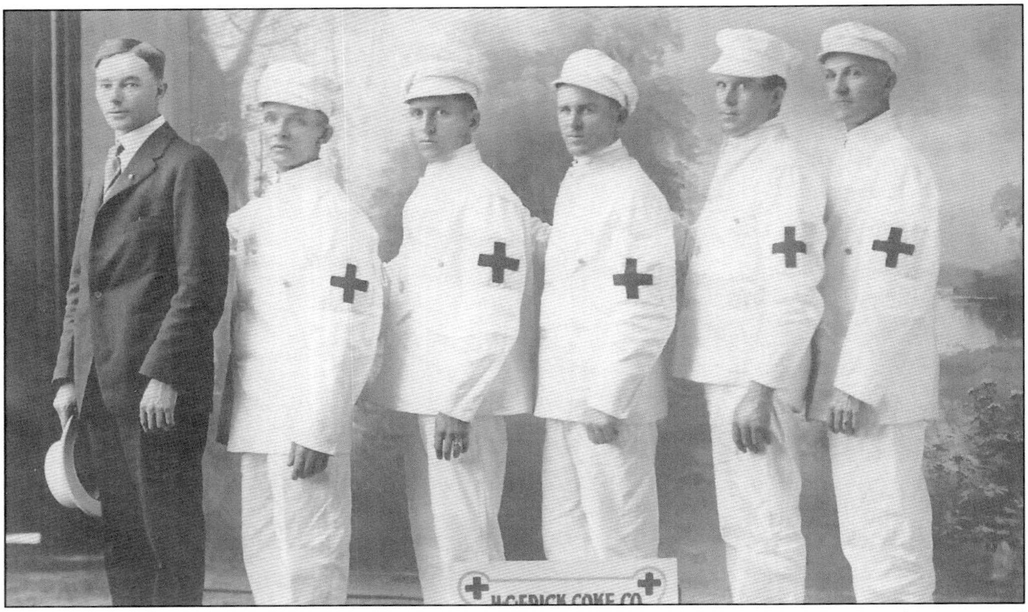

There was a Medic Corps at each large plant of the H.C. Frick Coke Company. Each consisted of five men, who were trained in first aid and rescue work. The proposed 11-point constitution of the United Mine Workers was to provide safety for miners in 1890. This necessitated that all operations use the latest technologies to preserve lives. (Courtesy of James Vaughn.)

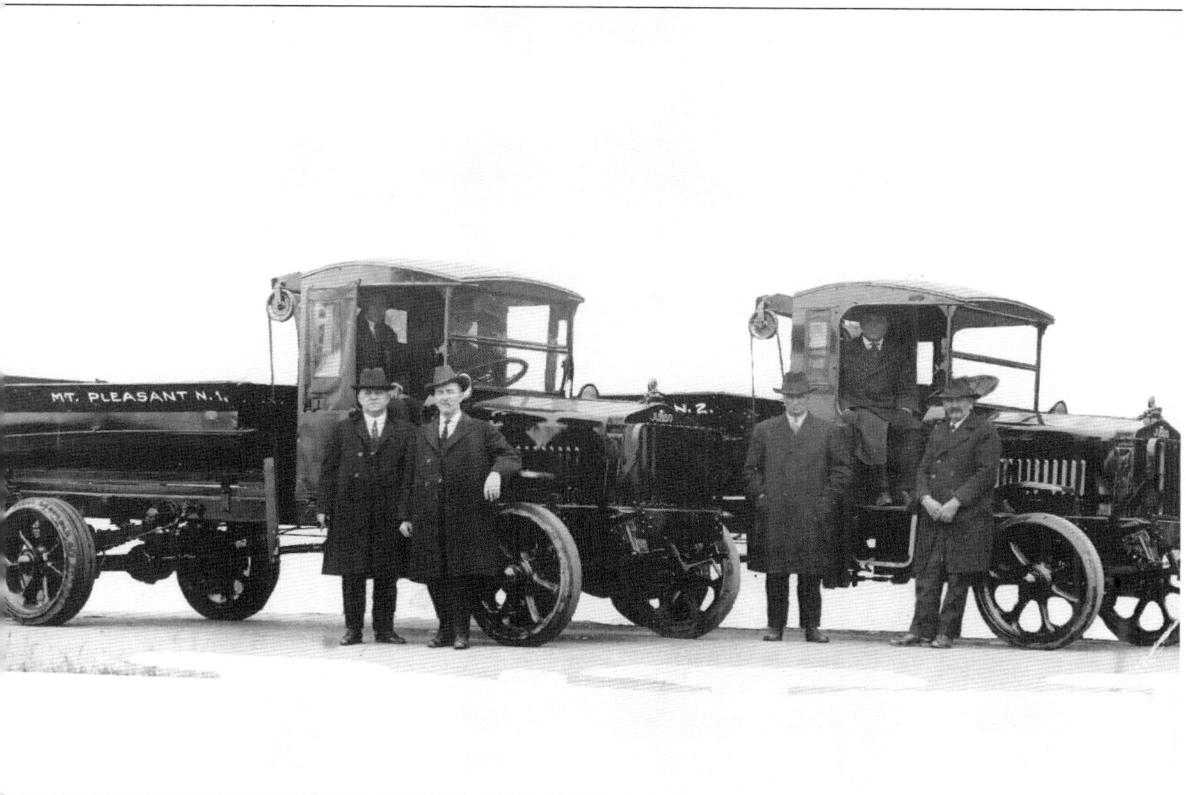

Mount Pleasant mine officials proudly displayed the newly purchased Jumbo motor trucks, which were manufactured by the Nelson Motor Truck Company of Saginaw, Michigan. These fine trucks were guaranteed for one year and the basic chassis price was $2,250. The Jumbo truck was manufactured from 1918 to 1932. (Courtesy of the Mount Pleasant Public Library Archives.)

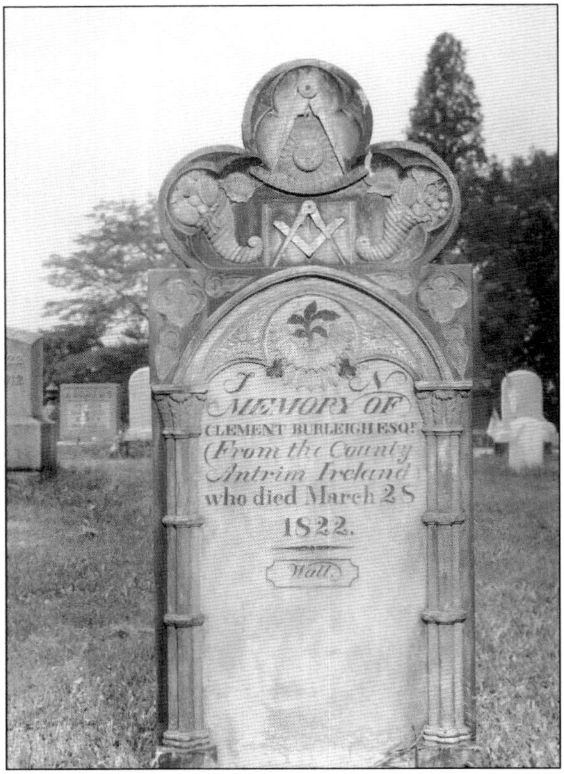

William Wall, a gravestone carver, was born in England. In 1821, he moved his family to Mount Pleasant. The gravestone of Clement Burleigh, Esq., was intricately carved in fine-grained sandstone and is found in Mount Pleasant Cemetery. The gravestone was anything but conventional—William Wall inscribed his name on the stone, and it was as large as the name of the deceased. The gravestone of Rev. Dr. James Powers, who was a circuit minister, was also carved by William Wall and can be found at the Middle Presbyterian Church Cemetery. Wall's signature on each stone is written with a great flourish found with the "W." He passed on his artistic talent to his sons, who became famous artists in their time. (Both photographs courtesy of the Mount Pleasant Public Library Archives.)

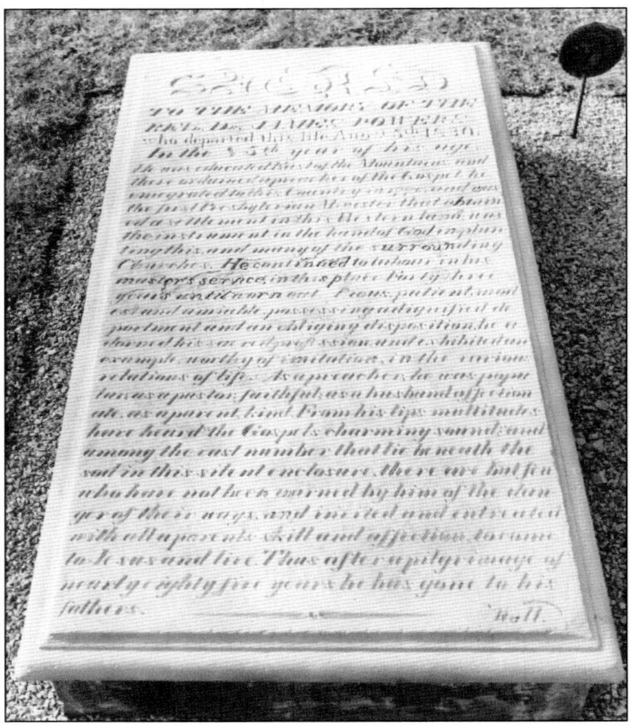

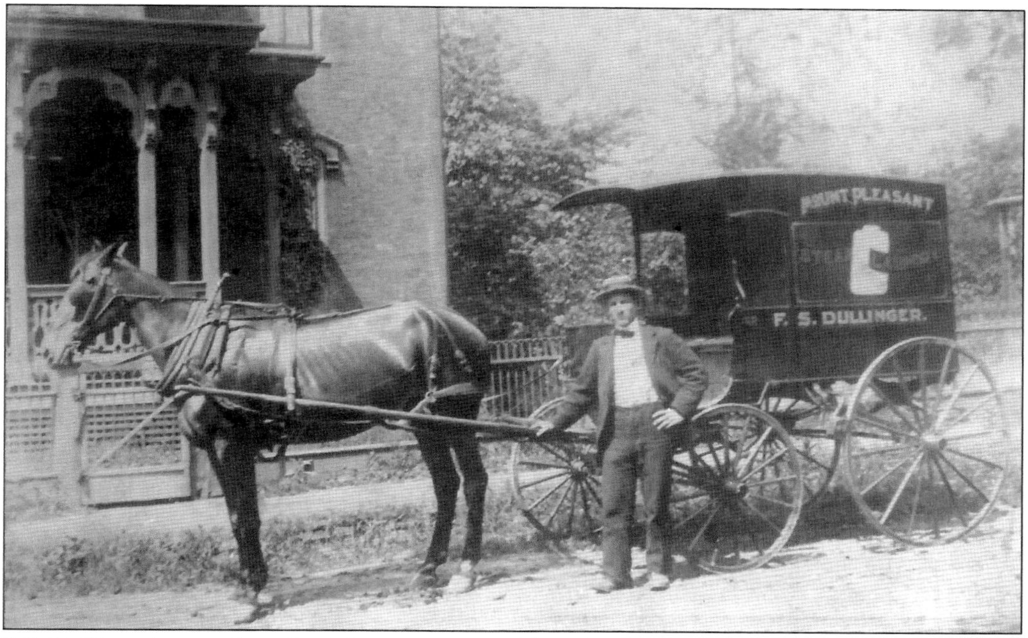

F.S. Dullinger's steam-laundry delivery van resembles a large baker or bread van. It had rear doors, which, when opened, had wickerwork laundry baskets inside. Some vans like this survived until the 1940s. There was a driver's seat or cross bench spanning the entire width of the front with a low footboard and extended canopy. (Courtesy of Kathy Stanislaw.)

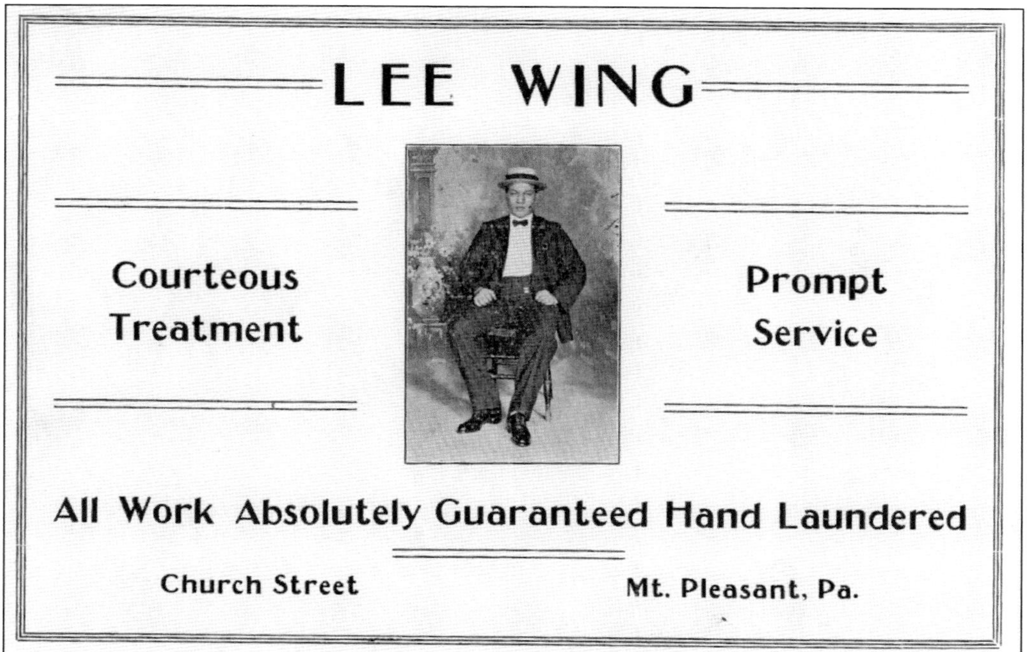

The advertisement pictured above was featured in the July 4–9, 1910, *Old Home Week, Mount Pleasant, PA, Souvenir Book*. Pictured is Lee Wing, the proprietor of a laundry service once located on Church Street. (Courtesy of the Mount Pleasant Area Public Library Archives.)

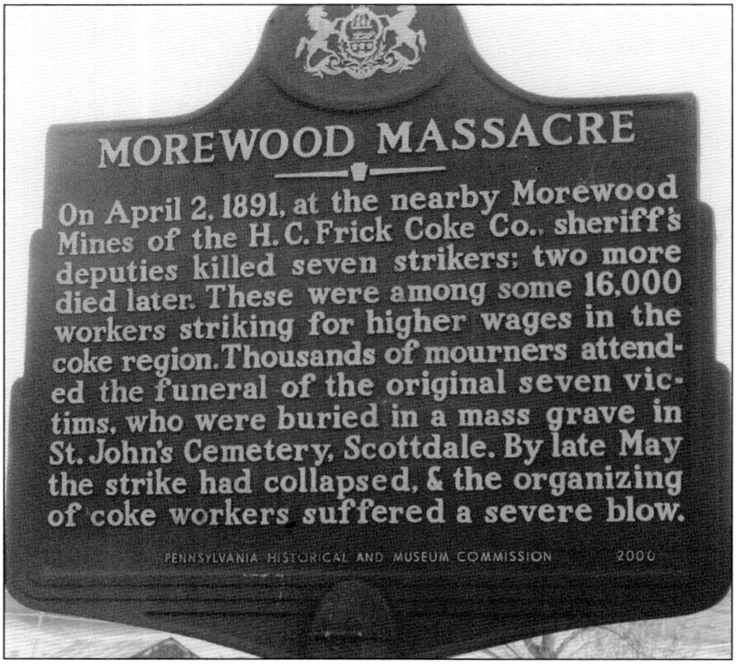

This historical marker is situated on Route 981 along Morewood Street going toward Alverton. It commemorates the strike of 1891, when the deputies of the H.C. Frick Coke Mining Company killed nine miners. Seven of the miners were buried in a common grave in St. John's Cemetery in Scottdale, Pennsylvania. (Courtesy of Bonnie Wilson.)

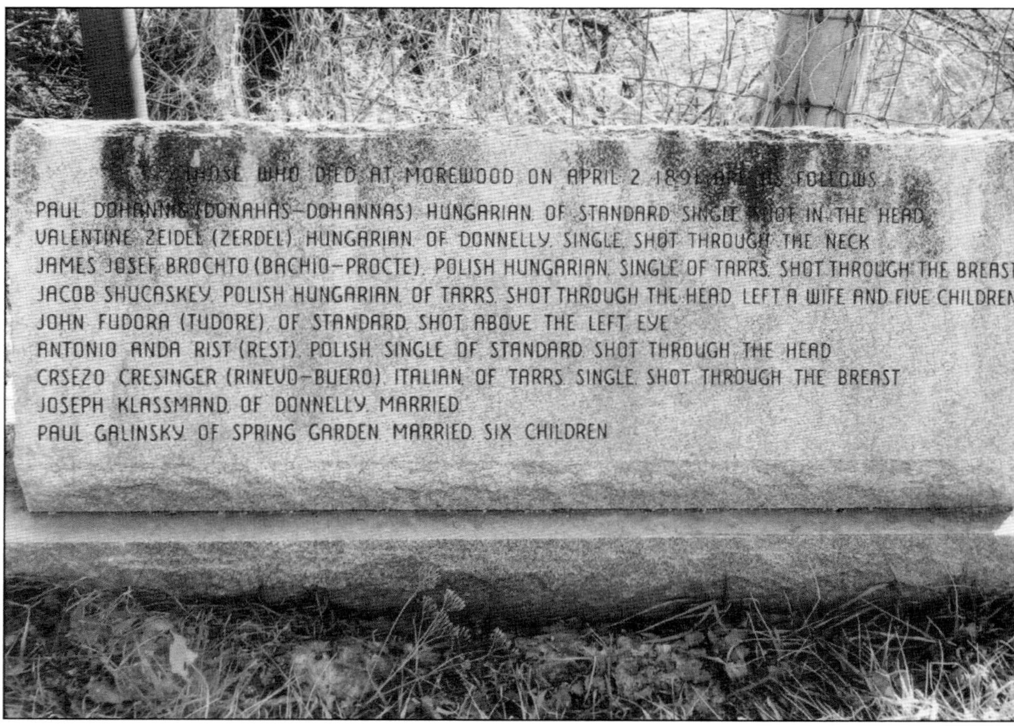

This large granite memorial can be found directly below the marker of the Morewood Massacre on Route 981. Each man's personal life and a description of his injuries are distinctly displayed as the casualties of the massacre. A month after the shooting, the coke-workers strike ended. (Courtesy of Bonnie Wilson.)

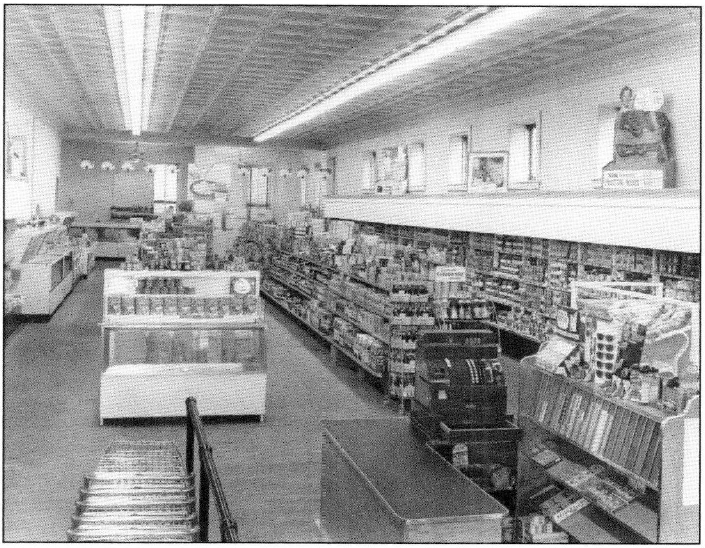

The Union Supply Store, pictured around 1950, was located at Diamond and High Streets. Note the cash register and the items behind the counter, including Wrigley gum, Luden's cough drops, candy, playing cards, De Nobili cigars, and Tareyton cigarettes. Originally, this was the company store used by the miners to purchase everyday staples. The store later became Oppman's Auto Supply. (Courtesy of the Mount Pleasant Public Library Archives.)

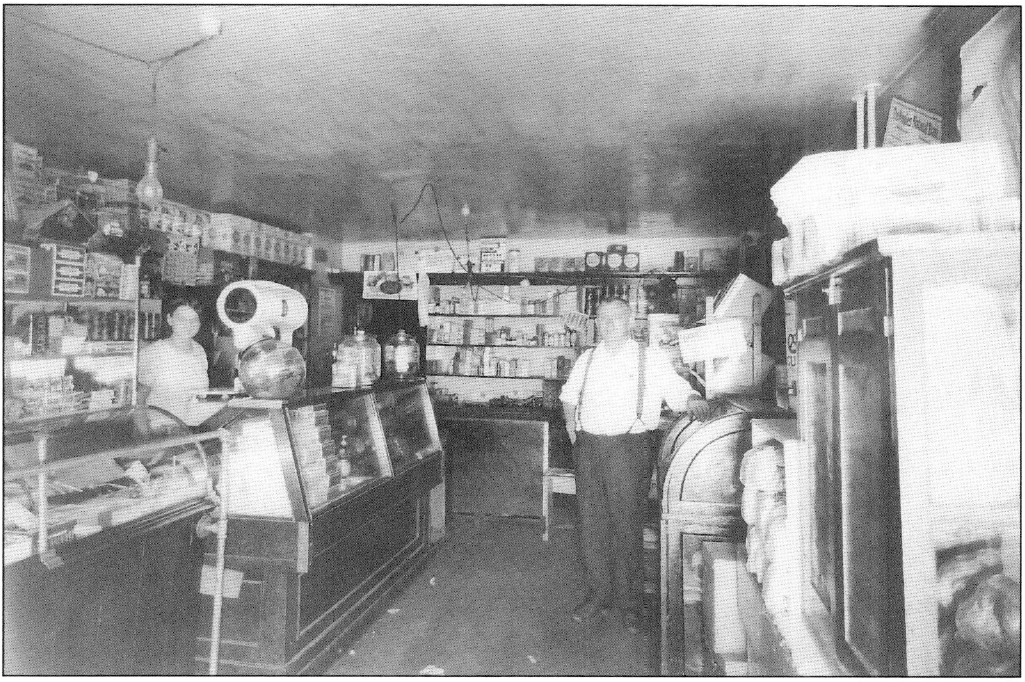

Mom-and-pop store Hribal's Market was located on East Main Street in the home of proprietors Emanuel and Albina Hribal, who are shown in the store in the summer of 1929. Among the items pictured are Baby Ruth candy bars, Hershey bars, Super Suds soap powder, and a People's National Bank calendar (in the right-hand corner of photograph). (Courtesy of Kathy Stanislaw.)

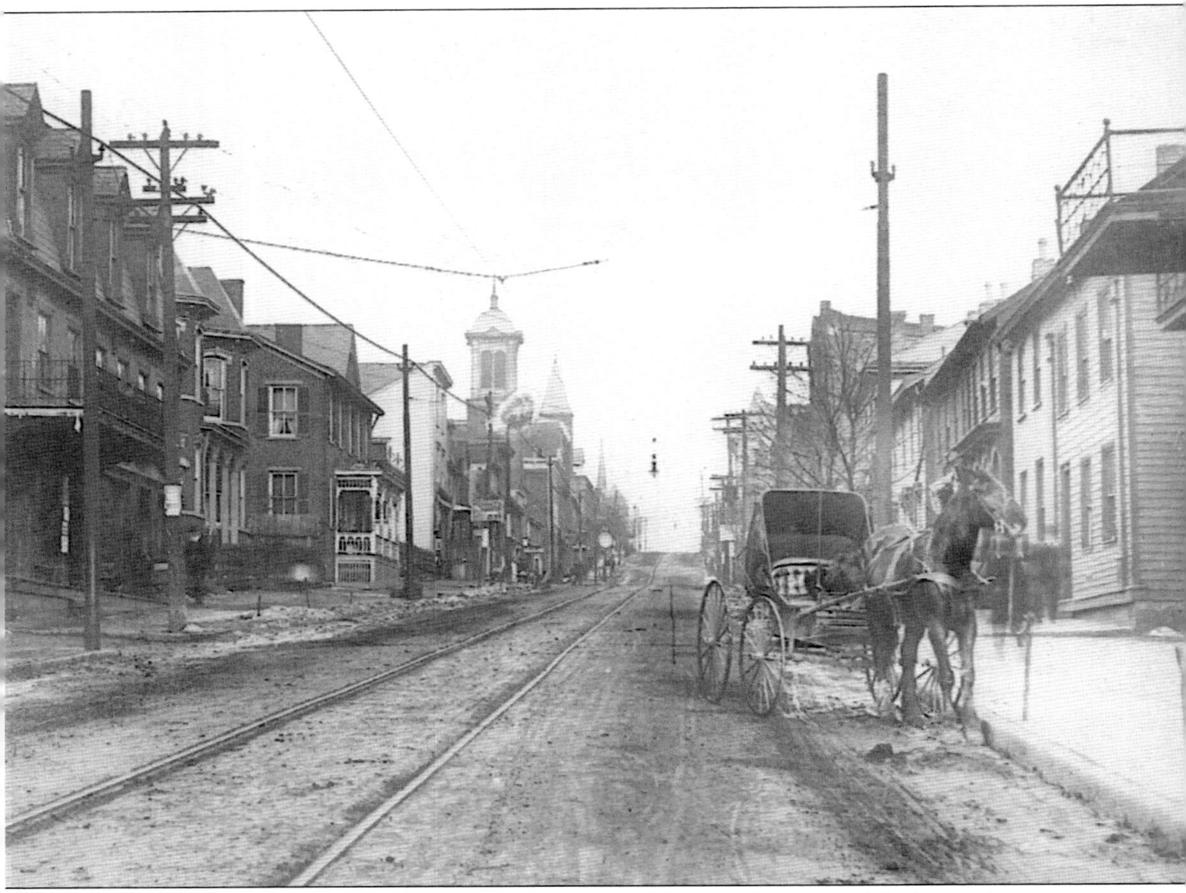

This c. 1900 photograph of Main Street in Mount Pleasant faces west. The horse-drawn carriage in the photograph would have traveled over the brick-lined road and trolley tracks. Individuals used this type of carriage for personal transportation. In the distance, one can see the steeples of three churches: the Evangelical United Brethren Church (now the United Methodist Church of Mount Pleasant, commonly known as the "Town Clock Church"), the First Baptist Church, and the Reunion Presbyterian Church. The architecture of this era is demonstrated in the style of the buildings. Many buildings had balconies and large front porches, which gave the families a full view of the happenings in the street. (Courtesy of William Dolan.)

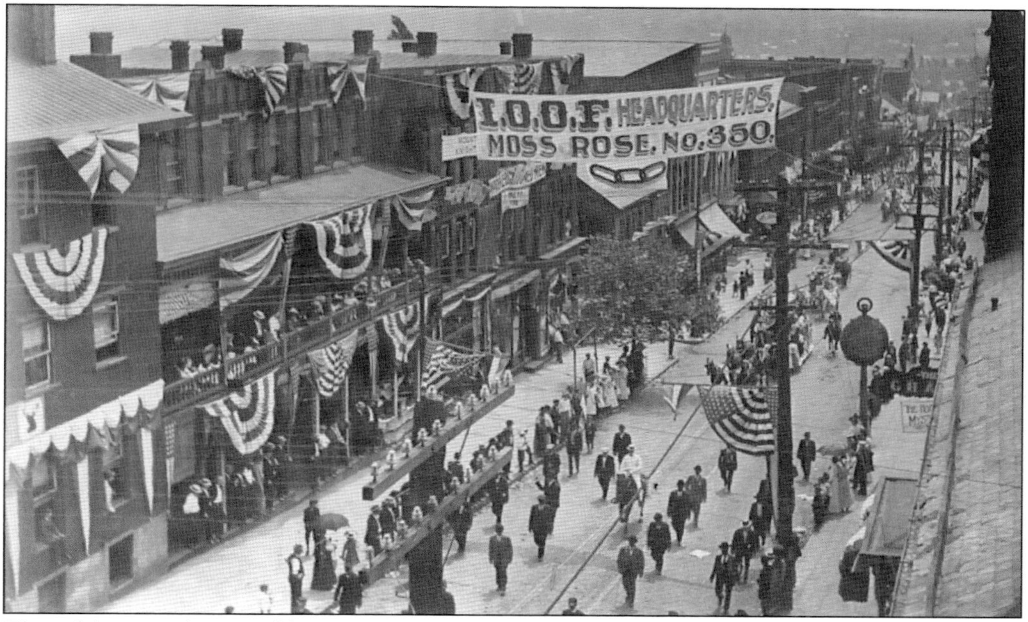

The celebration during Old Home Week in 1910 included a banner of Moss Rose Lodge No. 350, the Independent Order of Odd Fellows (IOOF) local headquarters, located on Main Street in Mount Pleasant. The IOOF started in the United Kingdom. Established to assist members of a community at a time when insurance was unavailable, they sponsored local fundraising. (Courtesy of the Mount Pleasant Area Historical Society.)

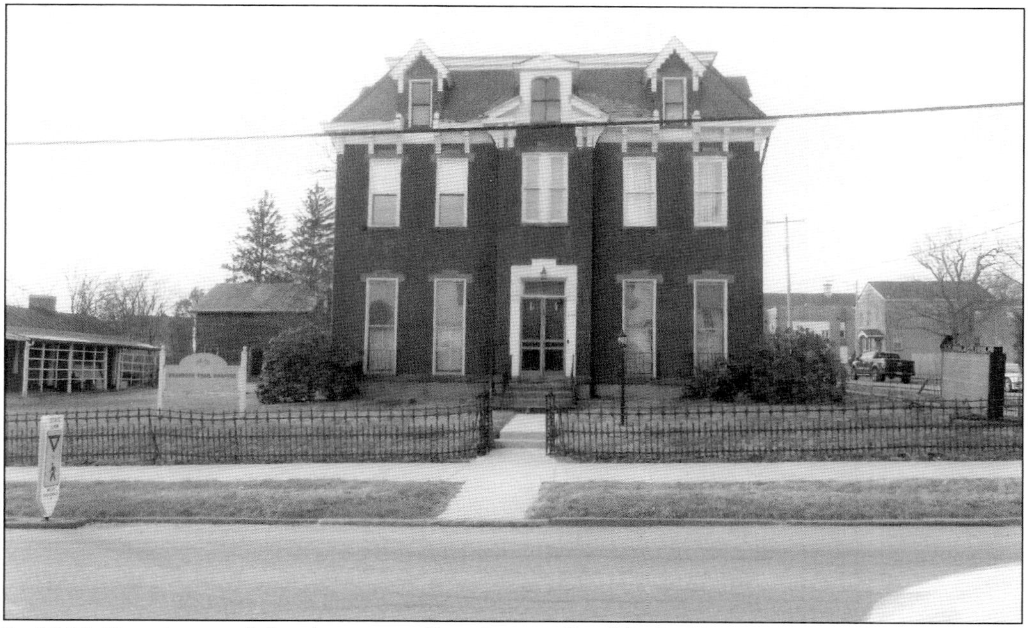

In 1960, Daughters of the American Revolution, Braddock Chapter, secured a permanent headquarters by purchasing Samuel Warden's residence. This was accomplished through a bequest from the Bess Campbell-Cook estate. Mrs. James S. Braddock and her sister Mrs. R.E. Beard organized this chapter in 1943. (Courtesy of Nancy Sebek.)

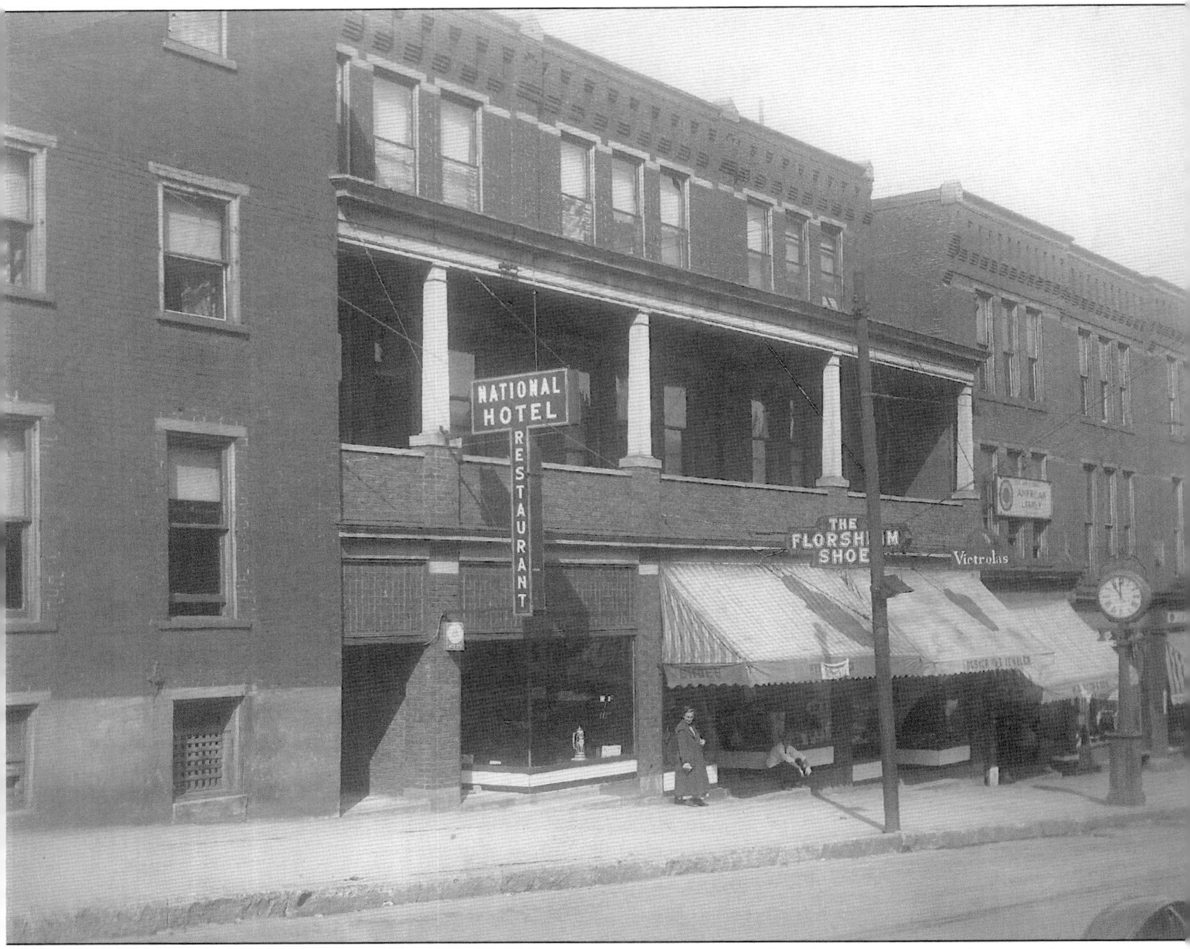

The National Hotel was located on Main Street next to the former post office building. A Pennsylvania Wine & Spirits Store and office building occupy this location today. This photograph was taken in 1946, when the hotel was leased by Harry and Mary Pfeifer and a Mr. Burkholder. The National Hotel had been in operation for about 78 years before it was closed. The original proprietor of this establishment was H.J. Jordan. From March 5, 1906, until December 21, 1906, a guest hotel ledger was handwritten for the names of the lodgers, which included entertainers from Pennsylvania and other states. This library material is located in the Mount Pleasant Public Library and may be viewed by appointment. (Courtesy of Steve Billey and Brian Billey.)

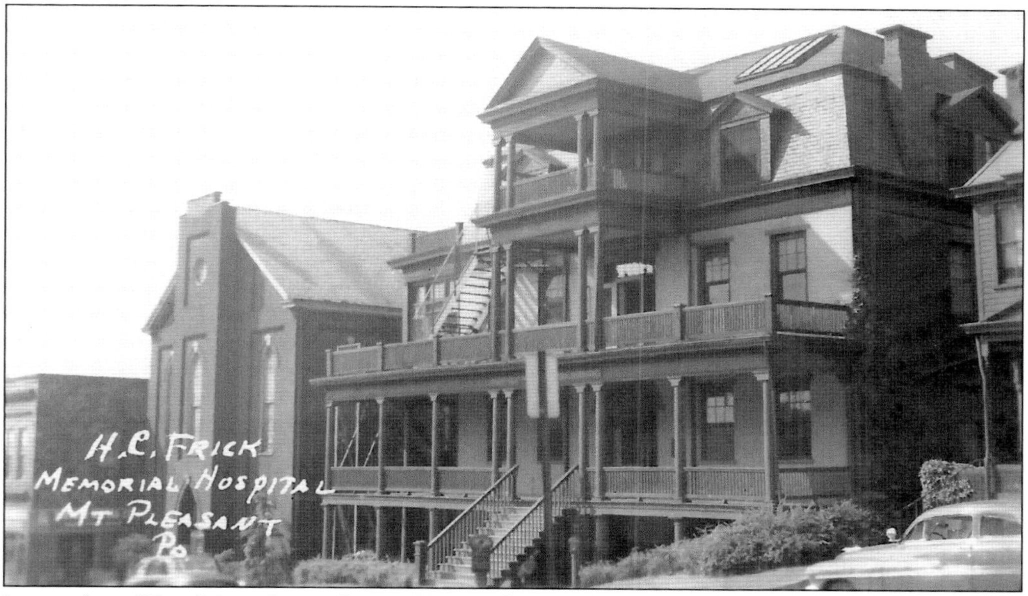

Located on West Main Street from 1904 until 1965, Mount Pleasant Memorial Hospital had a capacity of 67 patient beds. A school of nursing was soon added to provide for much-needed support staff. The first nursing class graduated in 1907, and this educational facility remained open until 1950. This site is currently a parking lot, which displays the Mount Pleasant Borough sign. (Courtesy of Kathy Stanislaw.)

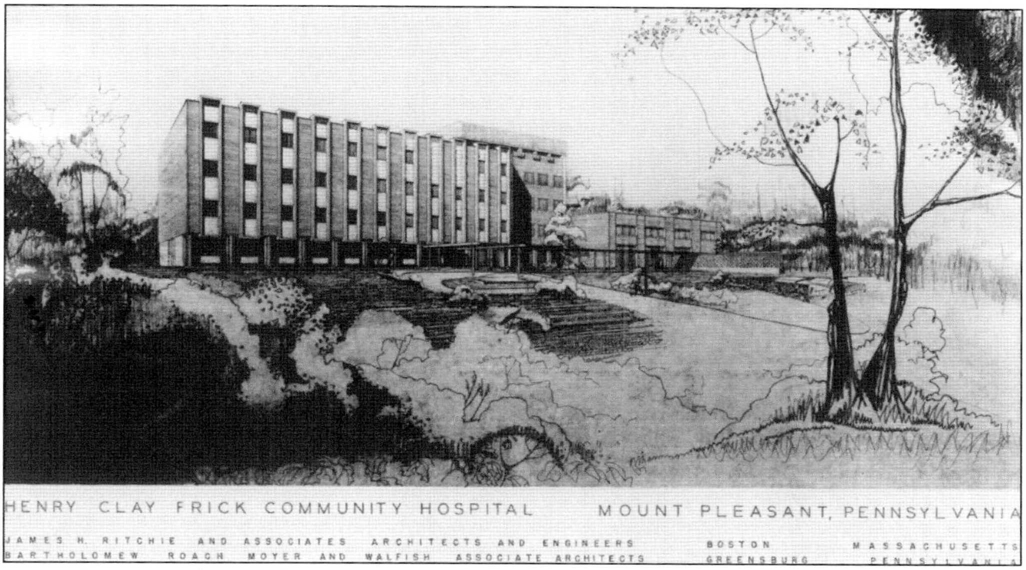

In 1965, Henry Clay Frick Community Hospital, now Excela Frick, was opened at its current location at 508 South Church Street. The current facility is a licensed 102-bed hospital, offering acute care services, surgical services, a sleep center, outpatient rehabilitation, full laboratory, and imaging and diagnostic services. This architectural drawing credits James H. Ritchie and Associates of Boston, Massachusetts, as architects and engineers, with Bartholomew, Roach, Moyer and Walfish of Greensburg, Pennsylvania, as associate architects. (Courtesy of the Mount Pleasant Public Library Archives.)

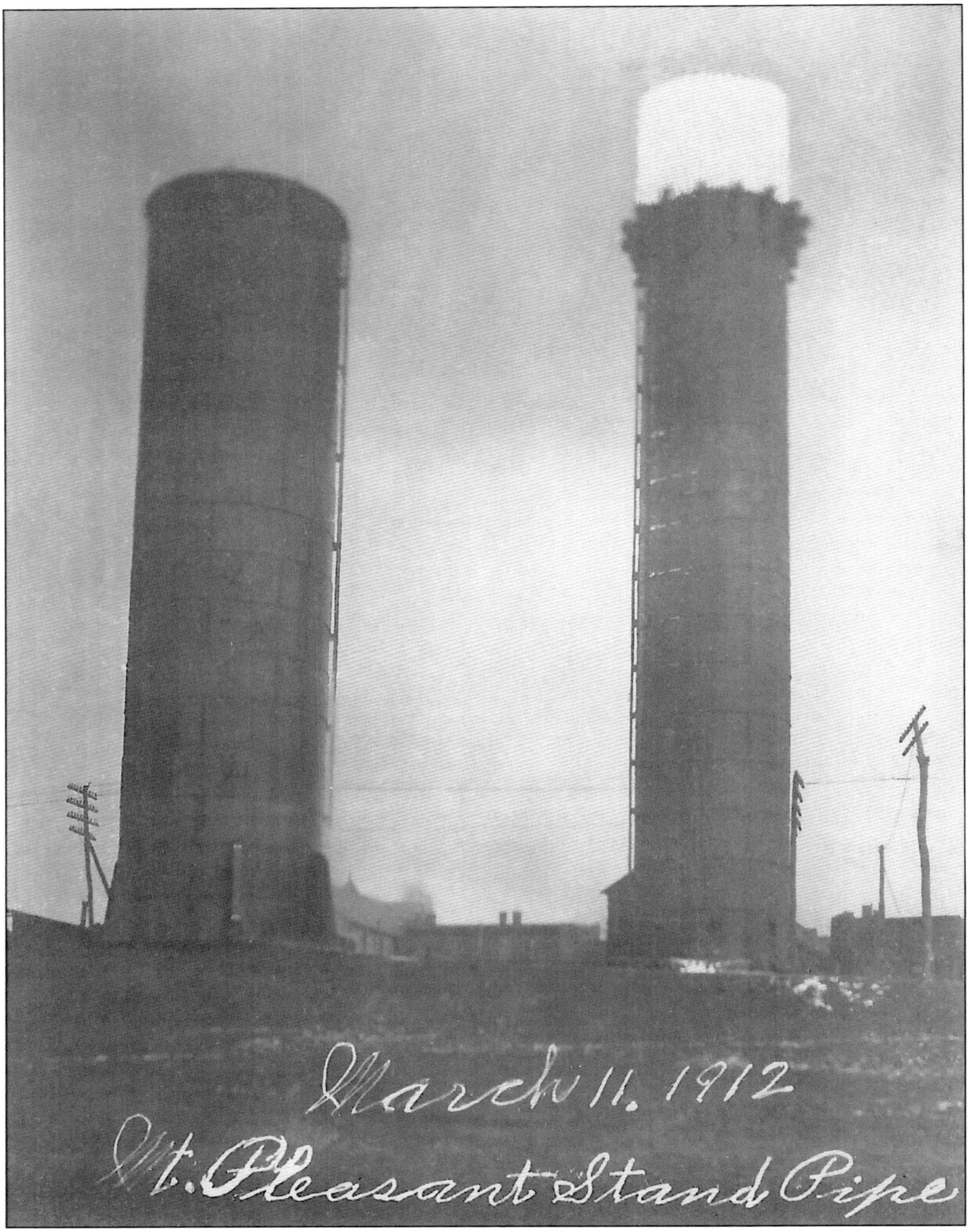

The standpipe stacks, a prominent feature of the Mount Pleasant Borough skyline, held water for the community. On March 11, 1912, the weather had been so cold that ice had formed on the top of one of the stacks, creating this interesting image. Today, a visitor can still find the street sign bearing the name "Standpipe Ally." (Courtesy of Margaret Milliron.)

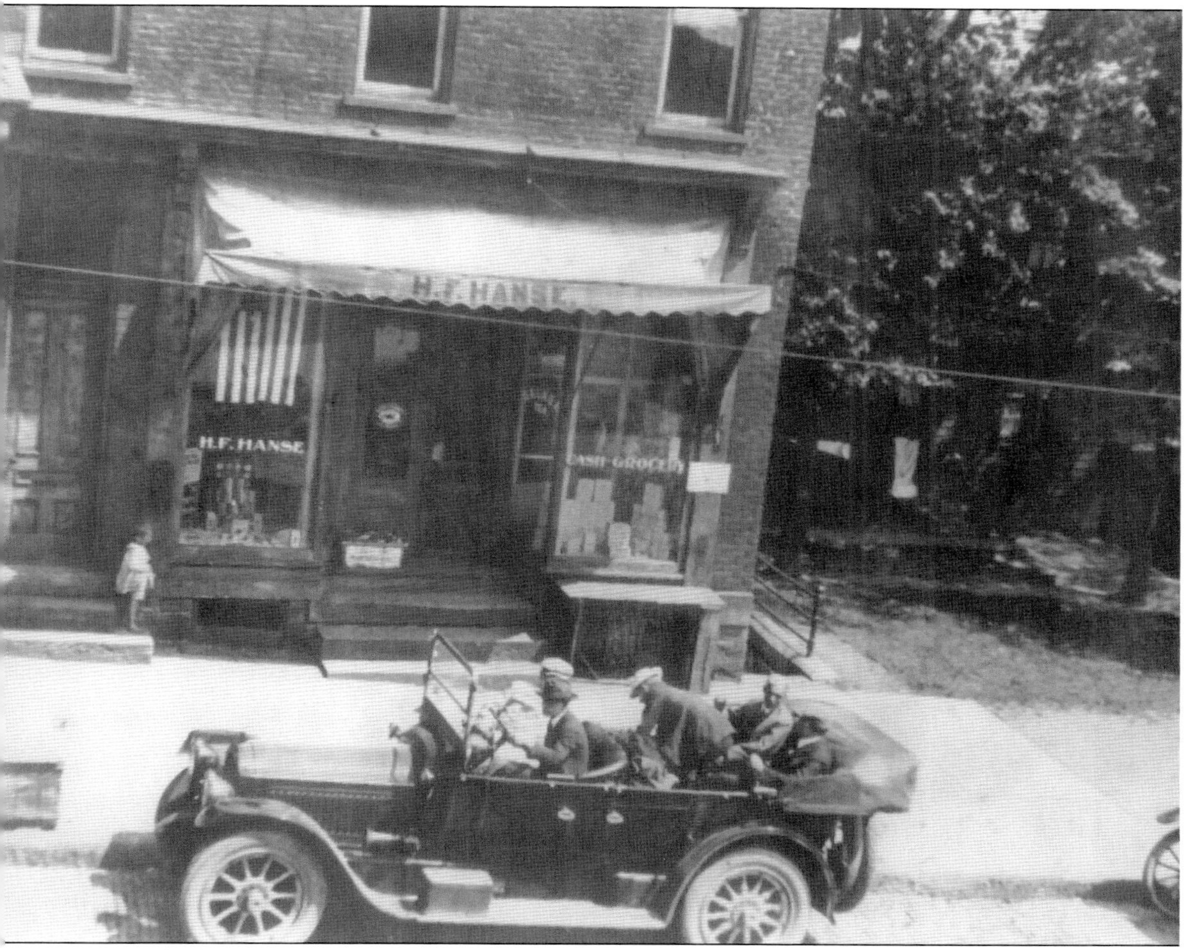

Henry Ford, Thomas Edison, and Harvey Firestone are among the passengers in the car, which is seen passing Hanse Store (now Saloom's Department Store). The party of travelers passed through Mount Pleasant on their way to Lincoln Highway. Incidentally, the glass for the headlights of the Model T Ford was manufactured at the L.E. Smith Glass Company in Mount Pleasant. Examples of these headlights are on display at the Mount Pleasant Glass Museum. (Courtesy of Charlotte Saloom Mowry.)

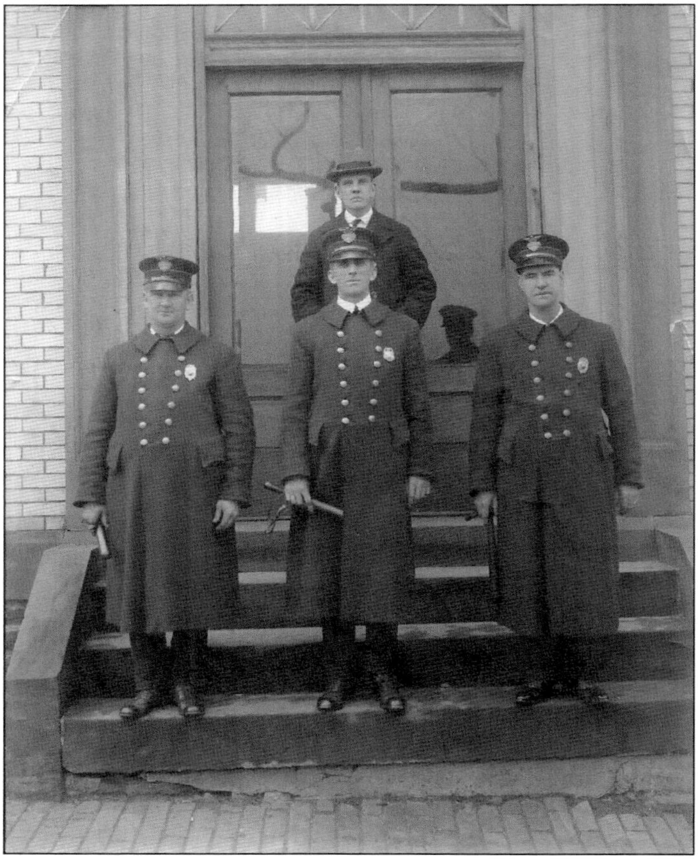

Standing on the municipal building steps in 1922 are (in front) police officers Joe White, Robert Smith, and "Red" Nugent; and (top step) William Overholt, burgess. The office of burgess was the head of the governing body for early Mount Pleasant Borough until 1961, at which time the elected position of mayor became the head of the borough. (Courtesy of Steve Billey and Brian Billey.)

Two Mount Pleasant borough police officers are pictured with four of the horses that they rode in their daily duties during the 1930s. This photograph was taken in front of the town's livery stables. (Courtesy of James Vaughn.)

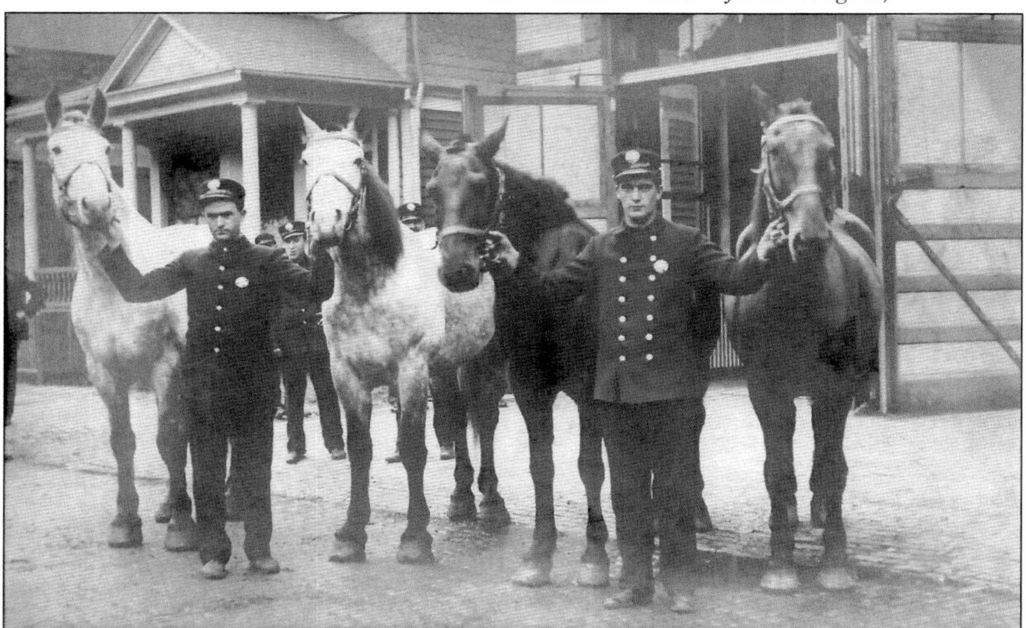

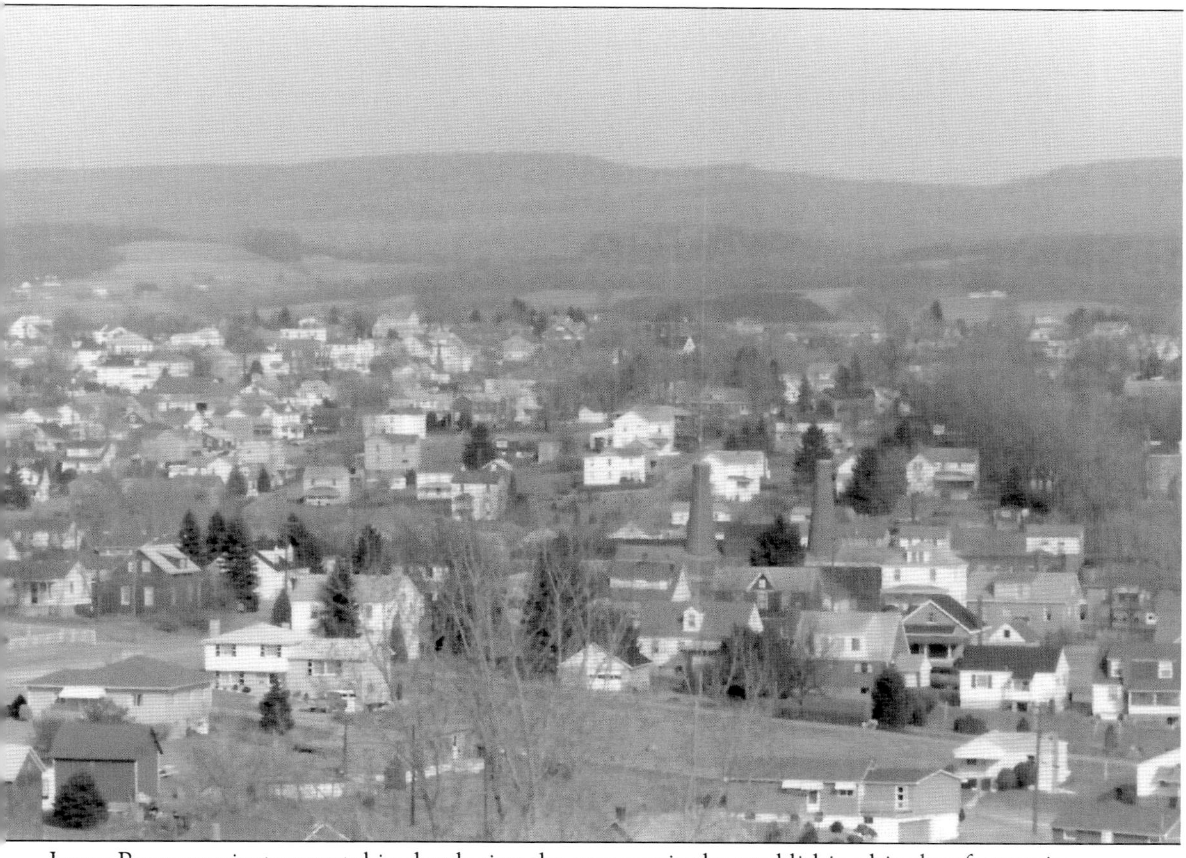

James Bryce was instrumental in developing the community by establishing his glass factory in Mount Pleasant in 1896. At one time, the plant employed as many as 1,000 workers. In 1965, the Bryce Glass Company was sold to the Lenox Co. In this 1980s view of Mount Pleasant, the twin stacks of the Bryce Glass factory still stand. Also visible in this photograph, taken from the hill near Visitation BVM Cemetery, are Jack Bobbs Park and the Laurel Mountains. (Courtesy of Ann Marie Grzywinski.)

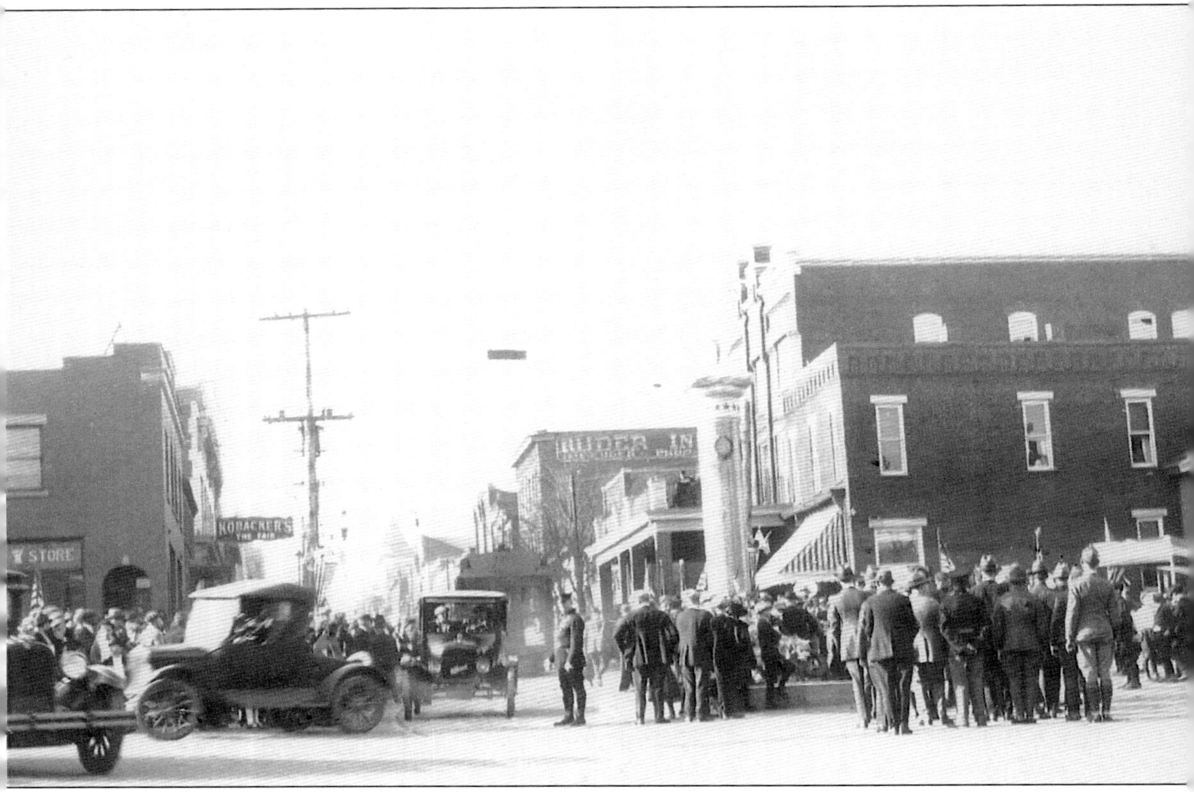

The Doughboy unveiling on November 11, 1924, was one of the biggest patriotic celebrations in Mount Pleasant history. This monument stands in the center of town and was dedicated to the sacred memory of the soldiers who fought in World War I for freedom in America and the world. This served as a memorial for Mount Pleasant and nearby vicinities. Ceremonies included a parade and an address by US senator Frank B. Willis. (Courtesy of the Mount Pleasant Area Historical Society.)

Artic Doncaster Stevenson Swartz of Mount Pleasant was the daughter of Richard and Alice Doncaster and sister to Paul Doncaster. Several weeks after her marriage to William Stevenson, he was killed in action in France during the early part of World War I. Artic participated in the dedication of the World War I memorial *The Doughboy* that was erected following the war. Artic later married Otto P. Swartz, who had served in France in the Army Corps of Engineers. (Courtesy of John Doncaster.)

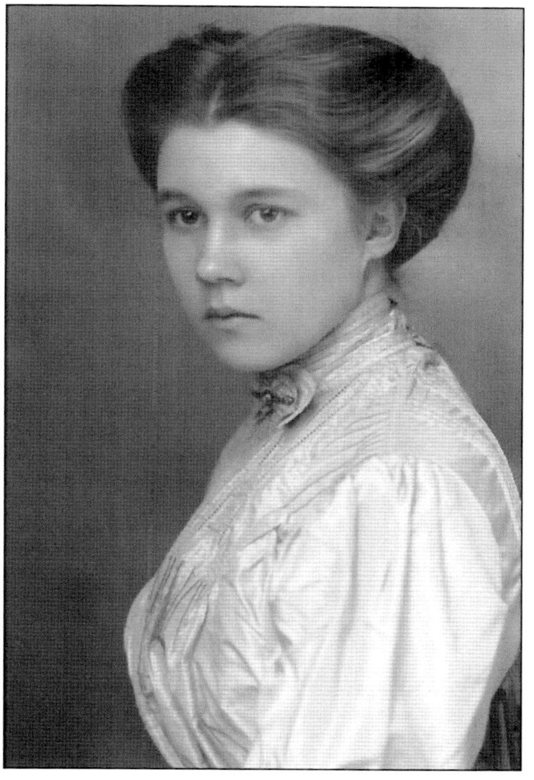

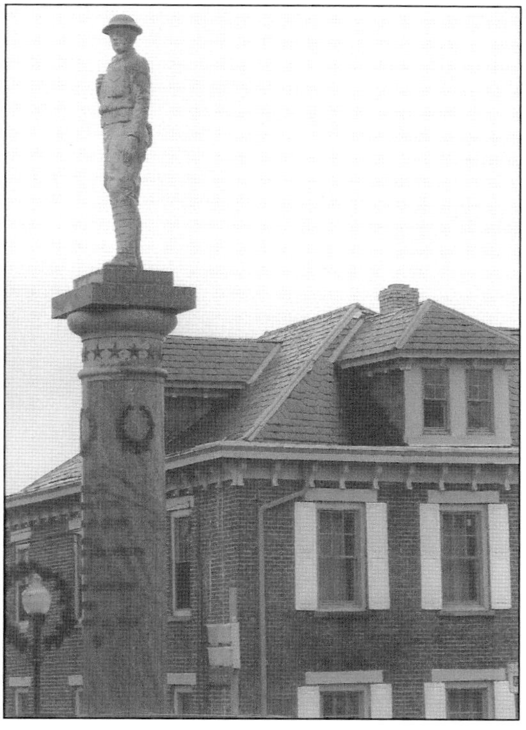

The close-up of the World War I memorial (now the Mount Pleasant Monument) was taken in December 2013. *The Doughboy* continues to be a symbol of Mount Pleasant today and an ongoing tribute to service men and women in all conflicts past, present, and future. (Courtesy of Rose Eckman.)

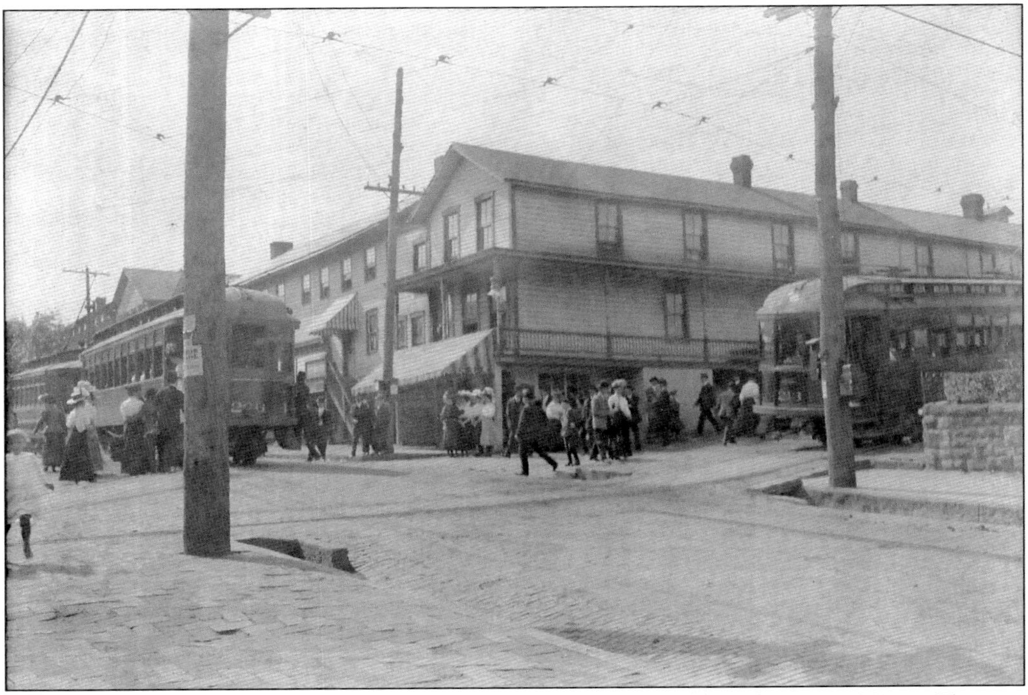

The east end of Mount Pleasant featured a trolley turnaround and boarding stop. Mount Pleasant was a significant destination on the trolley line because many were employed in the coke works in the borough and, later, in the glass factories. The employees of these industries and the businesses that supported the town's residents benefited from daily use of the trolley line, which was an extension of the Pennsylvania Railroad. (Courtesy of John Doncaster.)

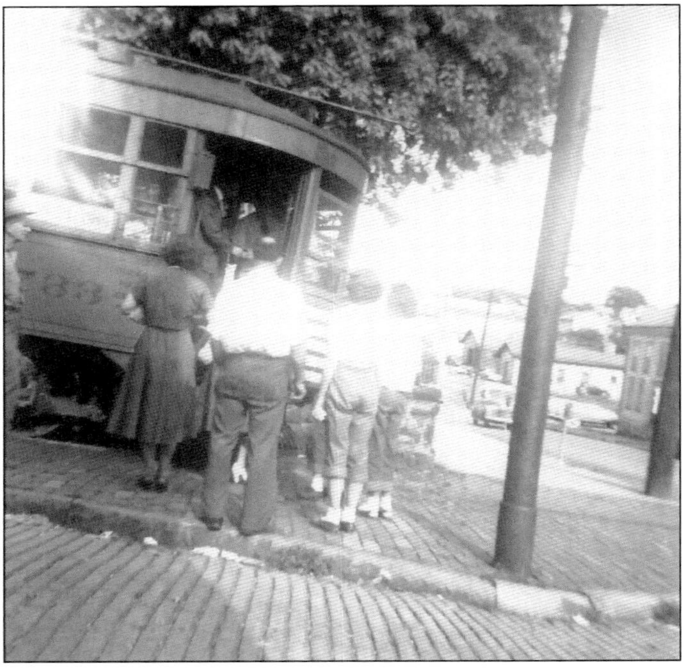

Passengers waited to board the trolley for the last streetcar ride in 1952 before the line closed. Note the attire of those pictured, especially the young women. The cuffed jeans are a big change from the hobble skirts worn by women who rode streetcars in times past. These skirts fastened at the bottom to prevent being blown about by the breeze created by the moving trolley. (Courtesy of Ruth Kauffman.)

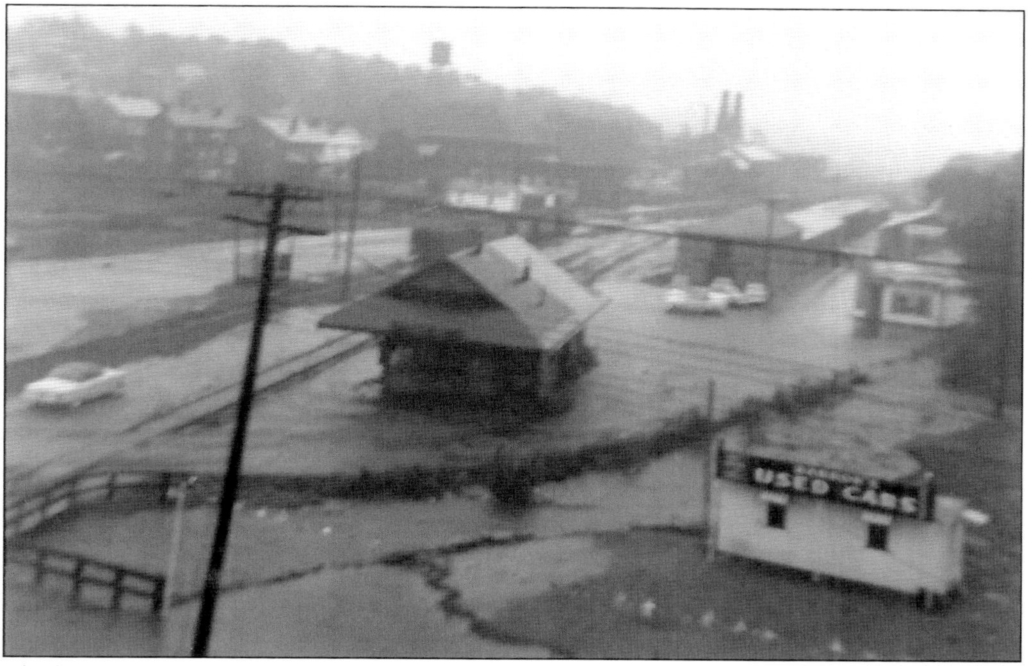

The lower end of Mount Pleasant has a memorable moment in its history. On October 16, 1954, Western Pennsylvania experienced significant flooding as a result of Hurricane Hazel making landfall on the East coast. In Mount Pleasant, cars were waterlogged or washed away while the railroad tracks and power lines were flooded. The towers of the Bryce Glass factory are visible, along with a used car dealership located across from Pritts Feed Mill. In the 1980s and 1990s, IGA and Cook's Lumber occupied this location. (Courtesy of Ruth Kauffman.)

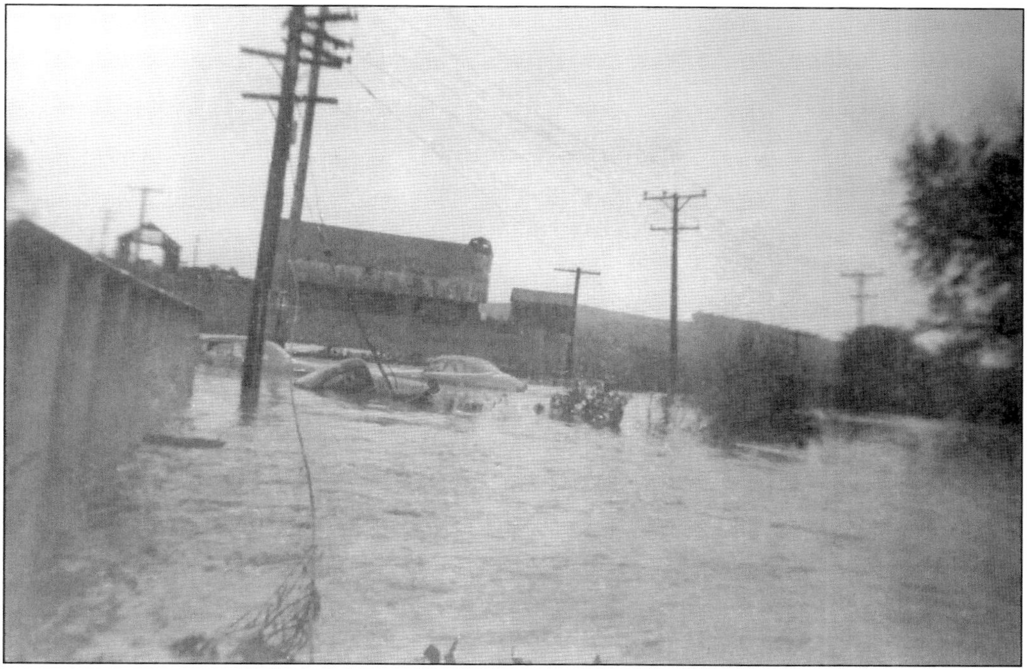

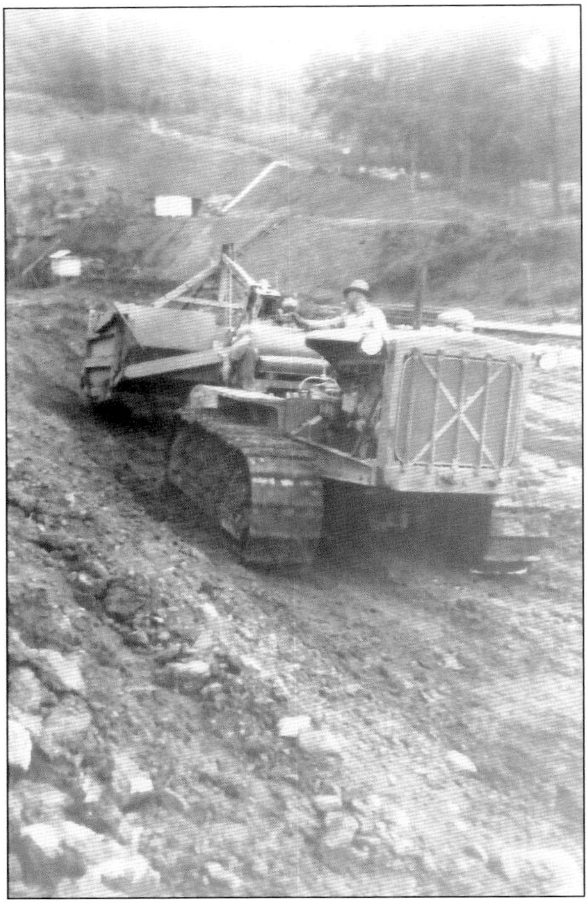

Mount Pleasant is a town that has always been in the midst of many means of transportation. Originally built at the crossing of two Native American trails, Mount Pleasant has hosted many forms of roadways, including dirt wagon trails, planked roads, bricked streets, trolley tracks, railways, and Route 31 East, which became an extension of Main Street. Route 31 connects Routes 119, 819, and 982 as handy passages to nearby communities and destinations. These roads also bring many visitors to our town and the surrounding area. Here, an earth-moving machine is preparing the grade that will become the two-lane highway leading out of town and into the Laurel Highlands. Traveling Route 31 East eventually links travelers to the Pennsylvania Turnpike exit in Donegal. (Both photographs courtesy of Kathy Stanislaw.)

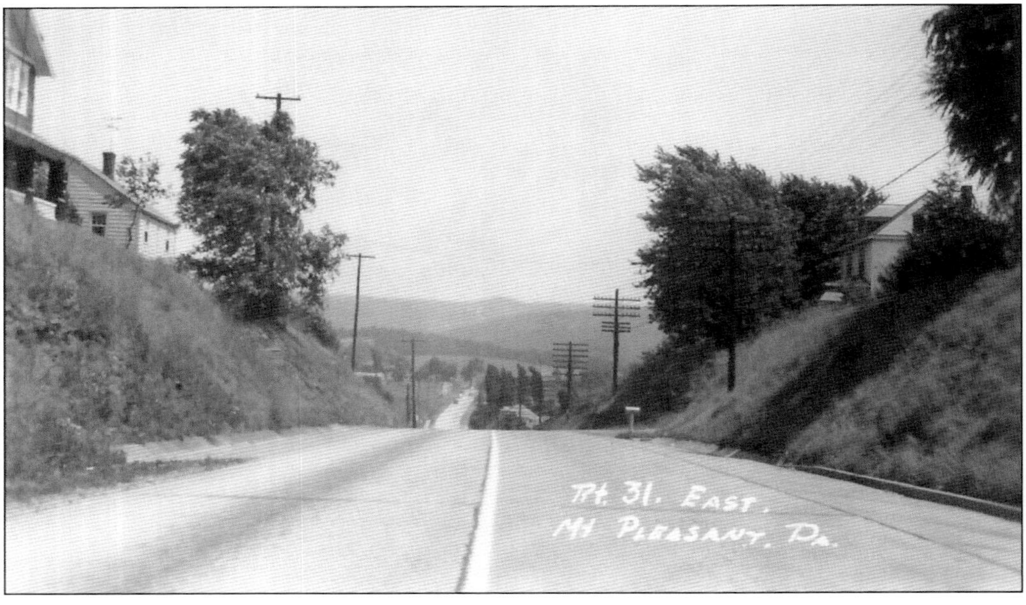

Two

Building a Community

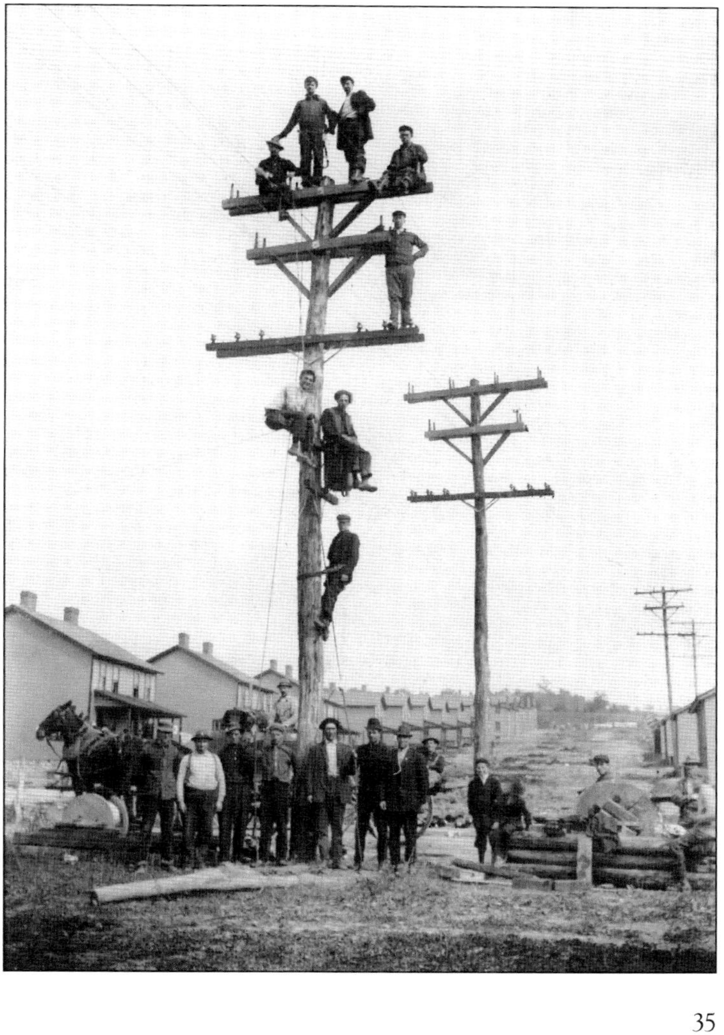

As depicted in this Standard Shaft photograph, electrical workers put in long hours with primitive equipment to bring electricity to Mount Pleasant Borough. Mount Pleasant has a long-standing tradition that hard work does pay off in building a community, and families worked together to improve their future. (Courtesy of the Mount Pleasant Public Library Archives.)

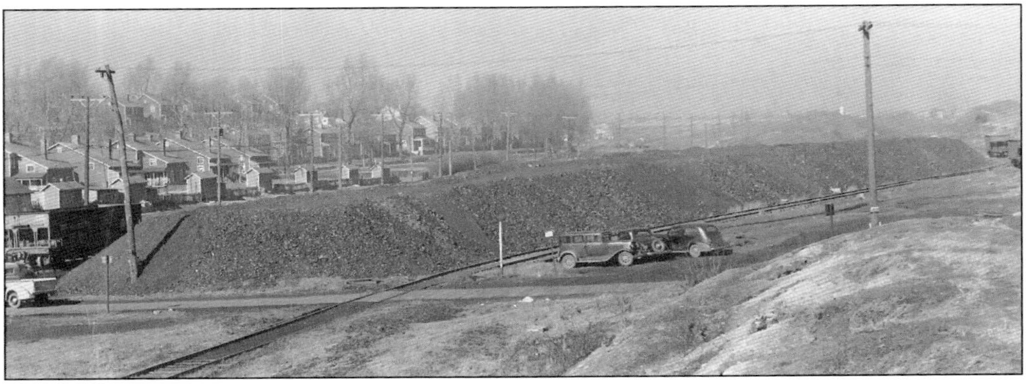

Mining was one of the major occupations for many residents. Families of the coal and coke workers had their own residencies in a series of company houses located at Standard. These dwellings were two-story wood-frame double houses, which rested on stone foundations. This close-knit community of miners became the face of laborers who made a difference in the community. Working long hours, these miners provided the delivery of coal through the use of trains. The view of the railroad tracks located in Spring Garden behind Low Street shows one track that carried coal and coke from the ovens at Standard Mines to various locations within the United States. (Both photographs courtesy of the Mount Pleasant Public Library Archives.)

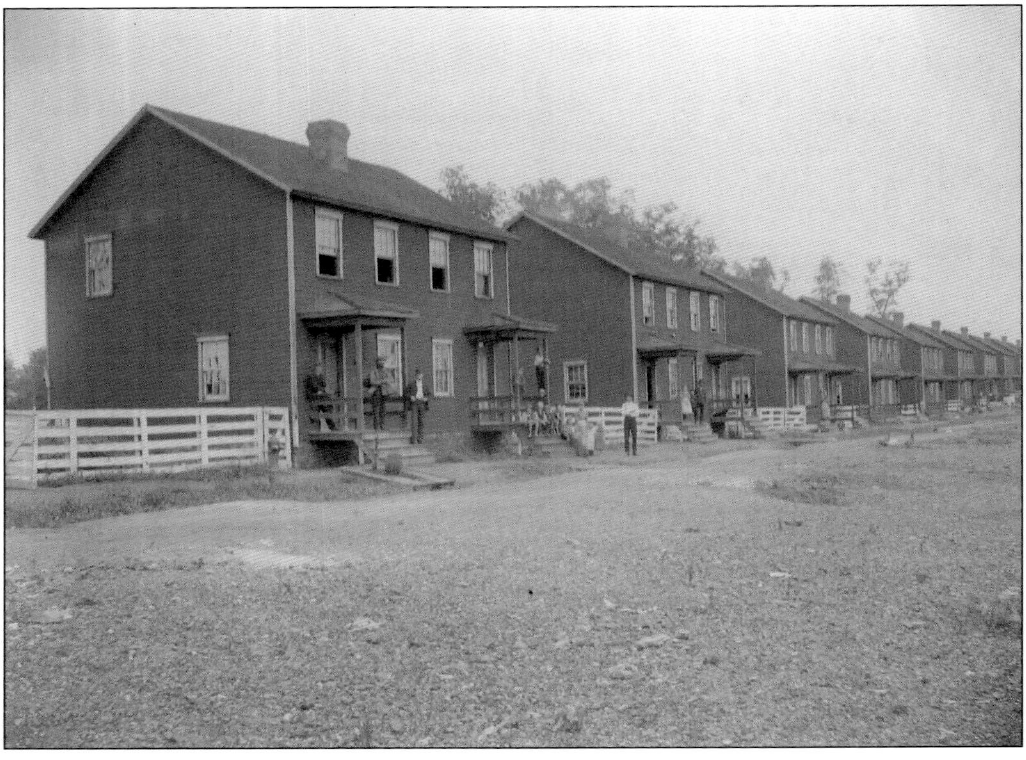

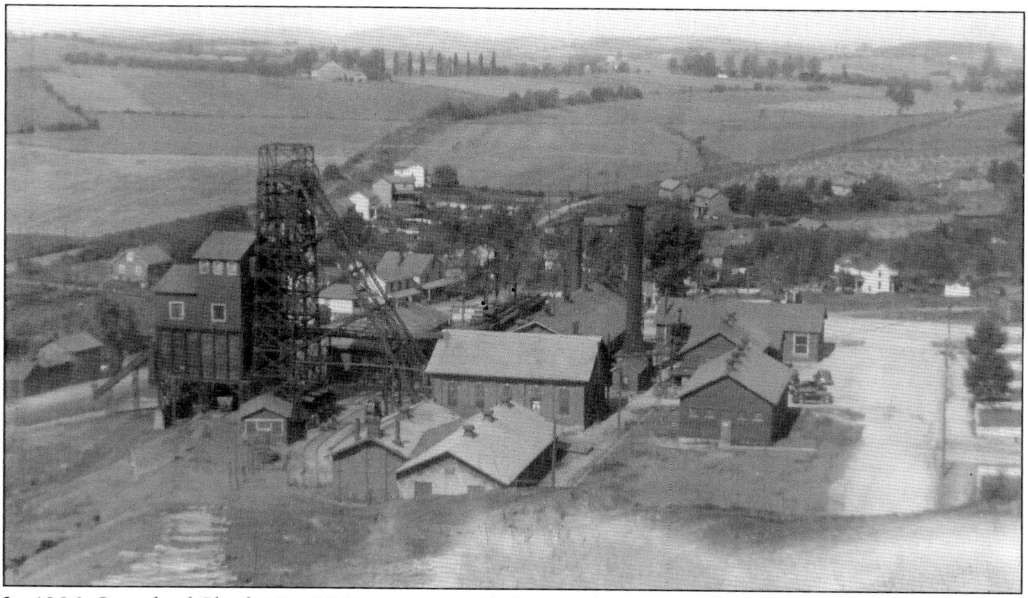

In 1886, Standard Shaft No. 2 Mine was established and was one of the largest coal mines in the United States. It included an engine house, boiler house, machine shop, and blacksmith shop. The Standard Shaft No. 2 Mine extracted between 52,000 and 56,000 tons of coal each month. There were more than 936 men and boys employed at the shaft mines during 1888. Production continued until 1922, when the coal industry hit a slump. (Courtesy of the Mount Pleasant Public Library Archives.)

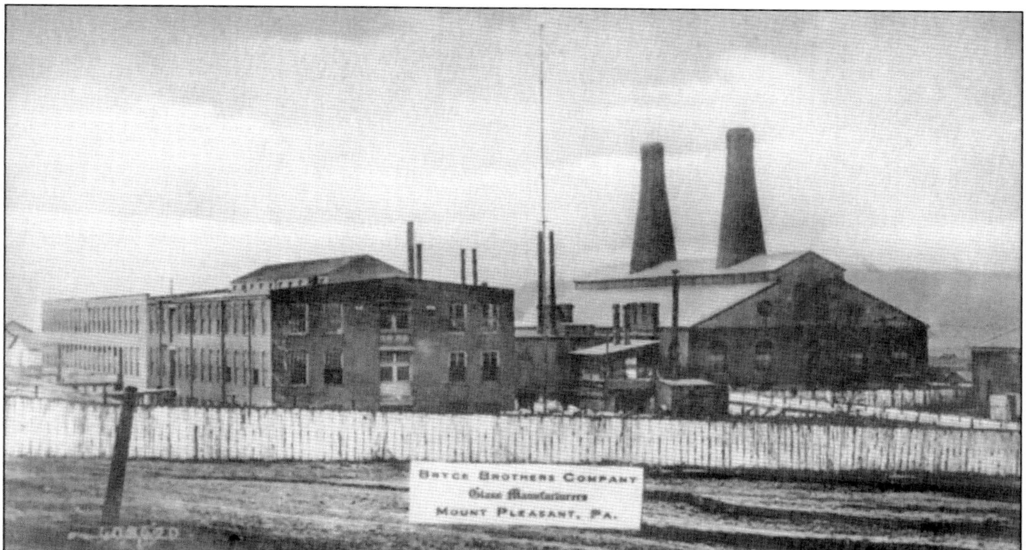

Employment was available in the glass plants, which were under the supervision of the Bryce Brothers Company in 1896 and L.E. Smith Glass in 1907. The art of making handblown glass was a process, which included making a batch of molten glass and etching designs into specific patterns, brilliance, color, and beauty for a finished product. The handiwork of these talented glassblowers has been displayed in hotels and ocean liners. (Courtesy of the Mount Pleasant Public Library Archives.)

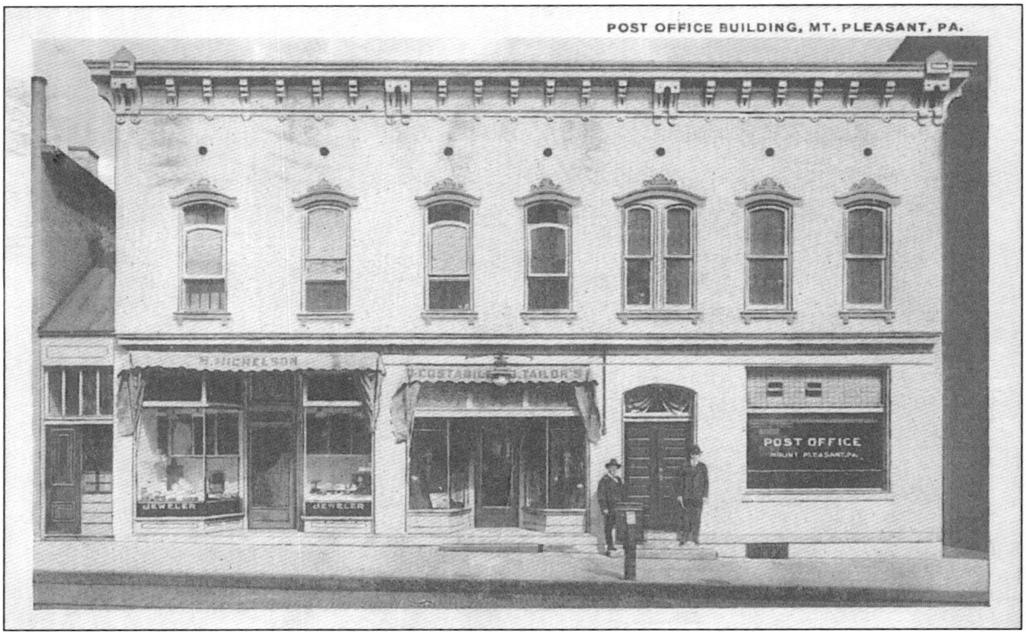

Building relationships and communication with family members was central to the community. Through the establishment of the first US post office in Mount Pleasant, which was located on Main Street, residents were able to communicate with others far and near. In this photograph, the simple storefront structure of the post office is nestled next to Costabile's Tailor (a family-owned business) and jeweler M. Michelson. (Courtesy of the Mount Pleasant Public Library Archives.)

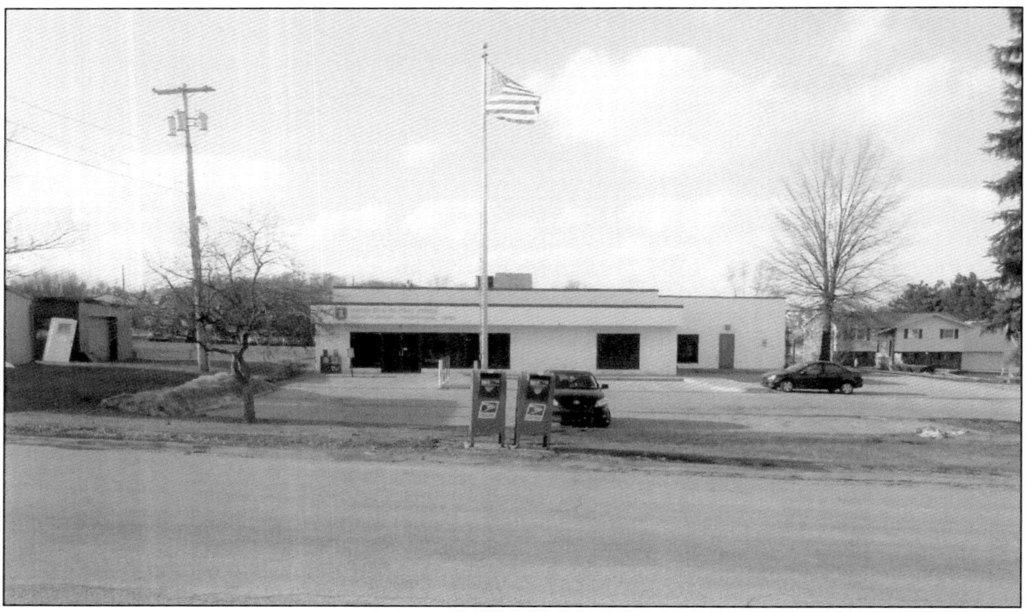

As the population grew from 534 registered residents in 1850 to an estimated 4,457 in 2012, Mount Pleasant's communication structure expanded to the present US post office, located at 24 Rumbaugh Avenue. This long building has individual post office boxes and a mailing center. Residents benefit from the expanded mail services and accessibility. (Courtesy of Nancy Sebek.)

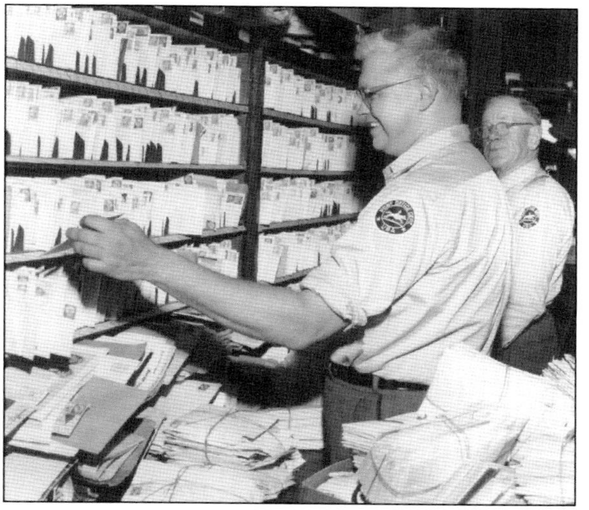

George Miller (left) and another former employee of the Mount Pleasant post office are shown sorting the mail by hand into different slots for delivery. Postal carriers are able to deliver the mail to individual homes each day. (Courtesy of the Mount Pleasant Public Library Archives.)

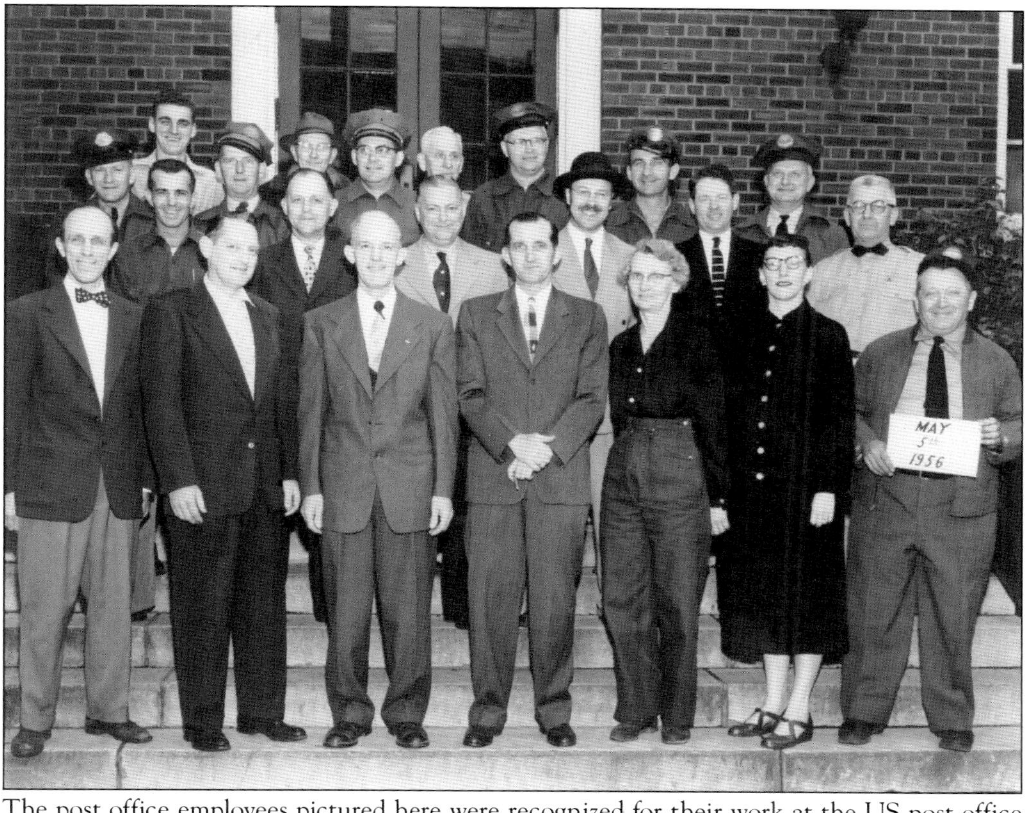

The post office employees pictured here were recognized for their work at the US post office on May 5, 1956. From left to right are (first row) Claude Harrer, Bob ?, Lloyd ?, Charles Fencil, Helen Pyle, Mary Louise Clausner-Roman, and R.C. ?; (second row) Vernon Nicolette, Louis Brown, Joe Miller, Roy Sweitzer, Robert Stahl, and Rob ?; (third row) Richard Crawford, Ernest Zundell, Lawrence Clausner, George Miller, Robert Whipkey, and Lloyd Zaronsky; (fourth row) Nelson Myers, Homer Pershing, and Harry Swartz. (Courtesy of the Mount Pleasant Public Library Archives.)

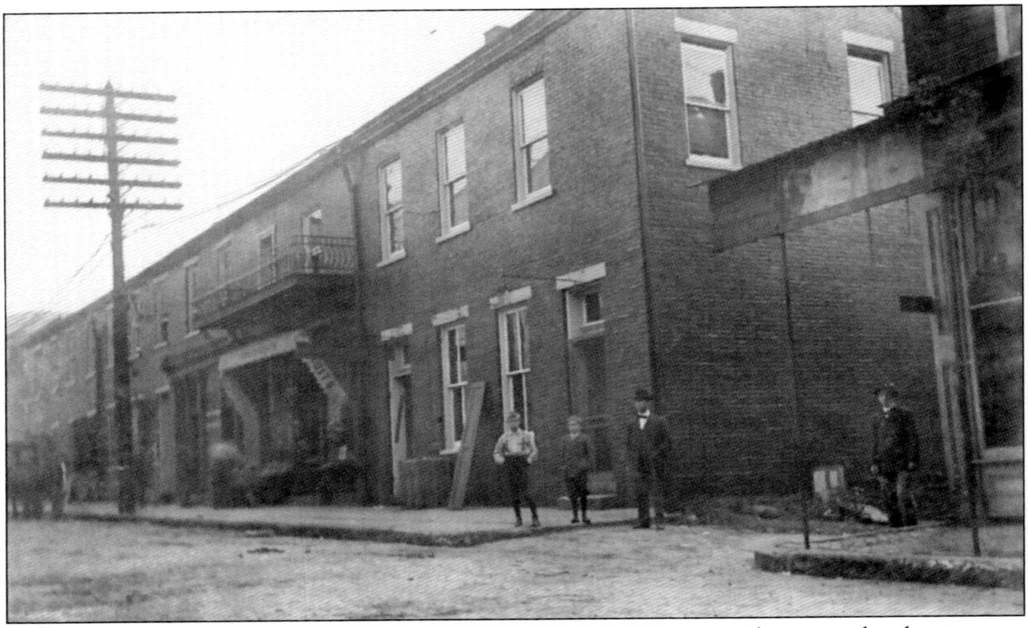

Businesses began to develop in the central areas of the borough. In the early 19th century, Freed's Store, a retail store specializing in clothing, was located on South Church Street. In 1978, this site became the home of a new Standard Bank, which is across from the Hauser Insurance agency. Groceries stores were also opened throughout the community, allowing residents to walk to them and get supplies for their families. At the far right of this building was Doncaster Grocery. (Courtesy of John Doncaster.)

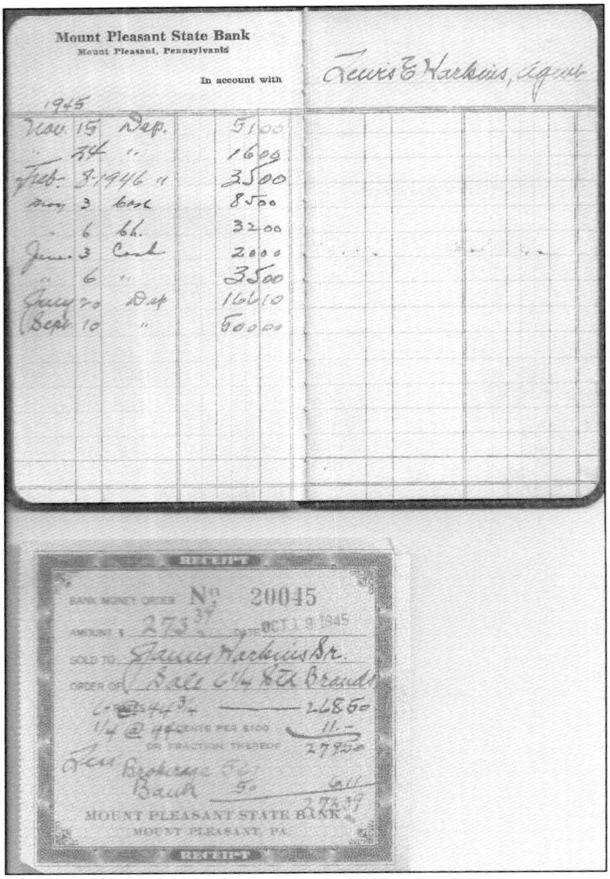

Residents would keep accurate banking records by hand. This 1945 banking ledger shows the deposits made by Lewis E. Harkius Sr. Also pictured is a bank money order from the Mount Pleasant State Bank. Note both the similarities and differences as compared to present-day banking statements. (Courtesy of Donald Baumann.)

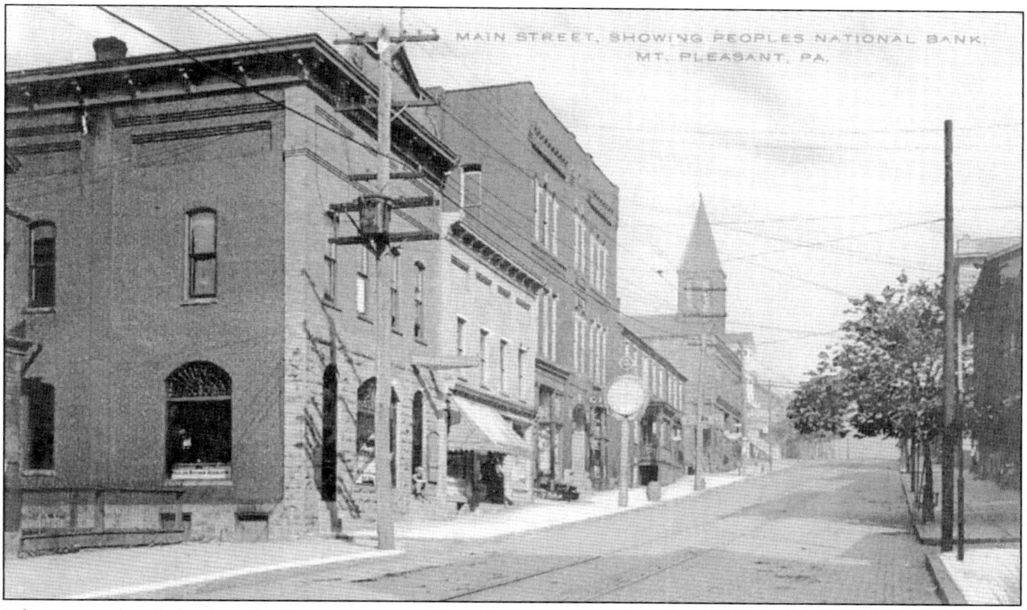

The growth of the banks is represented in this photograph of Peoples National Bank, located on Main Street. Presently, Mount Pleasant has three banks: Standard, First Niagara, and PNC. (Courtesy of the Mount Pleasant Public Library Archives.)

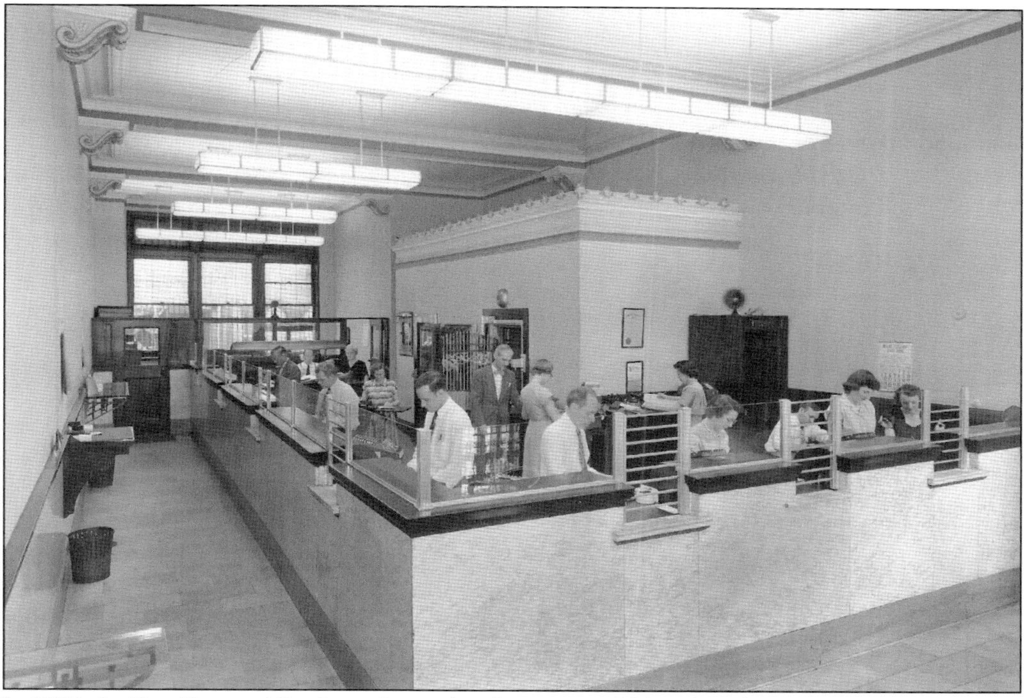

In 1905, the First National Bank was located at the corner of Church and Main Streets. Here, tellers at Mount Pleasant State Bank are hard at work in 1950. Among those pictured are Robert Weisel, Anna Mae Gearhart, Gilbert Clark, Lorraine Lessman, Frances Farrell, and Eleanor Brooks. The bank's name was changed to Pittsburgh National Bank in 1978. (Courtesy of John Doncaster.)

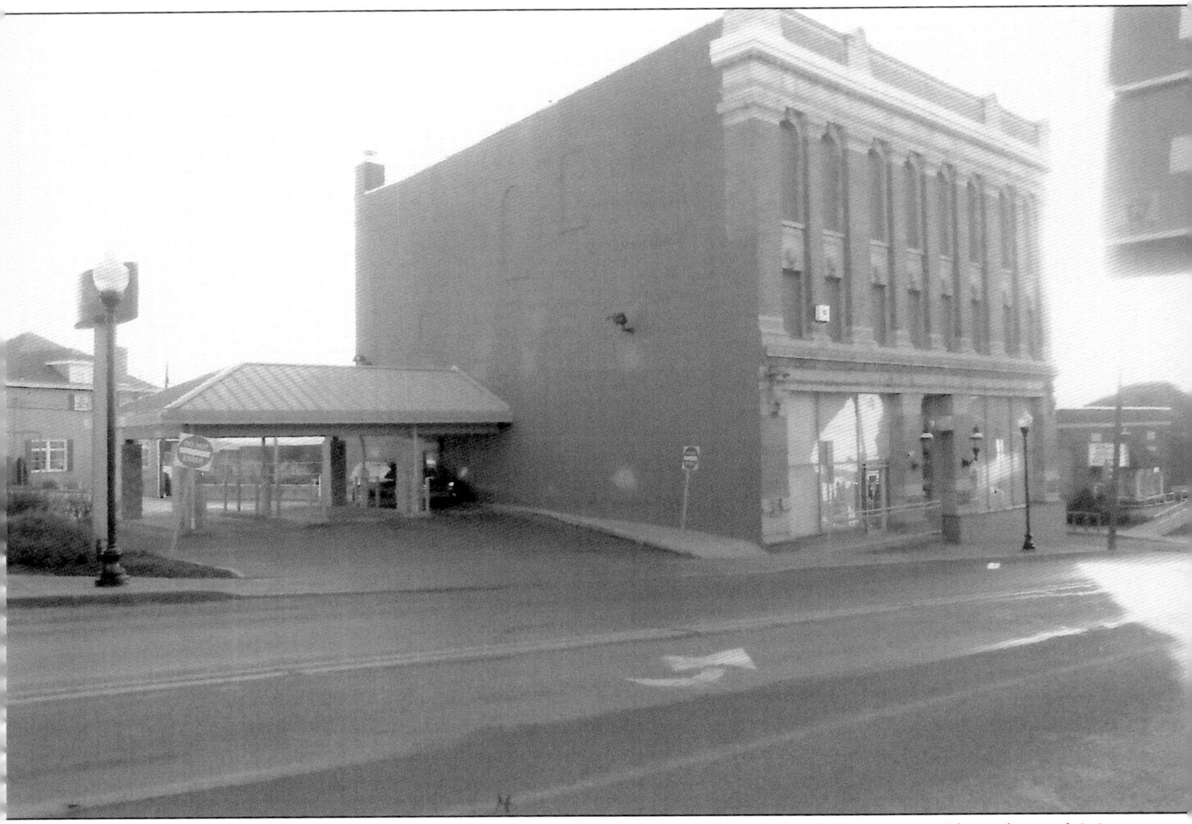

Presently, Pittsburgh National Bank maintains a multilevel structure at Church and Main Streets. The three-story building is the most architecturally decorated commercial building in the historical district. The canopy of the drive-thru facilitates financial exchanges between the customers and the teller or ATM. This demonstrates an advancement of banking resources for the patrons. (Courtesy of Nancy Sebek.)

Prominent floral shops were part of the thriving business community. Mrs. Echard spent many hours providing loving care to the flower buds and tender seedlings at Mount Pleasant Floral. This greenhouse, now owned by the Komarny family, can be visited at 208 Flower Way. (Courtesy of the Mount Pleasant Public Library Archives.)

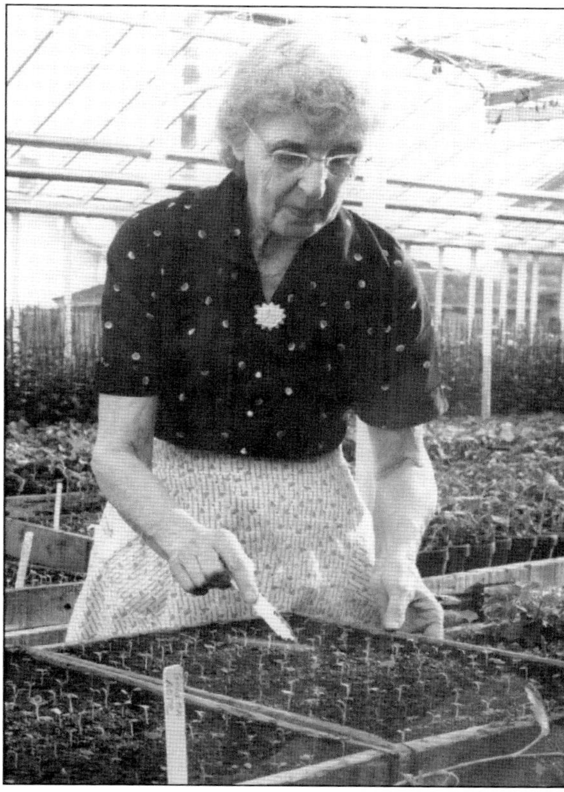

V. Rosso Florist has also served the community for many generations. They are currently located in the former post office on Main Street. Their future home will be located in the Diamond Mini Mall in the center of town. Both of these florists have been part of the 100-year history that makes up FTD's tradition of providing beautiful flowers. (Courtesy of Nancy Sebek.)

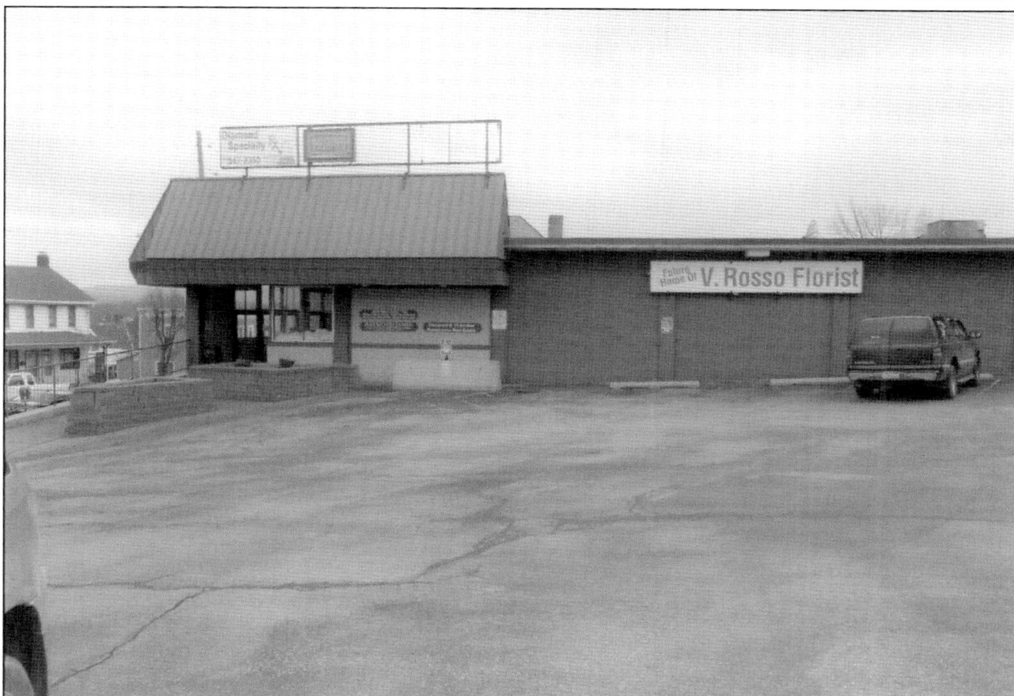

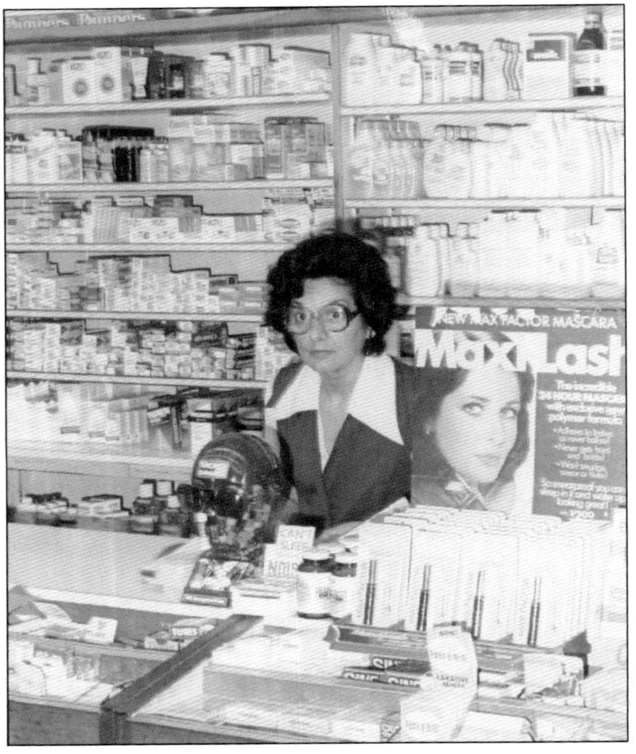

Serving the community's needs for many years, Burns Drug Store held a prominent place on Main Street. Employee Camille Fornal was a familiar face to many who frequented the pharmacy throughout the years. (Courtesy of Maria Macaluso.)

Located at 525 West Main Street, J.C. Penney provided department-style merchandise. From 1930 to 1940, the women's department carried Gaymore-brand hosiery, which was priced at $1.19 and 98¢. They also featured Cynthia-brand slips in crepe at 98¢ and in satin at $1.29. (Courtesy of the Mount Pleasant Public Library Archives.)

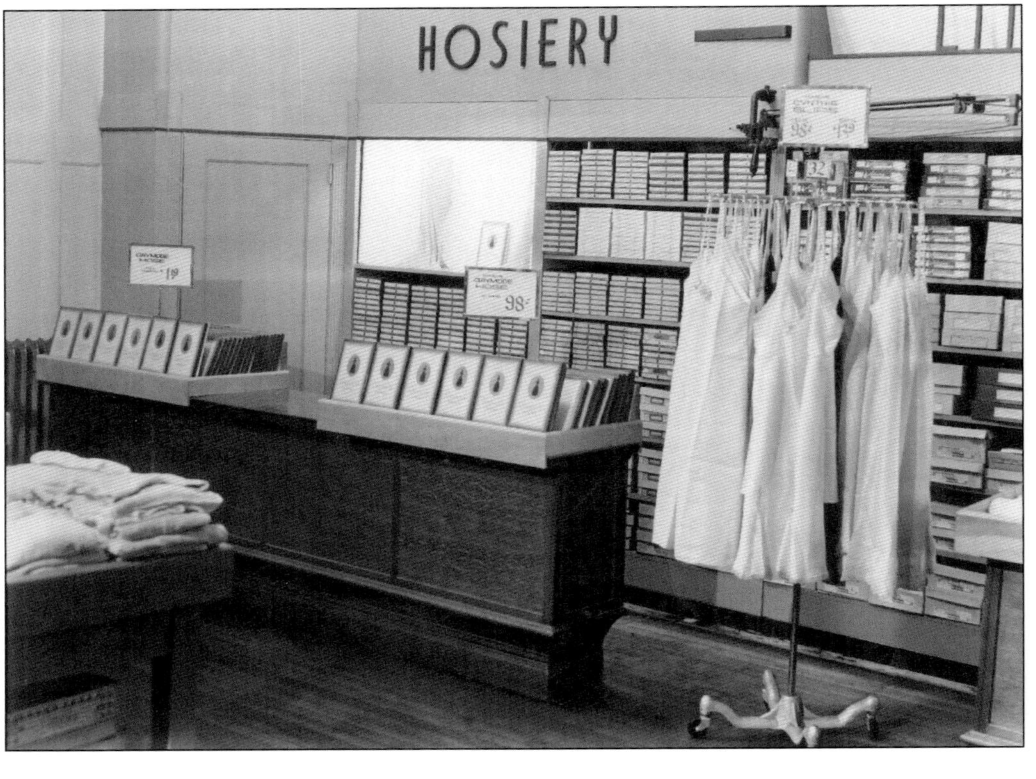

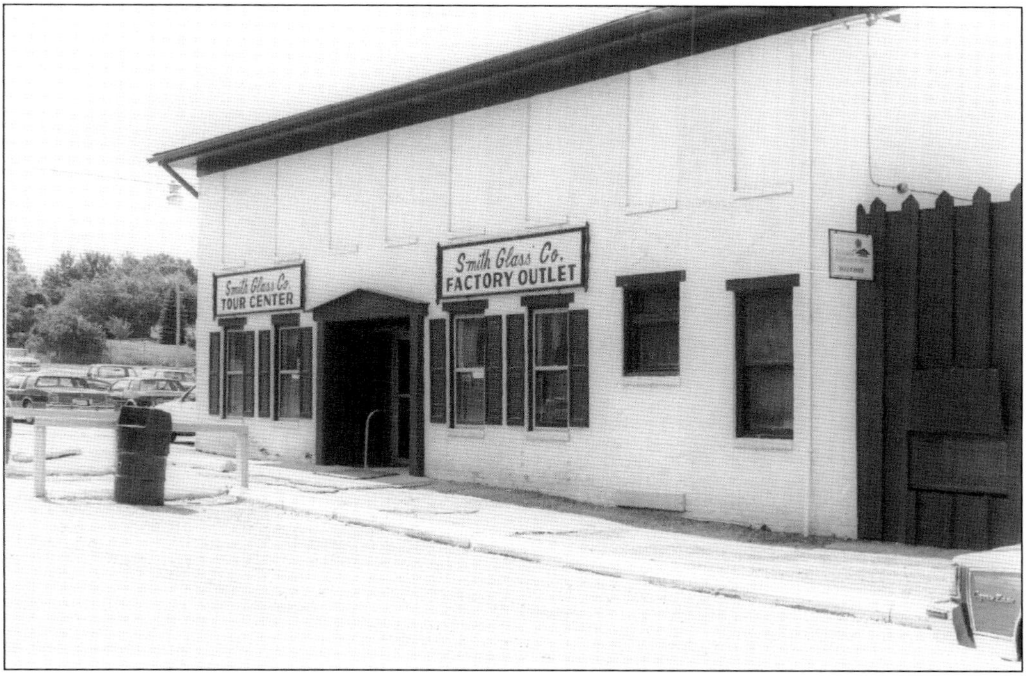

Having a long history in glassmaking, L.E. Smith was established in 1907. Smith Glass has long produced giftware and lighting fixtures, most notably with different colored glass, including green, amber, yellow, amethyst, and cobalt. Employees were recognized for their extraordinary craftsmanship and long history of service. Featured tours were held, and the factory outlet was a popular site for tourists and residents alike. (Courtesy of Debbie Brehun.)

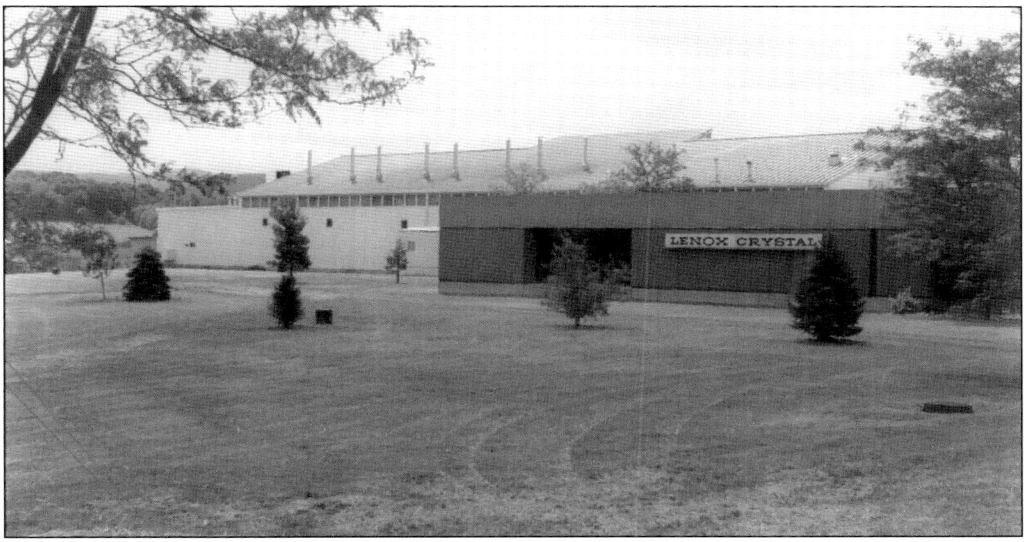

In 1965, the Lenox Corporation acquired Bryce Brothers Glass Company. Following over 75 years of tradition, Lenox Crystal has produced a large selection of china and crystal patterns that are treasured by many, including the White House. The former Lenox Crystal plant is located on a 50-acre track on Route 31 outside of Mount Pleasant. Currently, this plant houses the glass museum and outlet stores. (Courtesy of Debbie Brehun.)

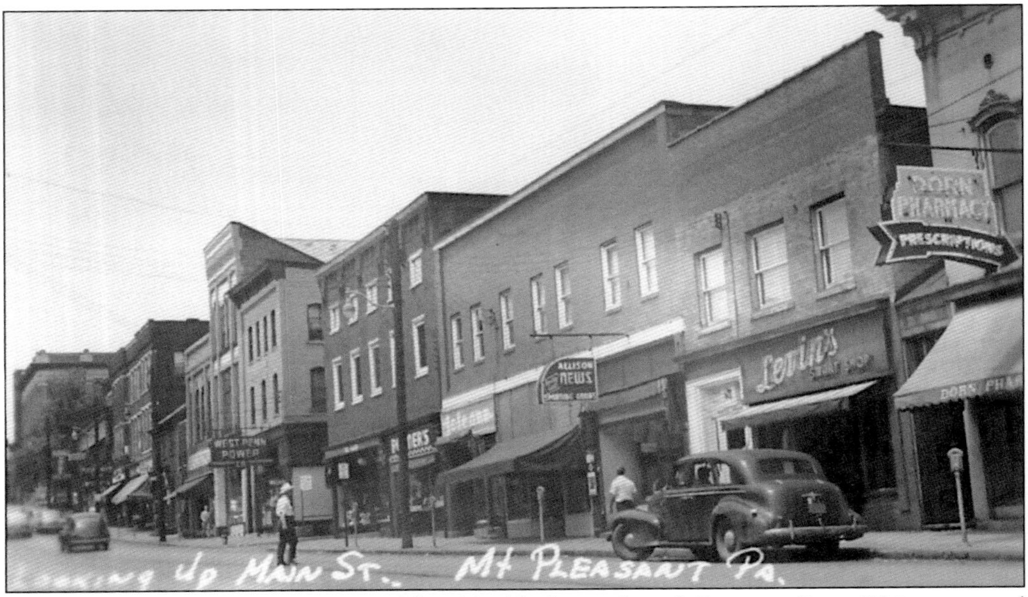

Allison News can be viewed in the middle of the block near Levin's Furniture Store. This newsstand provided a location to purchase newspapers, magazines, cards, and other stationery supplies. Utility bills could also be paid at this location. Storefronts visible in this vintage view of Main Street include West Penn Power, Jolene's, and Dorn Pharmacy. (Courtesy of Kathy Stanislaw.)

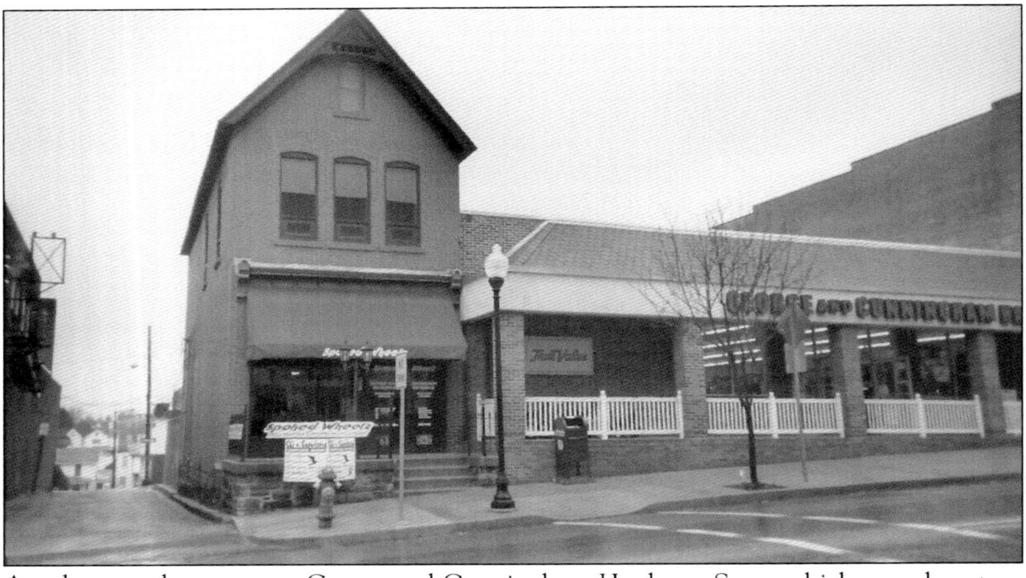

Another popular store was George and Cunningham Hardware Store, which served western Pennsylvania for at least 87 years, closing in 2011. This store was operated by two founding families and offered hardware supplies and gifts. This c. 2000 photograph shows the George and Cunningham building and Spoked Wheels, which specializes in biking equipment. (Courtesy of the Mount Pleasant Area Historical Society.)

At the lower end of Main Street near Shupe Street, Coppula's Meat Market and Grocery provided residents with many food supplies, home-baked goods, quality meats, and fresh cold watermelon. The friendliness of the owners lent much charm. Folks patronized the store because it had a long history of service to the community. Near the grocery store, one can see Coppula's bar, M.J. Rega Shoe Rebuilding, and the Village Restaurant and Hotel. (Courtesy of Vincent Coppula.)

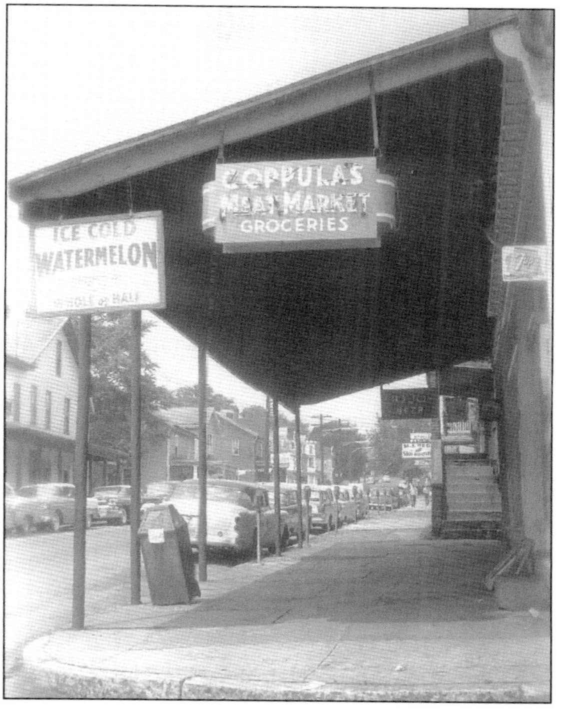

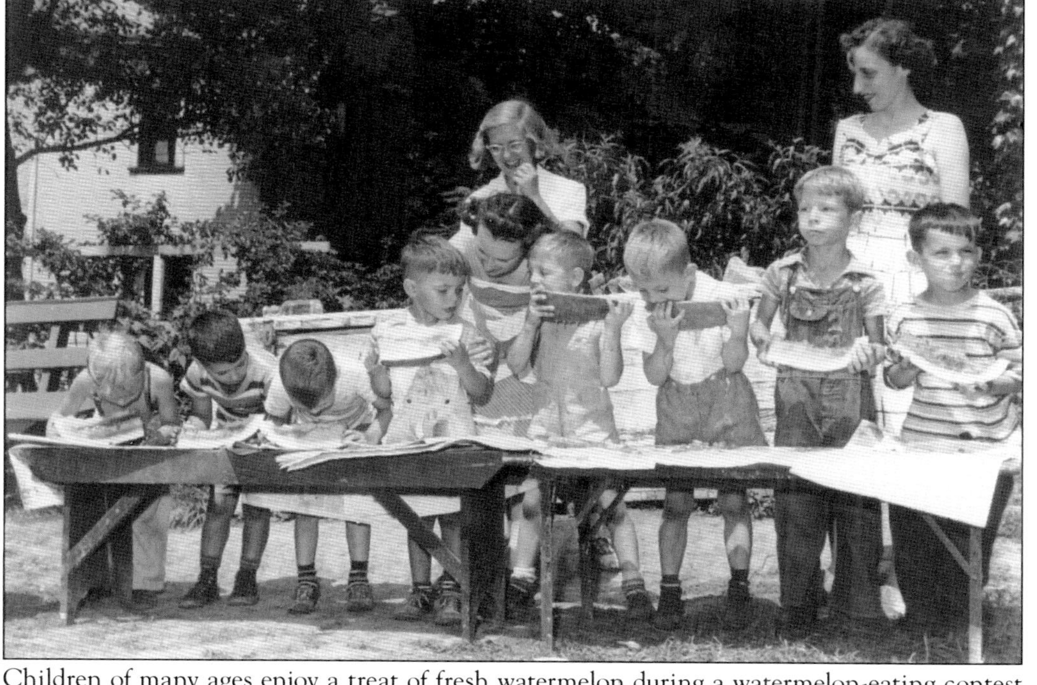

Children of many ages enjoy a treat of fresh watermelon during a watermelon-eating contest around 1950. This contest was one of the many festivities organized by the Mount Pleasant Parks and Recreation Committee during the summer months. (Courtesy of the Mount Pleasant Public Library Archives.)

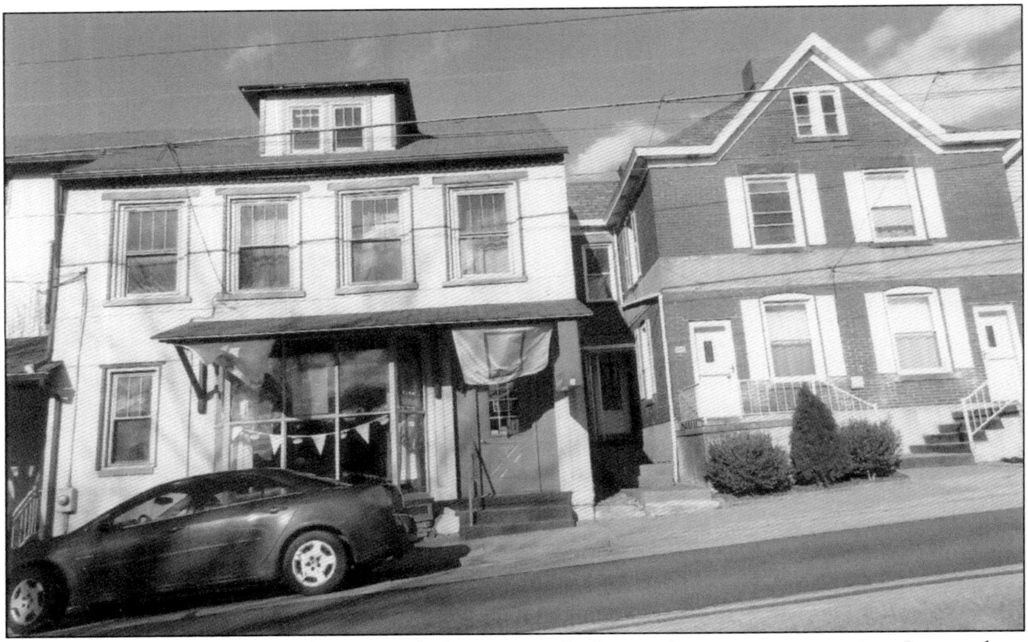

In 1870, Cooper's Harness Shop provided resources for horse-drawn transportation. Located on Main Street, this shop was later converted into a 2.5-story painted-brick apartment building. In 1920, windows and dormers were added near the roof. Presently, it houses Nationwide Insurance Company, which is owned and operated by David Stairs. (Courtesy of Bonnie Wilson.)

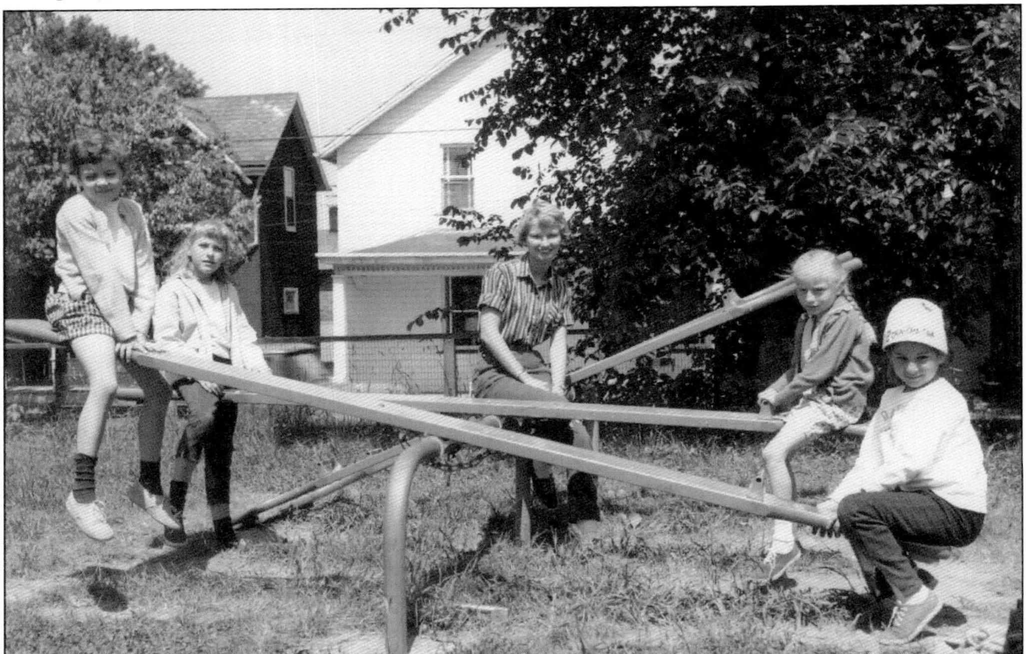

From the early days, children enjoyed the simple pleasures at Frick Park, such as playing on a seesaw and spending the day with friends. (Courtesy of the Mount Pleasant Public Library Archives.)

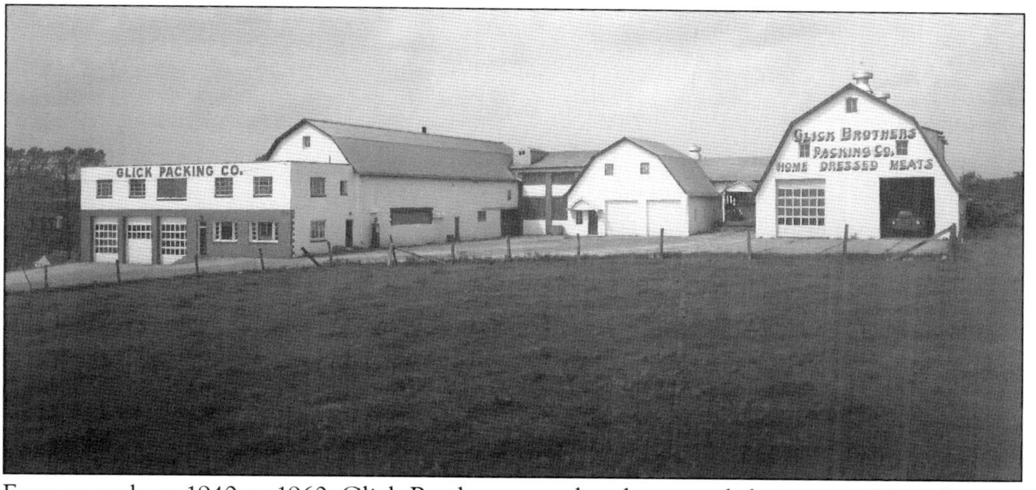

From as early as 1940 to 1960, Glick Brothers owned and operated the meatpacking plant on Route 31 just west of Mount Pleasant Borough. The three farms bordering the town provided doorstep delivery of milk from the Maple Glen Dairy from the 1930s to the 1960s. In the pre-tractor era of farming, there was an active workhorse trade to supply the farm communities. For more than 75 years, Glick Brothers actively participated in the Mount Pleasant Main Street economy, supplying merchants like Marne's and Devorak's markets with quality home dressed meats and Holiday Brand processed meats. The Glick family owned and leased the Main Street properties occupied by the National Hotel, Pennsylvania State Store, the Hub, and Allison's News. (Courtesy of Richard Glick.)

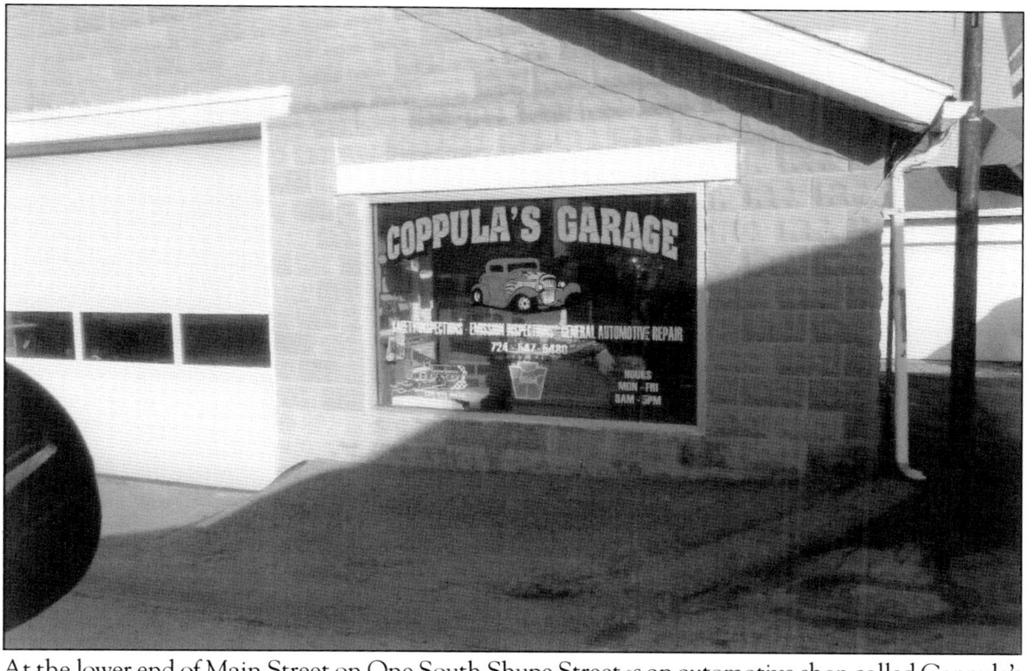

At the lower end of Main Street on One South Shupe Street is an automotive shop called Coppula's Garage, which continues to deliver auto maintenance, repair service, and state inspections to car owners. Under the ownership of Jim Sebek, Coppula's Garage continues to thrive today. (Courtesy of Nancy Sebek.)

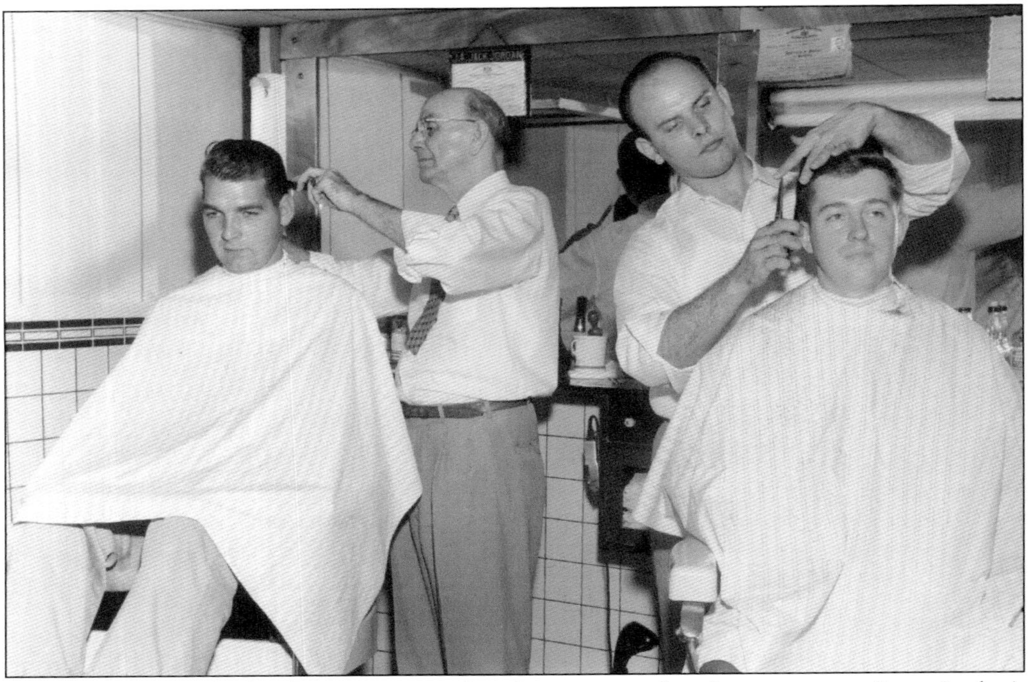

During the 1950s, barbershops were popular places to socialize for many men. From Jordan's Barber Shop to Jerry Rega's Barber Shop, to name just a couple, one could find expert haircutters fashioning men for their daily work. Here, two men are getting their hair trimmed at Jordan's Barber Shop. One could find Jerry Rega and Nick Etze working at Jerry Rega's Barber Shop on Smithfield Street. In addition to the haircut, Jerry Rega would serenade patrons with violin songs. (Courtesy of the Mount Pleasant Public Library Archives.)

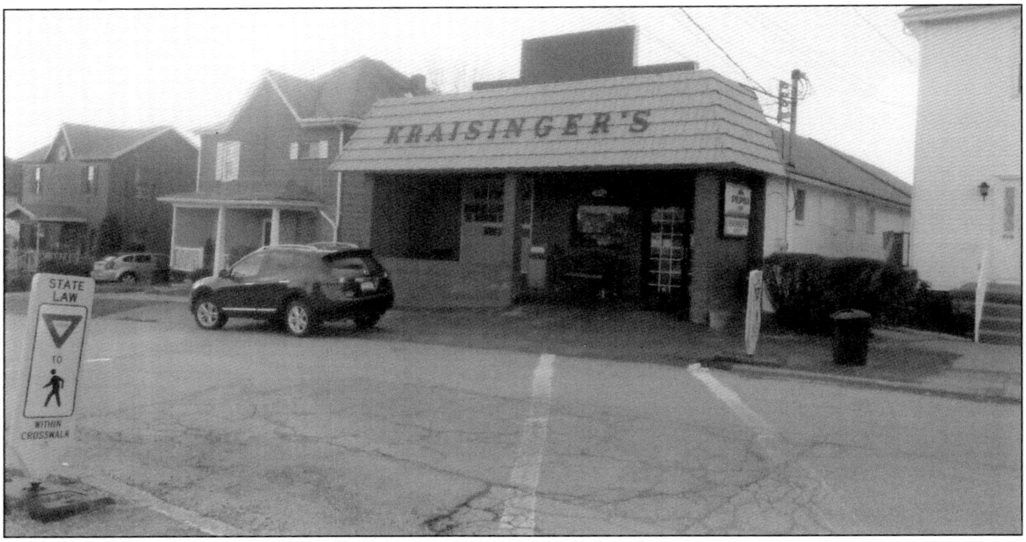

Located at 122 South Quarry Street, Kraisinger's Market is a local grocery store with a long history of service to the community. This grocery store is well noted for delicious deli foods and quality smoked meats. Most popular is its wide range of daily meal specialties, which have been a favorite of the community since 1937. (Courtesy of Nancy Sebek.)

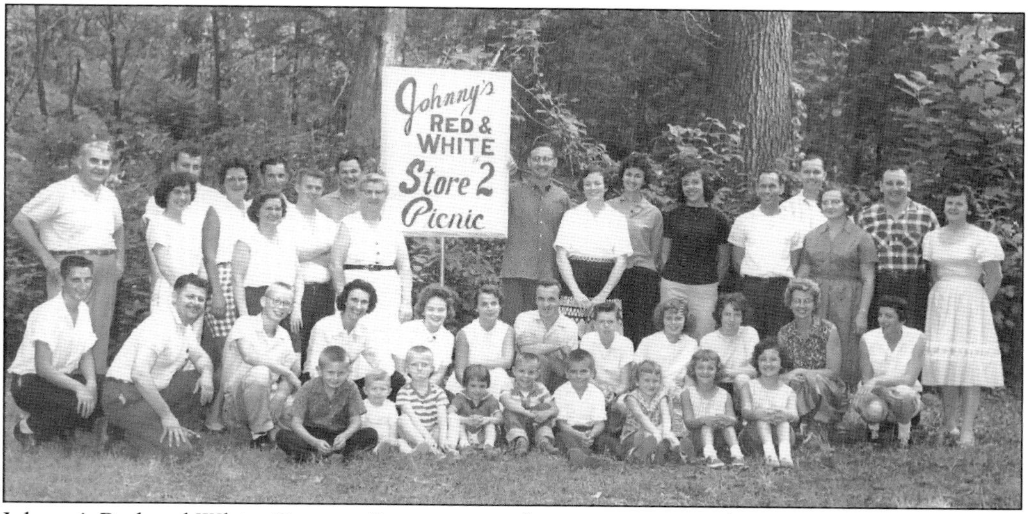

Johnny's Red and White Grocery Store grew as the community got larger. John Krystyniak and his father started with a small, local grocery store on Shupe Street and expanded to the thriving store in 1972. Many workers and their families gathered for their annual picnic. In the photograph above, John and his wife, Margaret, can be seen to the right of the sign titled "Johnny's Red & White Store 2 Picnic." Pictured below are some of the many people who enjoyed shopping at Johnny's for a wide variety of items, including bread goods, food mixers, heaters, and pet supplies. (Both photographs courtesy of Margaret Krystyniak and Theresa Gerson.)

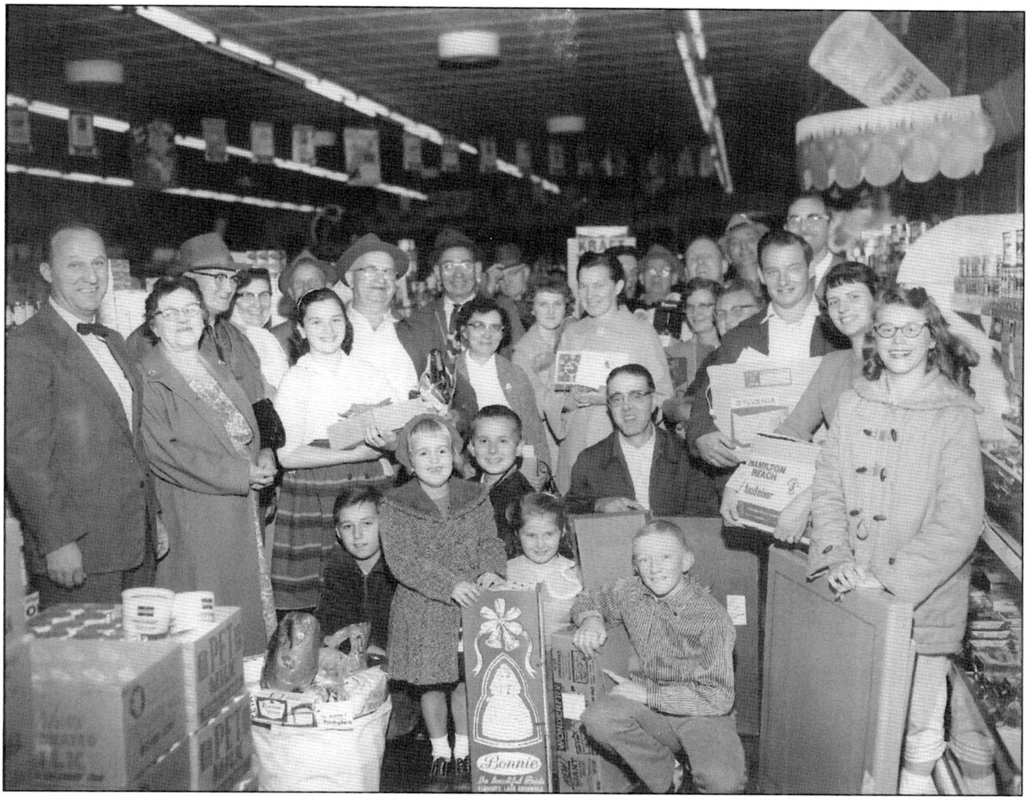

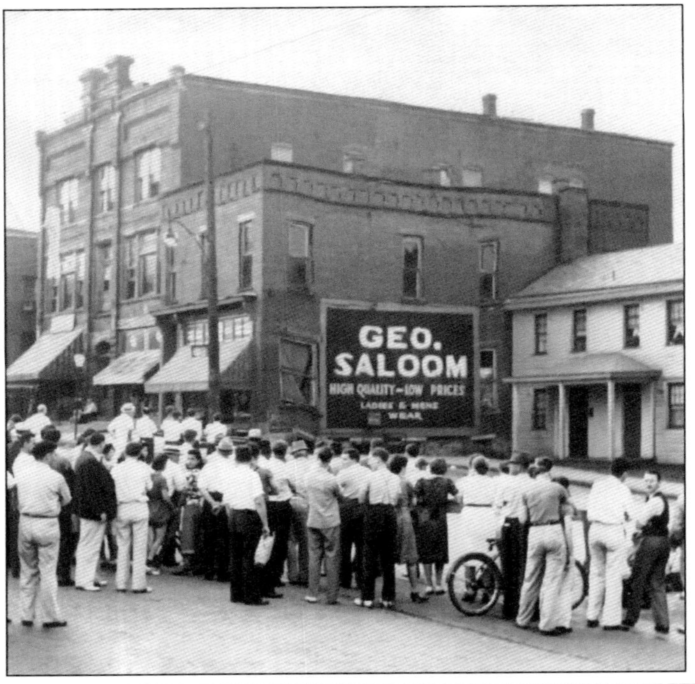

A prominent store in the center of town is the George Saloom Department Store. In the early 1940s, structural damage occurred during renovations to change the entrance from a step-up entry to ground level. The ground subsidence caused excitement in town, resulting in this photograph in the *Mount Pleasant Journal*. (Courtesy of Eugene Saloom.)

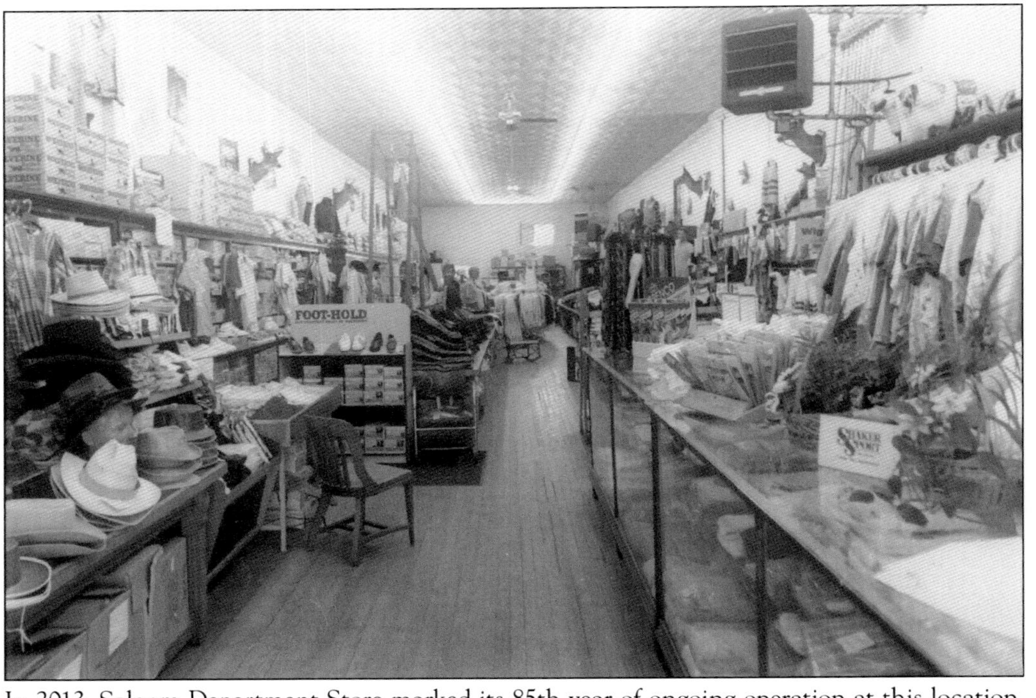

In 2013, Saloom Department Store marked its 85th year of ongoing operation at this location. This makes the store one of the oldest continuous businesses in the town of Mount Pleasant. George's daughter Charlotte and her husband, Leon Mowry, are the current proprietors. This store features clothing items—such as hats, shoes, and shirts—sporting goods, and an indoor archery range. (Courtesy of Debbie Brehun.)

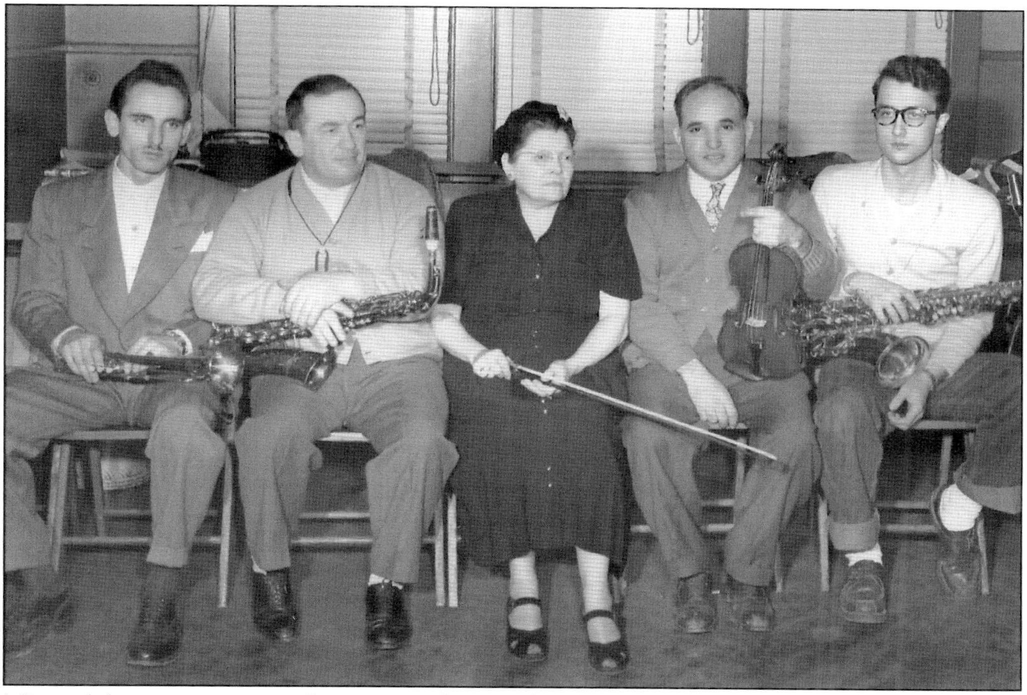

Minstrel shows were a musical treat, providing much entertainment in Ramsay Auditorium during the mid-20th century. Featured in the photograph above with their instruments are, from left to right, C. Herschberger (trumpet), H. Caruso (saxophone), Mrs. Semmey (director), J. Rega (violin), and R. Cost (saxophone). Music also flourished in family enclaves including Jerry Rega (violin), George Pologruto (mandolin), and Patsy Rega (bass tub). Another forerunner of musical history was George D'Amato, who still plays Christian and Oldies music at festivals and senior citizen homes. In the photograph below, the New Romanos include Mike, Terri, and their father, the group's founder, Louis Rega. (Above, courtesy of Mary Agnes Spinella and Gerri Spinella; below, courtesy of Louis Rega and Michael Rega.)

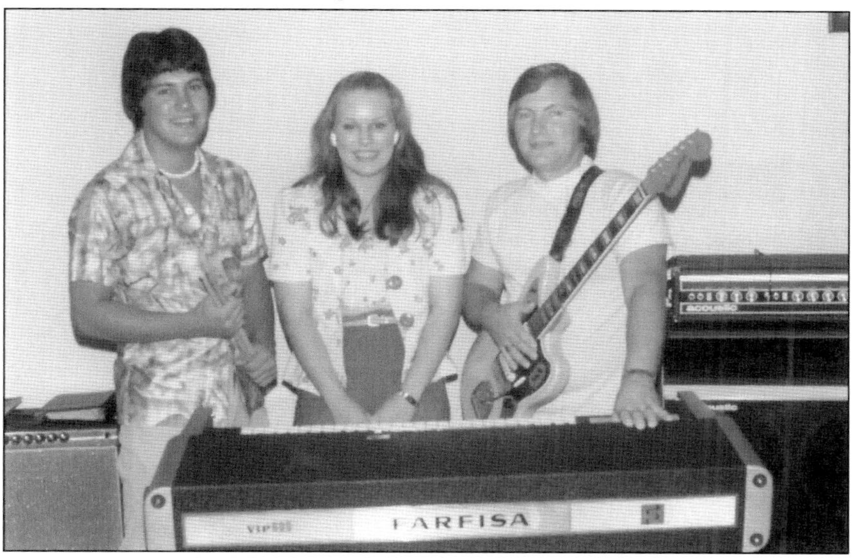

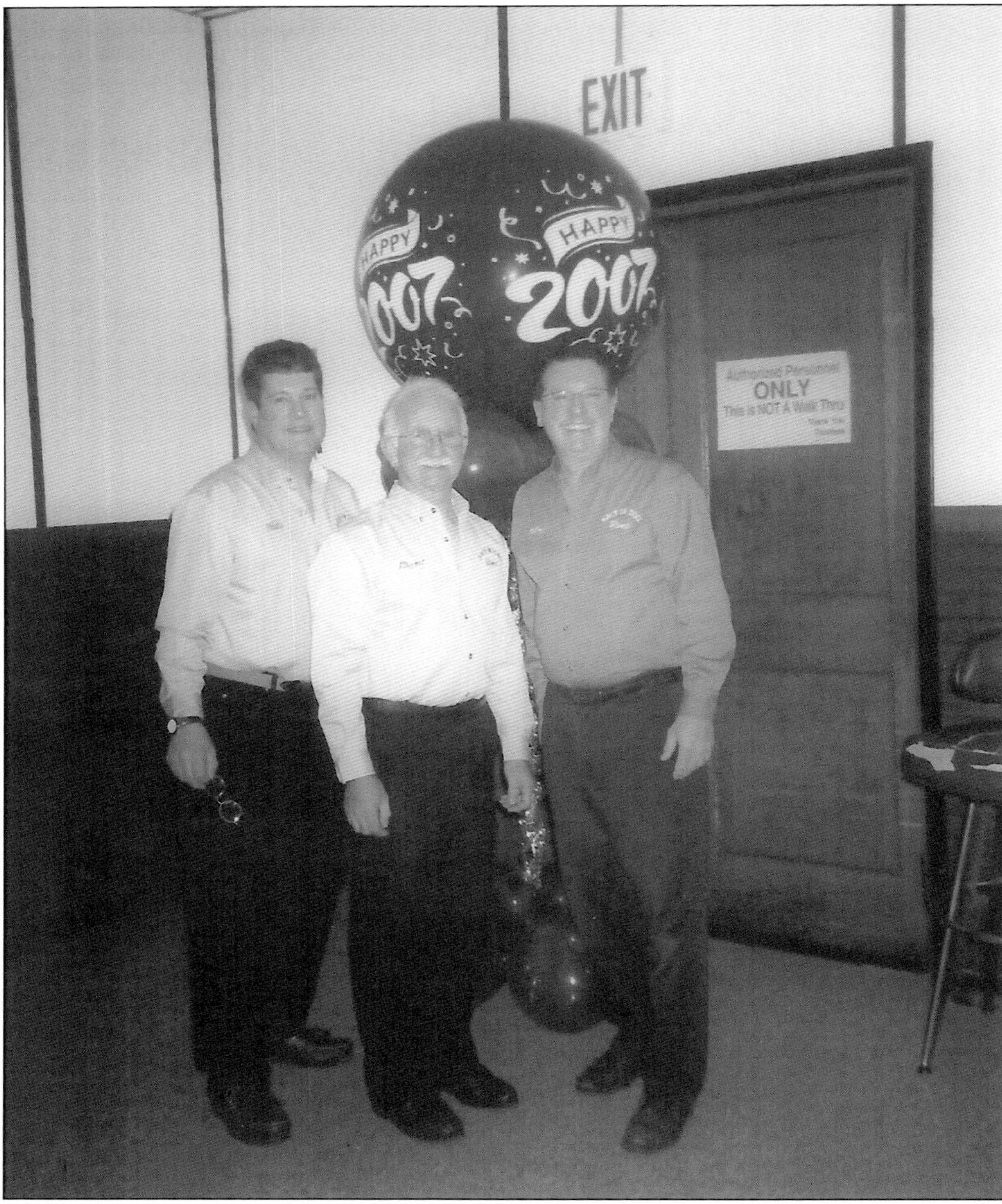

The Back in Time Band features, from left to right, musicians Mike Rega, Ron DiFilippo, and Paul "T-Bird" Kettren. The Ron DiFilippo family formed the Derons Band and Strawberry Hill Band, who performed oldies and traditional Italian music. The Herman Caruso family specialized in the clarinet, and the Vince and Mike Coppula family played the sax, bass, guitar, and drums. Panfield J. DiNicola played the accordion and the organ. Eddie and John Smartnick, who played the accordion, performed in polka bands. Frances Spinelli made her musical mark as a piano player during the silent movies and as an organist at Transfiguration Church. Frances (Rega) Spinelli (piano) and Jerry Rega (violin) were a popular brother-and-sister musical talent. Many family musicians flourished in sharing their artistic abilities. (Courtesy of Louis Rega and Michael Rega.)

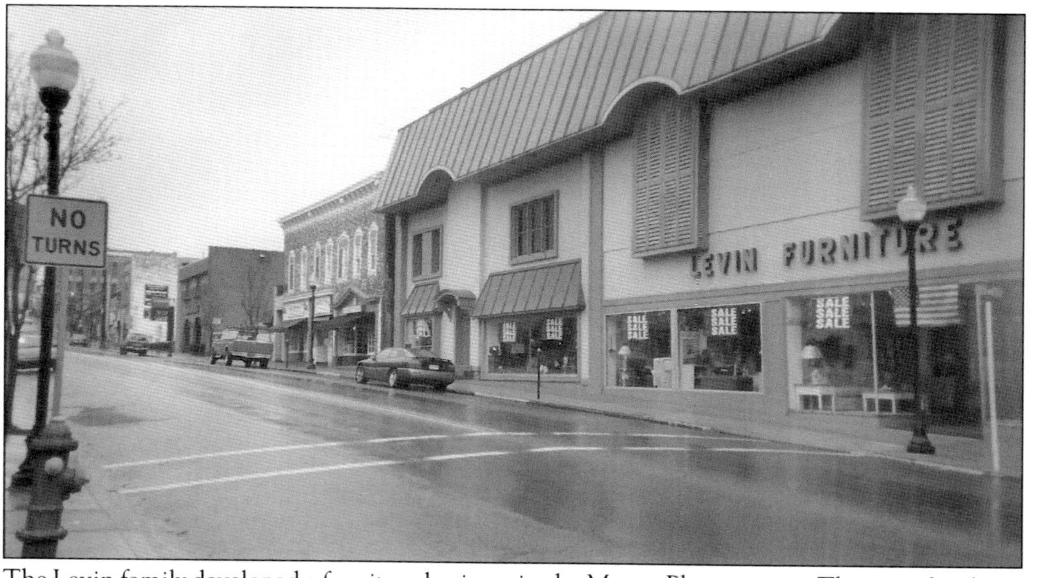

The Levin family developed a furniture business in the Mount Pleasant area. This store has been a landmark for over 80 years. Levin Furniture later expanded its business into the surrounding Pittsburgh area. The family has also played a prominent place in serving the community. (Courtesy of Nancy Sebek.)

Nino's Restaurant, located at 546 Three Mile Hill Road, is a converted farmhouse and former speakeasy. Nino Barsotti has featured seasonal Italian cuisine and an intimate setting since 1971. Sunday brunches have been popular throughout the years. Elizabeth Barsotti, the daughter of Nino and Linda Barsotti, now manages this establishment and has added a wonderful and engaging gift shop. (Courtesy of the Mount Pleasant Public Library Archives.)

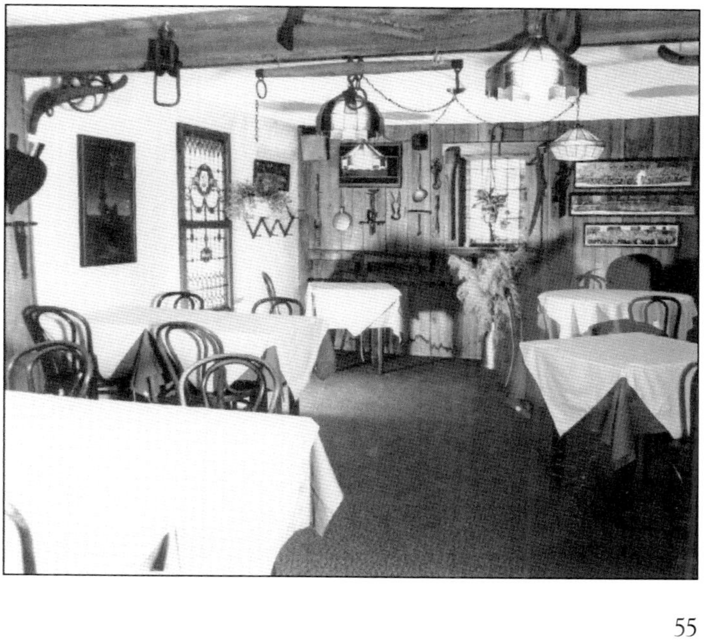

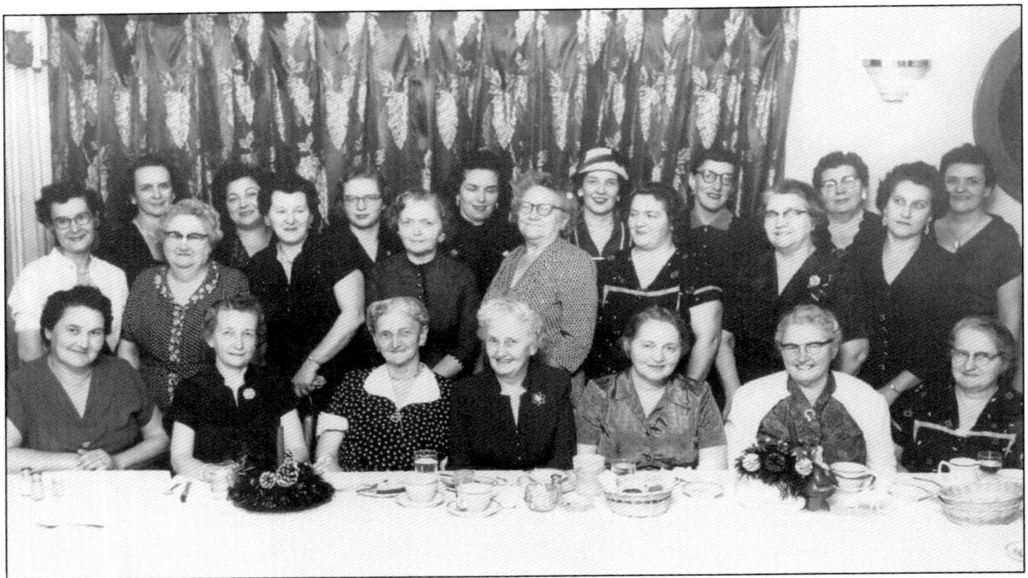

Community Aid Society of Bridgeport women provided an important service. These women cared for the honor roll, which listed the men and women who served in the military. Included in this photograph taken on December 21, 1956, are Mary Carlton, Missouri Clausner, Jessie Minick, Victoria Thomas, Anna Jones, Laura Slonecker, Mary Angle, Betty Zabrobsky, Evelyn Barnhart, Mazie Morgan, Jane Keefer, Emma Snyder, Margaret Bollinger, Marie Jones, Worene Minick, Louise Clausner, ? Carlton, Bonnie Clausner, Jessie Gowton, and Mildred Davis. (Courtesy of the Mount Pleasant Public Library Archives.)

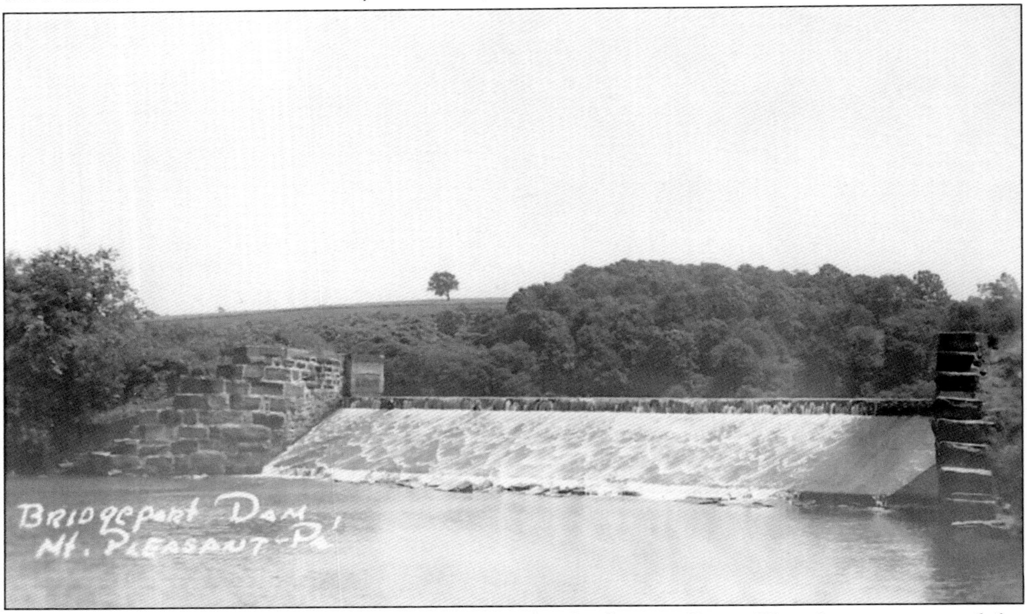

A popular destination for outdoor enjoyment is the Bridgeport Dam. This dam is a part of the Jacobs Creek flood control system and is popular with anglers of all ages. In the summertime, residents enjoy picnics and swimming. In 2014, a new bridge was built to cross Jacobs Creek below the falls area. (Courtesy of the Mount Pleasant Public Library Archives.)

All communities have their eccentrics. John Borchin was one such individual who joined Mount Pleasant's festivities from Labor Day to the Fourth of July. Here, he is dressed in prison garb with a sign that states, "Marked for Life!" Borchin demonstrated for a variety of causes and could often be found exercising his freedom of speech on street corners. (Courtesy of Mount Pleasant Public Library Archives.)

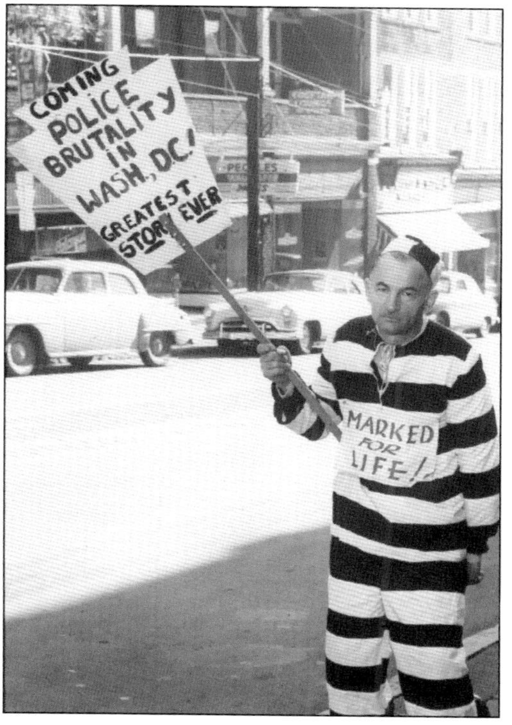

Contrasting this modern-day activism was the promotion of the Labor Day activities. From early history to modern time, residents promoted their allegiance for many causes. This included men and women proudly marching for the local union of American Flint Glass Workers Union (AFGWU), Branch No. 537. (Courtesy of the Mount Pleasant Public Library Archives.)

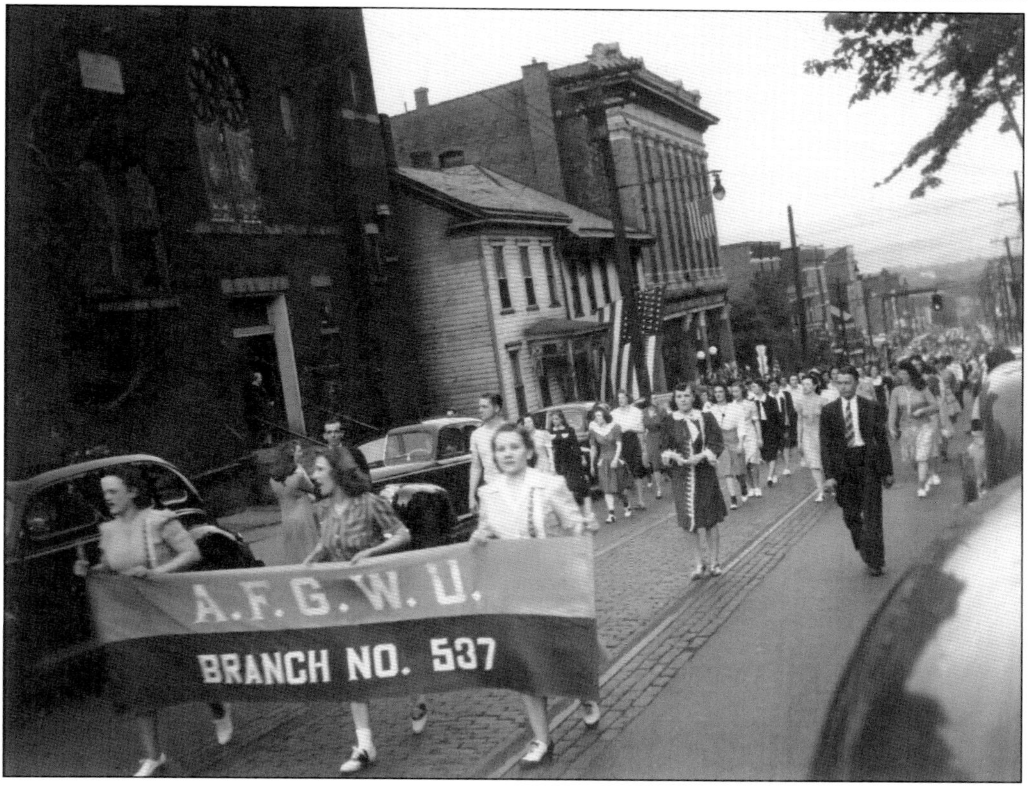

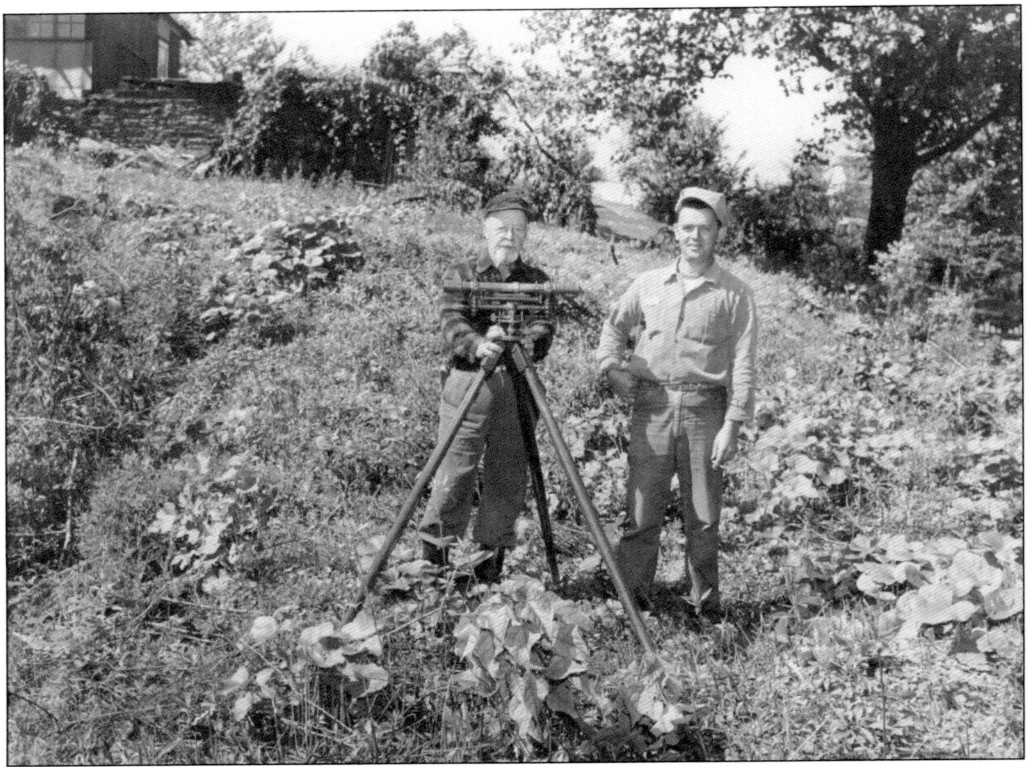

Transportation is important to a growing community. Depicted above are the surveyors from D.R. Wolkinshaw who provided resources for the Smithfield extension in 1956. (Courtesy of the Mount Pleasant Public Library Archives.)

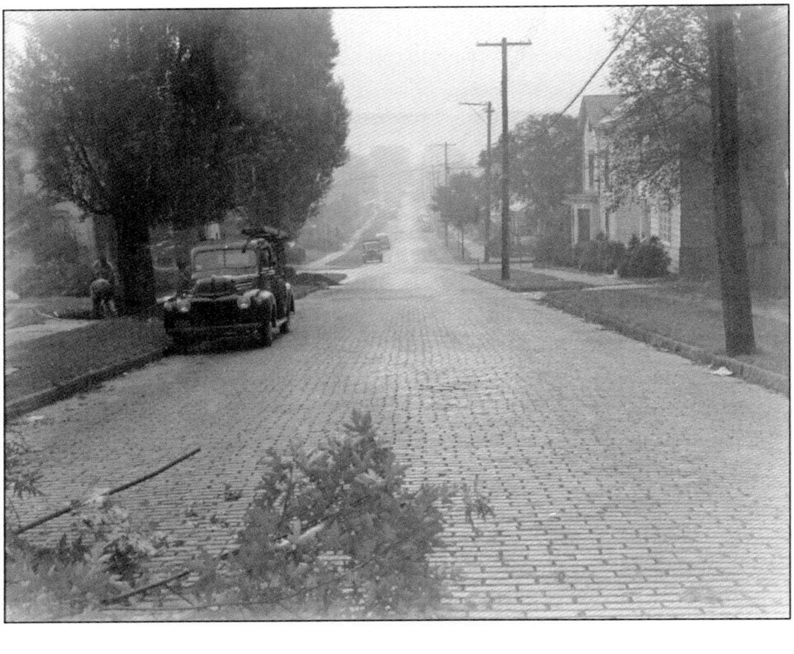

The brick-lined surface of Washington Street from the 1940s would be later transformed with the modern blacktop paving that still serves the community today. (Courtesy of the Mount Pleasant Public Library Archives.)

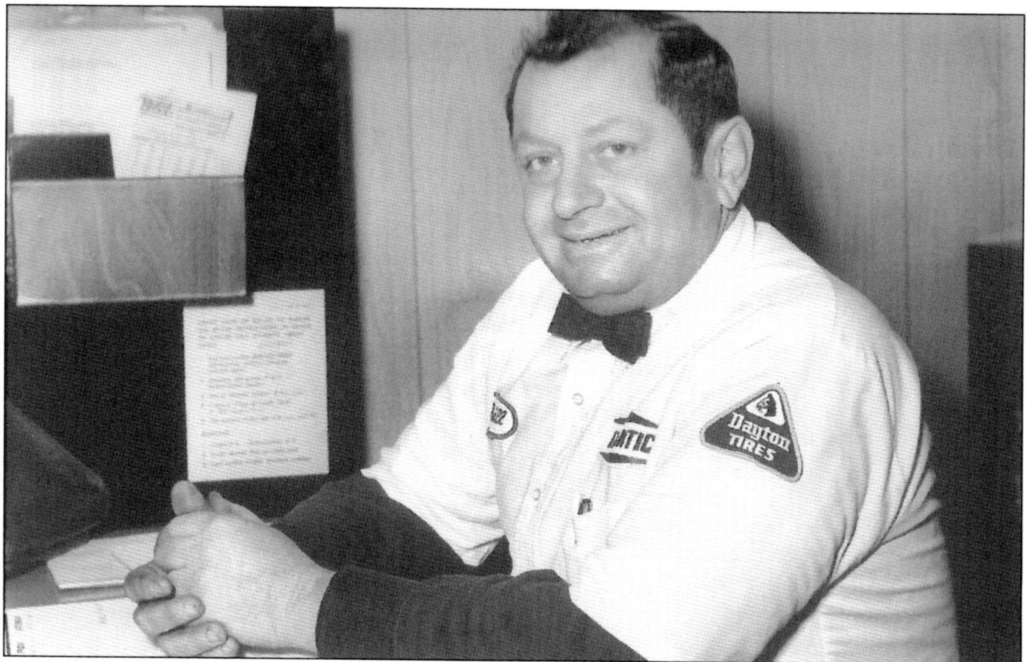

William Potoka presided as mayor of Mount Pleasant Borough for 16 years. He was the last school-board president of Ramsay High School and a member of the chamber of commerce, the bicentennial committee, and the fire department's rescue squad. Potoka also led a group that supported Iranian hostage Jerry Miele and was honored as Citizen of the Year in 1983. (Courtesy of Sandy Potoka Coppula and William Potoka Jr.)

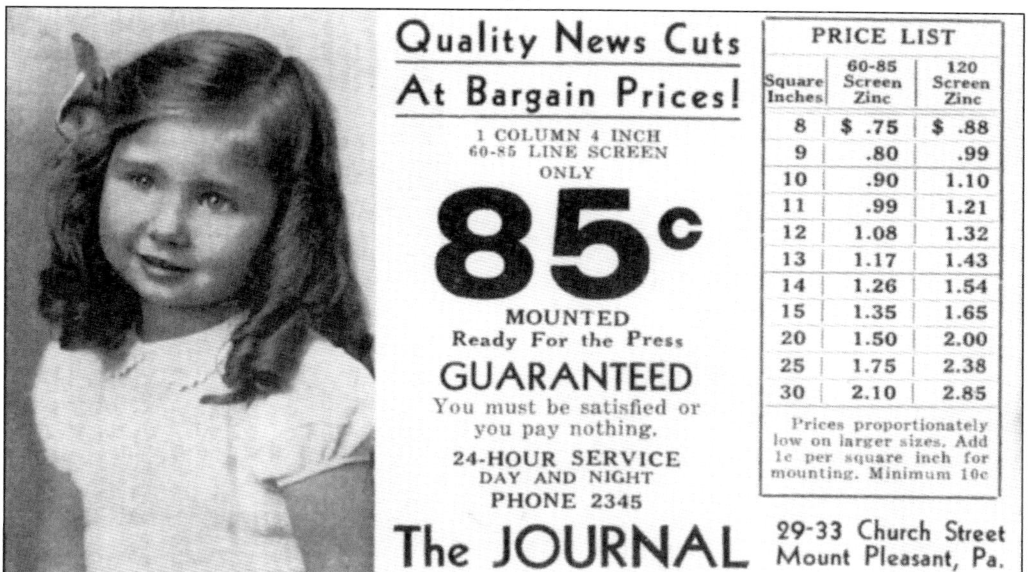

Since the late 1870s, the *Mount Pleasant Journal* has provided news for the community. Based on this ad, the cost for a one-column four-inch mounted section in the paper was 85¢. Additional prices per square inch are located on right side of the ad. The office is now part of Trib Total Media. (Courtesy of the *Mount Pleasant Journal*.)

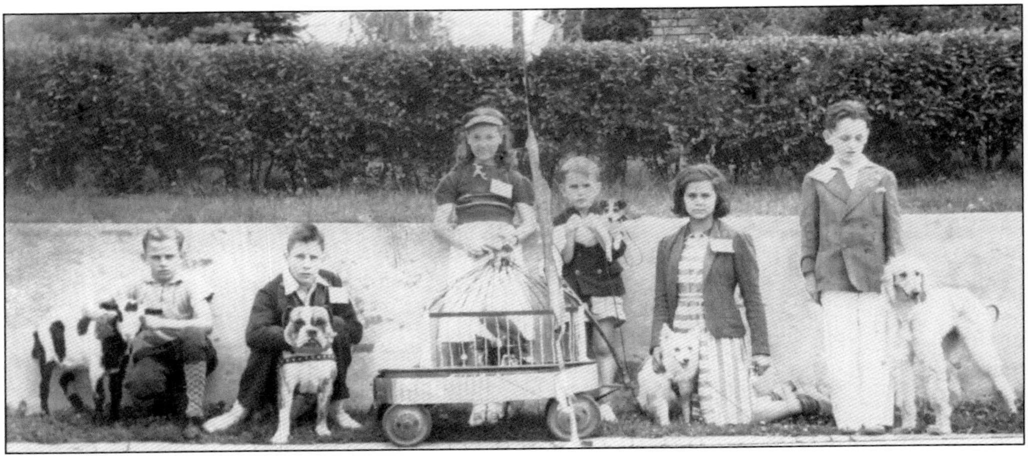

A community thrives when adults and children gather for its many local festivities. One of the most popular in Mount Pleasant was the annual Fourth of July celebration depicted in both photographs. This bonding experience for the community's youngsters has enabled them to show their talents and their appreciation for what they hold dear. The pet parade was popular. Here, children hold some of their favorite pets, including a goat! From the youngest to the oldest child, civic pride was always part of this display. In the photograph below, young boys compete in the annual bicycle race. Their determined faces show their enthusiasm for the event. (Courtesy of the Mount Pleasant Public Library Archives.)

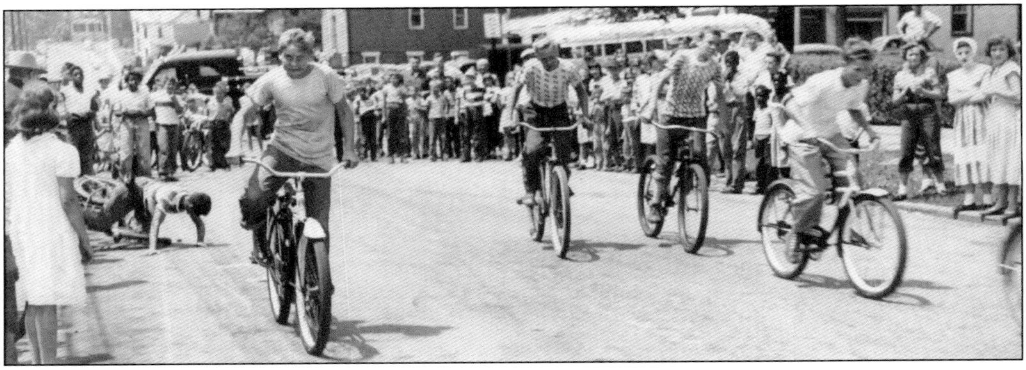

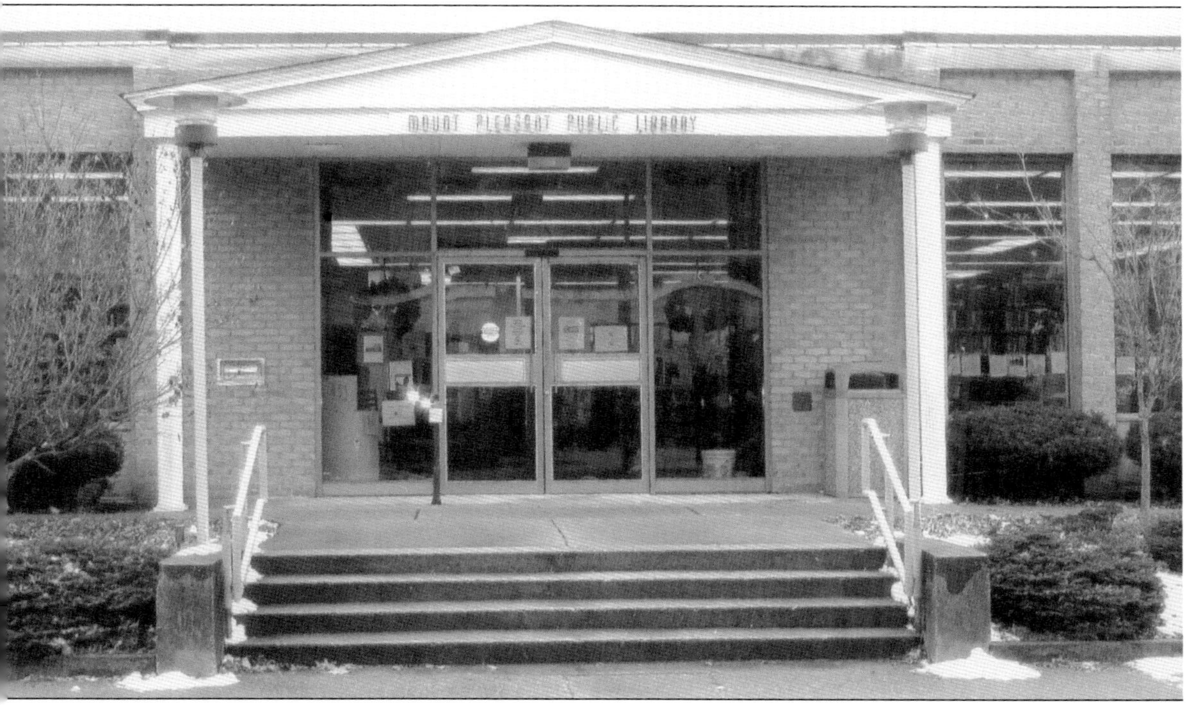

Learning is cultivated through many venues. The Mount Pleasant Public Library holds learning activities for children and writing experiences and book discussions for young and older adults. These engaging opportunities offer an experience to explore different areas of personal interest. Featured artists and speakers discuss topics ranging from invasive species to historical artifacts throughout the year. Friends of the Library also offer many book sales and other fundraisers in order to help all residents reach their reading and learning potential. (Courtesy of Nancy Sebek.)

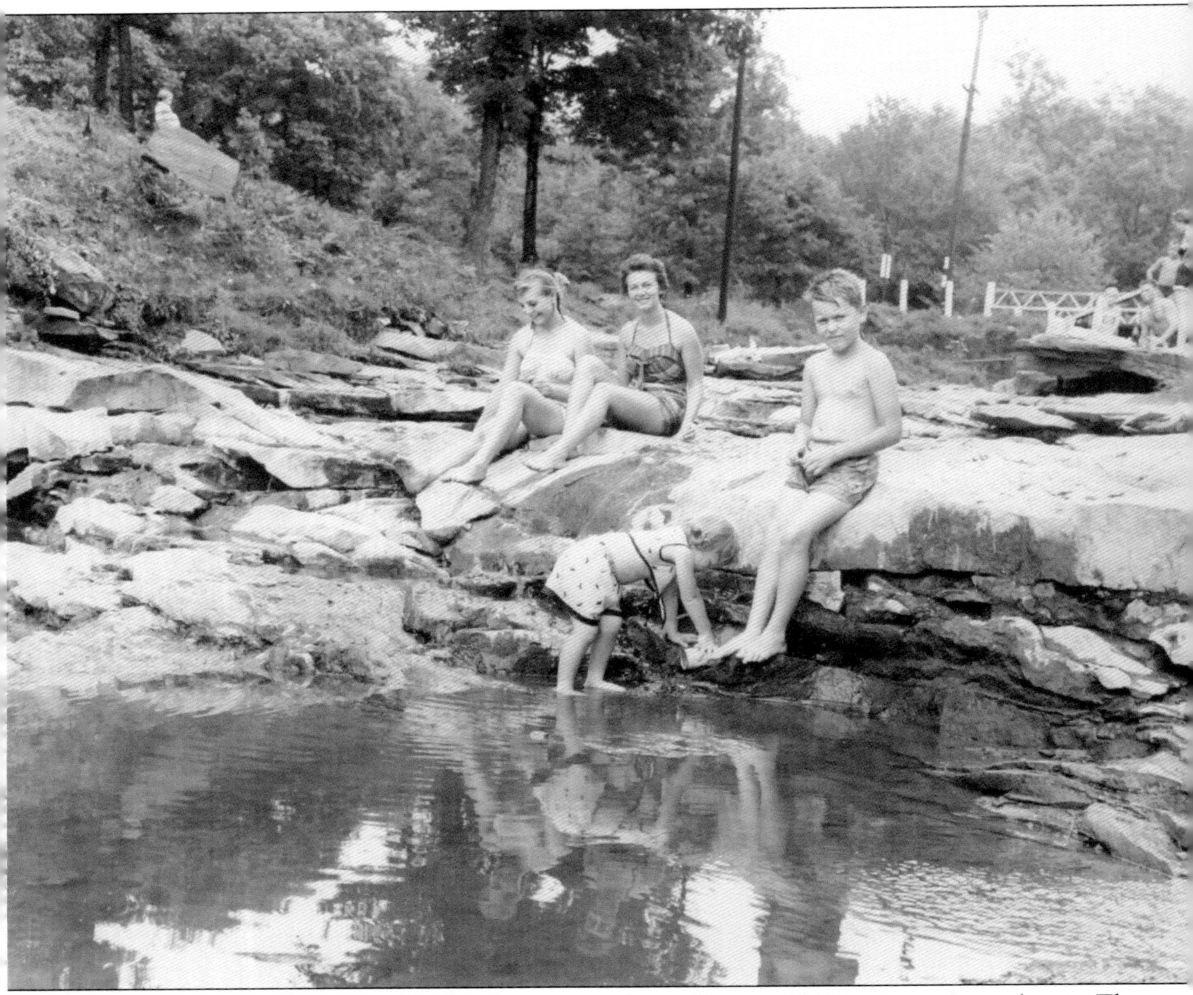

A favorite 1960 hangout of the local young people was Freeman Falls in Acme Pennsylvania. The falls had many huge rocks, which were great for climbing, exploring, and picnicking. Many families also came to wade, swim, or fish. The Mount Pleasant area features many engaging opportunities for visitors and locals alike, with entertainment, shopping, learning, and personal development. Most importantly, Mount Pleasant engenders a community feeling of being home. (Courtesy of the Mount Pleasant Public Library Archives.)

Three

Celebrating Mount Pleasant Pride

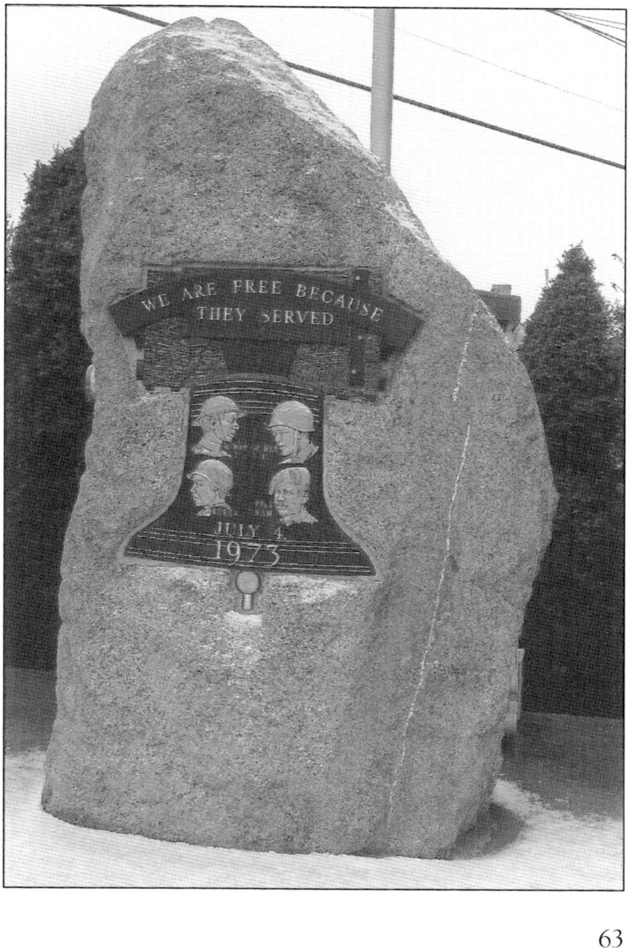

Mount Pleasant pride was built on a foundation of serving others in the community. Whether these individuals were military, athletes, educators, or community leaders, residents are indebted to them. Their attributes have left an indelible mark on the community. On July 4, 1973, this granite memorial stone commemorating soldiers was erected at Veterans Park. (Courtesy of Rose Eckman.)

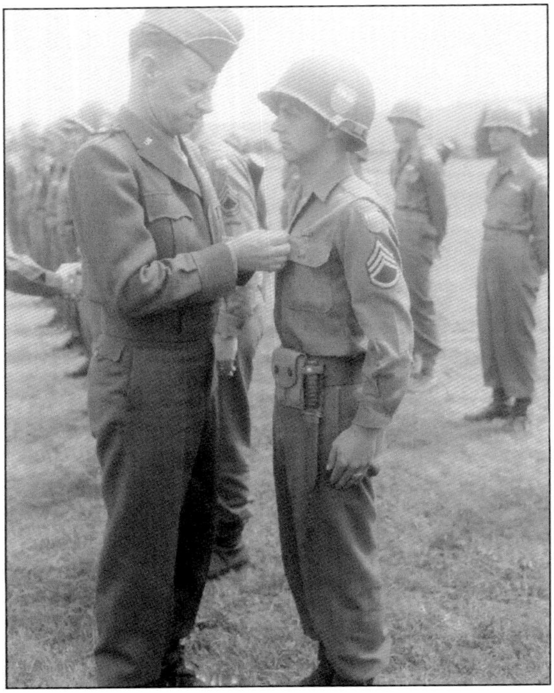

While serving in the Army in Germany during World War II, Sgt. William R. Barnhart, a Mount Pleasant resident, receives the Bronze Star from Brig. Gen. John B. Murphy for valor in the field on June 16, 1945. (Courtesy of the *Mount Pleasant Journal.*)

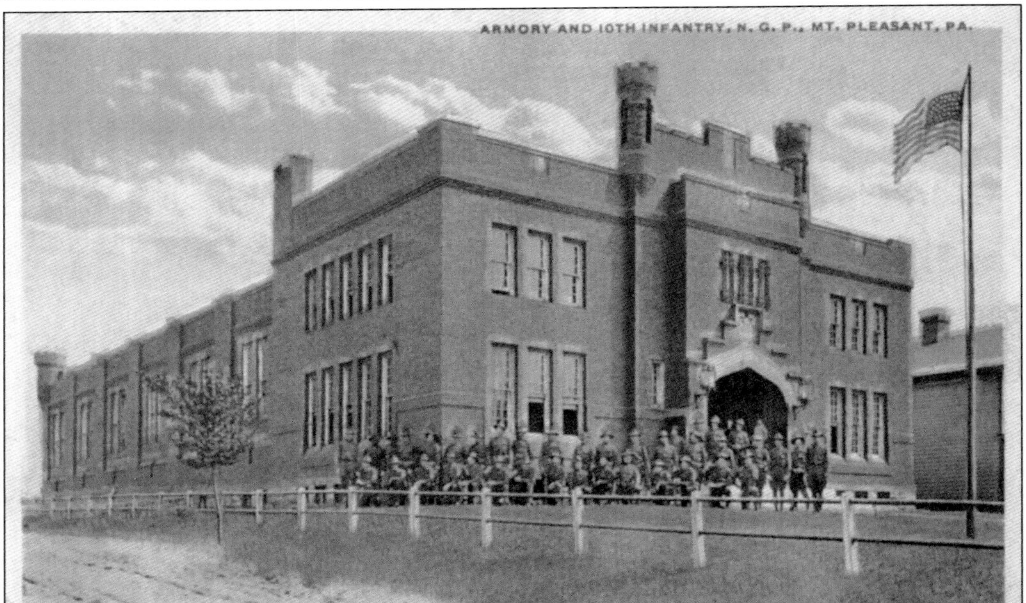

The Mount Pleasant Armory housed Company E of the 10th Infantry National Guard of Pennsylvania, which was formed pursuant to Special Order No. 96 on November 18, 1873. In 1906, the armory was a two-story, T-shaped brick building, built in the Romanesque style. It had a flat roof over the administrative section and a gambrel roof over the drill hall. It was added to the National Register of Historic Places in 1989. The armory was demolished in 1996. (Courtesy of the Mount Pleasant Area Historical Society.)

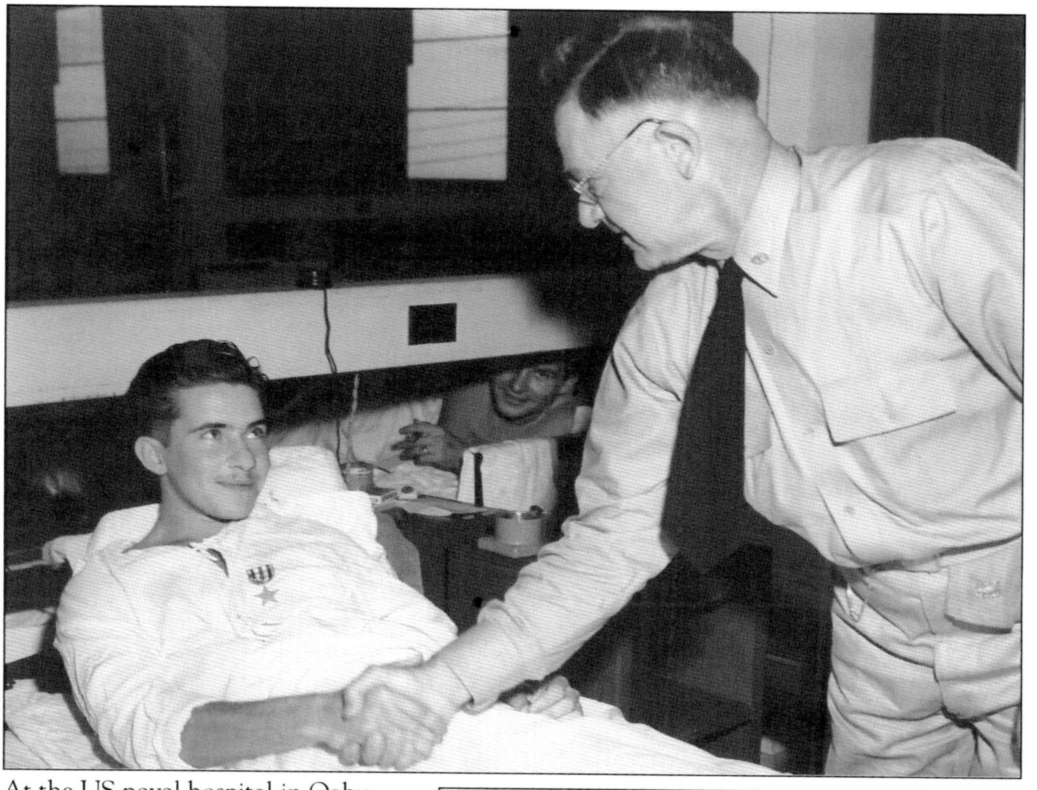

At the US naval hospital in Oahu, Hawaii, Pfc. Raymond Tedrow of Mount Pleasant receives the Silver Star Award from Capt. R.M. Lhanon, LMC USMP. (Courtesy of the Mount Pleasant Public Library Archives.)

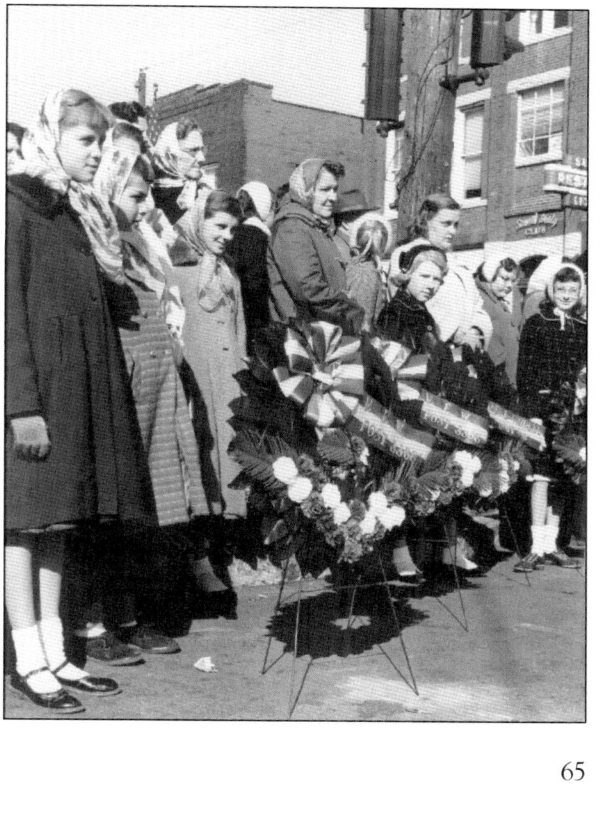

The Ladies Auxiliary from the Mount Pleasant VFW Post No. 3368 lay wreaths around the base of *The Doughboy* on a cold, blustery Armistice Day, November 11, around 1950. The Sons of Italy Club and Sann's Restaurant are visible on the right. (Courtesy of the Mount Pleasant Public Library Archives.)

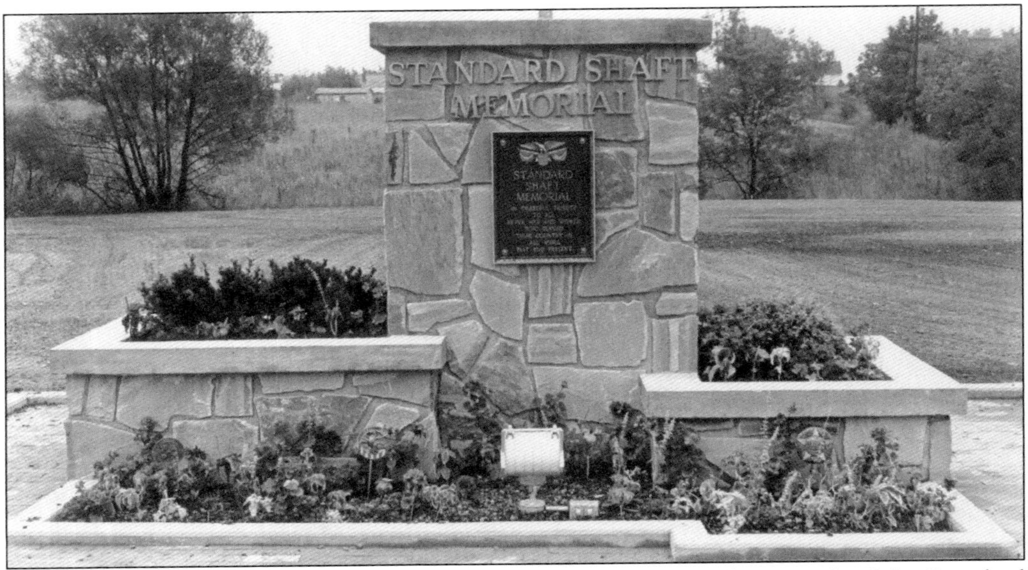

The bronze and stone Standard Shaft Memorial can be found on the grounds of the Standard Shaft Citizens Club. The inscription reads as follows: "In grateful tribute to all brave men and women who served their country in all wars past and present." (Courtesy of the Mount Pleasant Public Library Archives.)

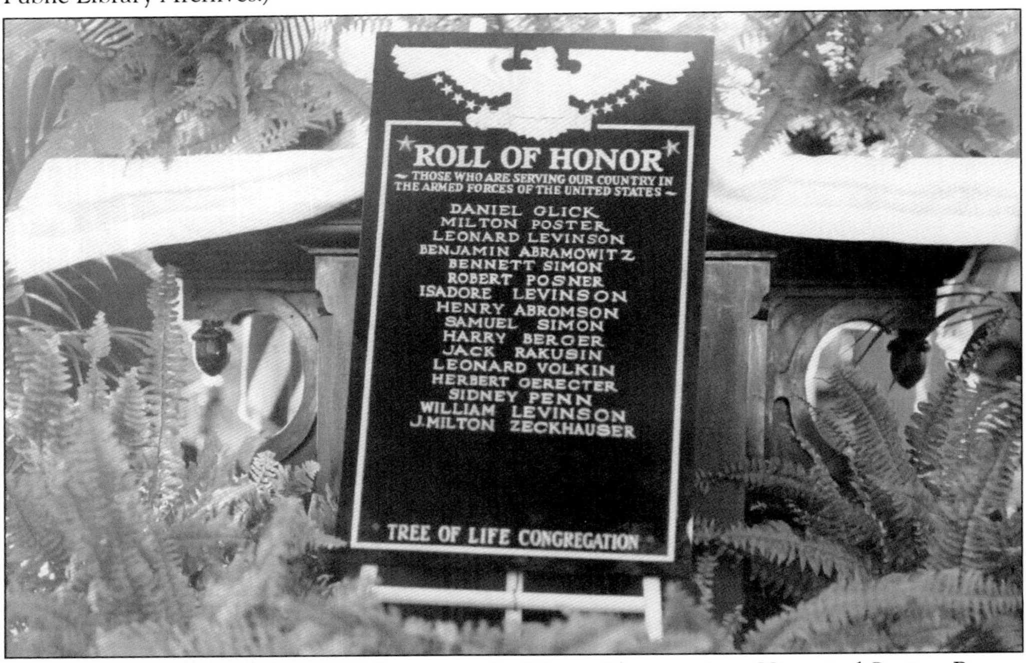

The Tree of Life Roll of Honor can be seen at the Mount Pleasant Area Historical Society Room. The memorial honors Jewish veterans who served in the armed forces of the United States. They are Daniel Glick, Milton Poster, Leonard Levinson, Benjamin Abramowitz, Bennett Simon, Robert Posner, Isadore Levinson, Henry Abromson, Samuel Simon, Harry Berger, Jack Rakusin, Leonard Volkin, Herbert Gerecter, Sidney Penn, William Levinson, and Milton Zeckhauser. (Courtesy of the Mount Pleasant Public Library Archives.)

Brig. Gen. William G. Walker presents Col. Alfred Dennison of Mount Pleasant with the Legion of Merit. He was recognized for his actions following the attack on Pearl Harbor. Dennison saved gasoline, rubber, and labor in Hawaii. Colonel Dennison was promoted to the rank of lieutenant colonel in 1944 in Washington, DC. (Courtesy of the Mount Pleasant Public Library Archives.)

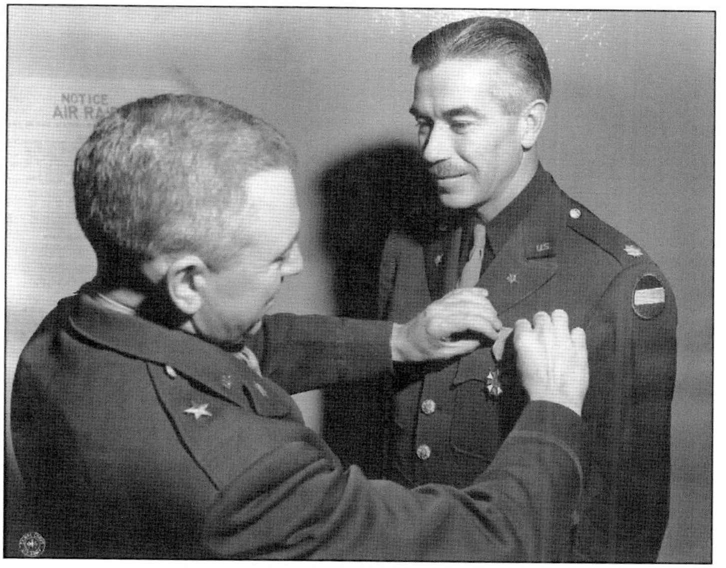

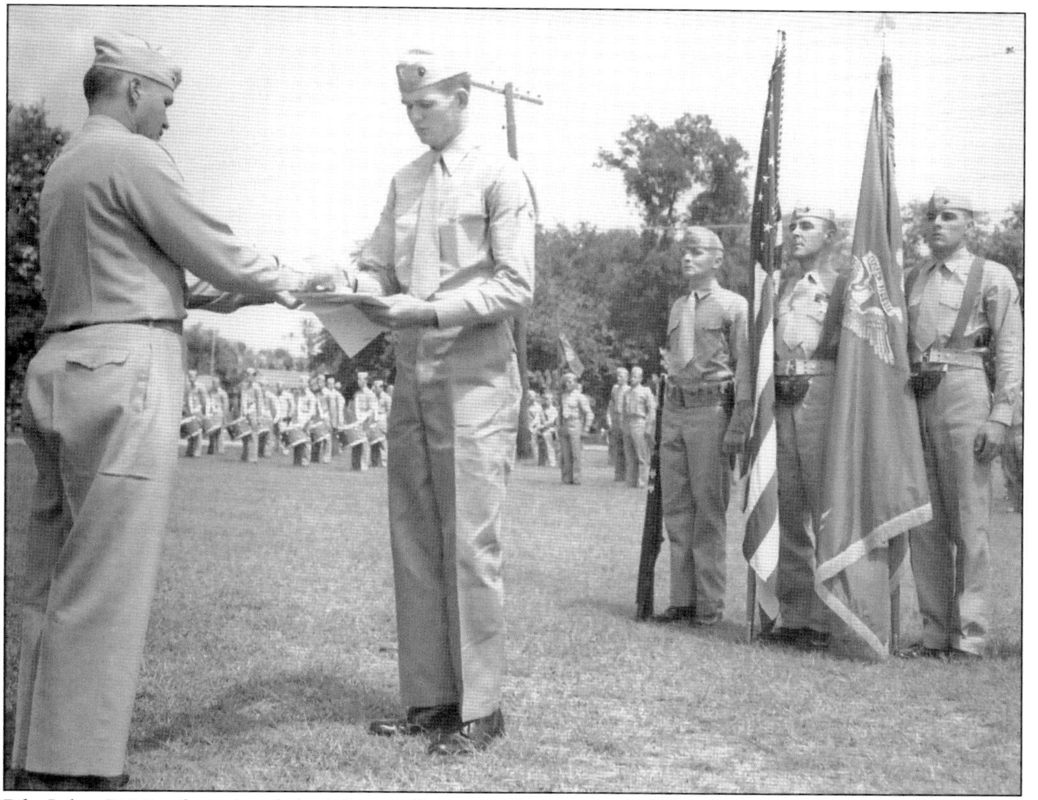

Pfc. John P. Murtha joined the Marine Corps and was awarded the American Spirit Honor Medal for displaying outstanding leadership qualities during training in 1953. He became a drill instructor at Parris Island and was selected for Officer Candidate School at Quantico, Virginia. Murtha represented Pennsylvania's 12th Congressional District in the US House of Representatives from 1974 to 2010. (Courtesy of the Mount Pleasant Public Library Archives.)

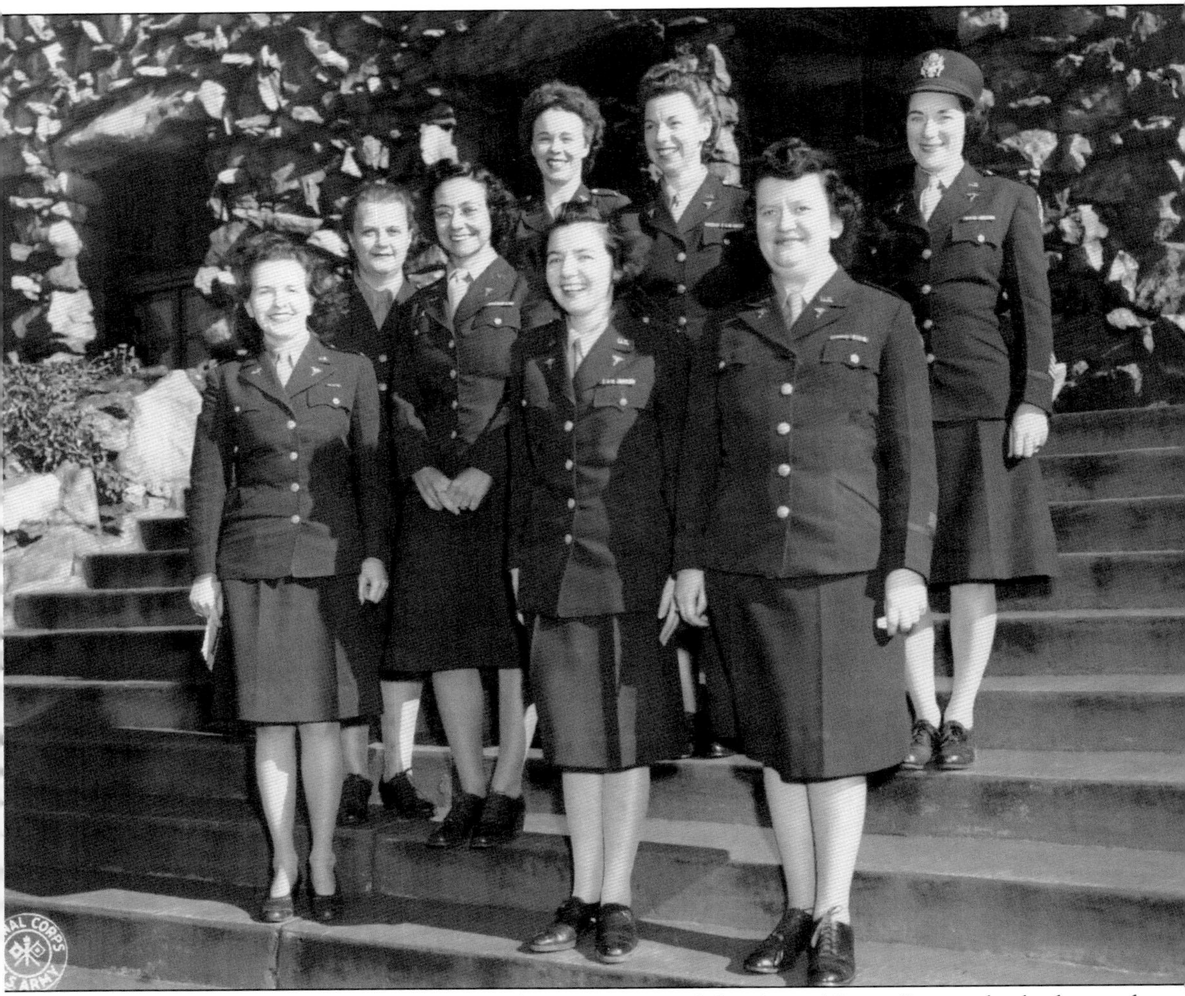

Pictured on the terrace of Grove Park Inn, women of the Army Nurse Corps who had served overseas during World War II await reassignment at Asheville, North Carolina. The nurses are, from left to right, (first row) Lt. Wanda Hargus, Lt. Doris Wilmes, Lt. Catherine Hayes, and Capt. June E. Lemmon of Mount Pleasant, Pennsylvania; (second row) Lt. Jeanette Roussle, Lt. Barbara Ochs, 1st Lt. Mildred Graham, and 1st Lt. Ester O'Connell. Captain Lemmon was the daughter of V.A. Lemmon of Mount Pleasant, Pennsylvania, and she served 20 months in the Mediterranean Theater. More than 59,000 American nurses served in the Army Nurse Corps during World War II. The skilled and dedicated nurses worked closer to the front lines than they ever had before. (Courtesy of the Mount Pleasant Public Library Archives.)

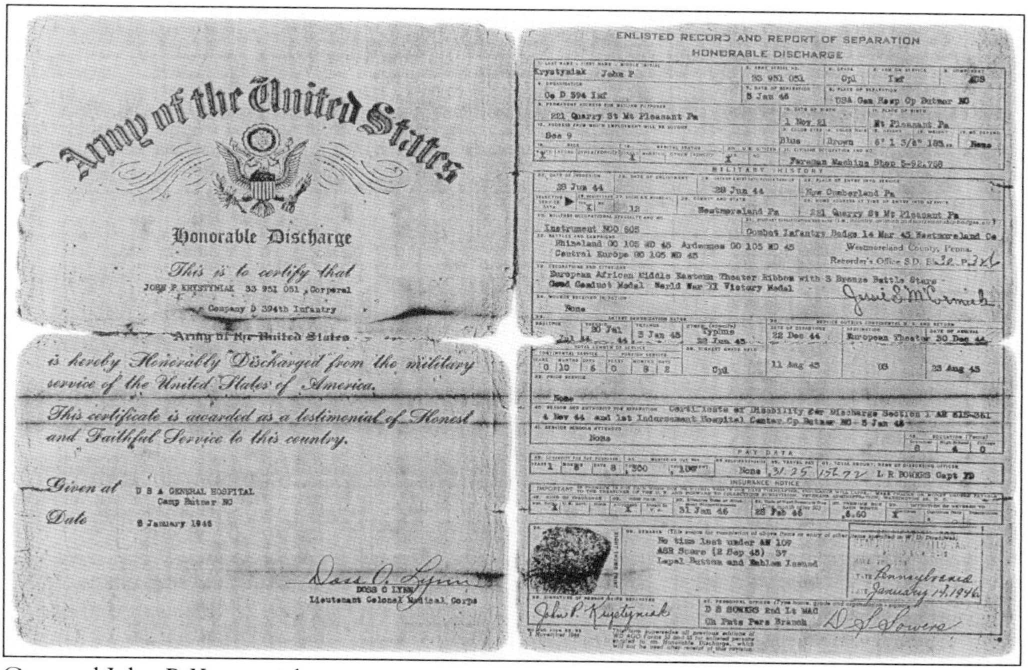

Army of the United States

Honorable Discharge

This is to certify that

JOHN P. KRYSTYNIAK 33 951 051, Corporal

Company D 394th Infantry

Army of the United States

is hereby Honorably Discharged from the military service of the United States of America.

This certificate is awarded as a testimonial of Honest and Faithful Service to this country.

Given at U S A GENERAL HOSPITAL Camp Butner NC

Date 5 January 1946

DOSS O LYNN
Lieutenant Colonel Medical Corps

ENLISTED RECORD AND REPORT OF SEPARATION
HONORABLE DISCHARGE

Krystyniak John P · 33 951 051 · Cpl · Inf

Co D 394 Inf · 5 Jan 46 · USA Gen Hosp Cp Butner NC

221 Quarry St Mt Pleasant Pa · 1 Nov 21 · Mt Pleasant Pa

Corporal John P. Krystyniak was honorably discharged from the US Army on January 5, 1945. His discharge was given at the USA General Hospital, Camp Butner, NC. This certificate is awarded as a testimonial of honest and faithful service to our country. (Courtesy of Margaret Krystyniak and Theresa Gerson.)

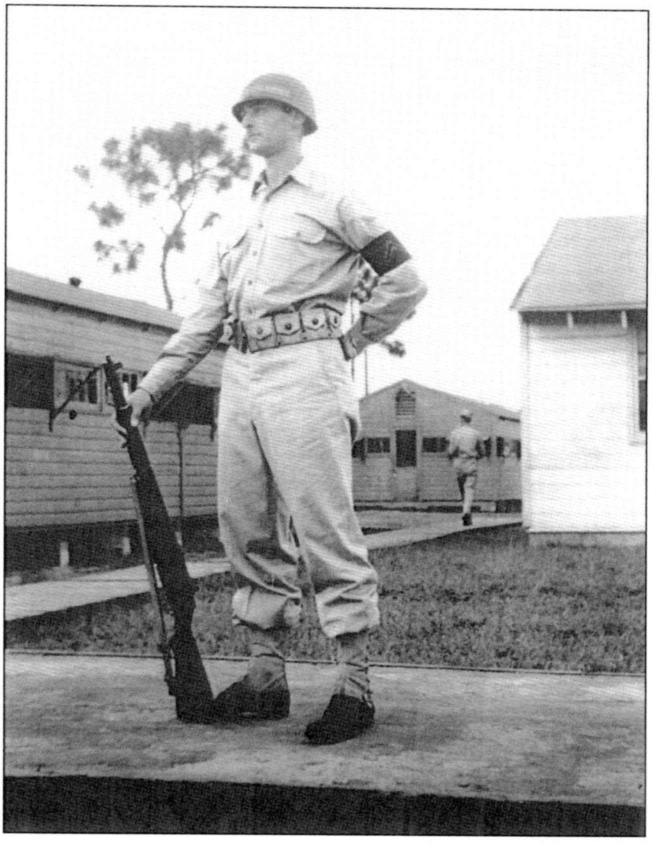

A young Cpl. John P. Krystyniak of 221 Quarry Street, Mount Pleasant, Pennsylvania, stands on guard outside the army barracks. Later, John married Margaret Rose and started a local business, the Red & White grocery store. He became very involved in the community and, in 1953, became president of the chamber of commerce. John was born in 1922 and lived until 1994 in Acme. (Courtesy of Margaret Krystyniak and Theresa Gerson.)

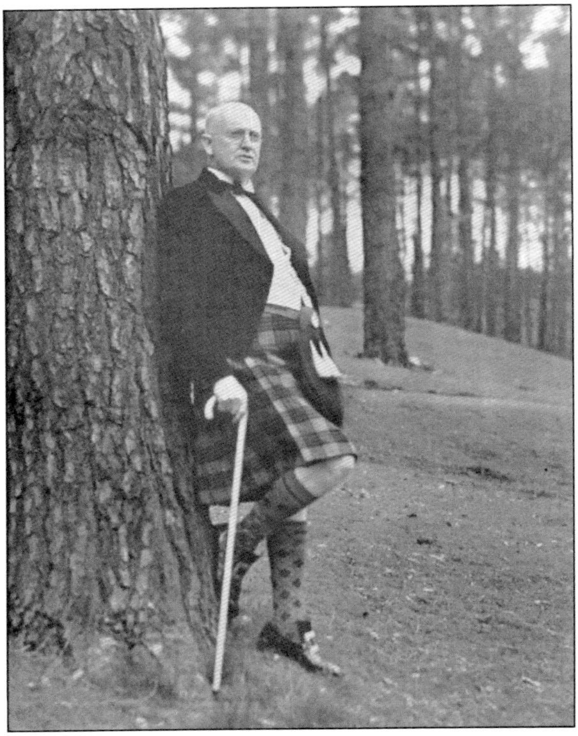

Erskine Ramsay, nicknamed "Sir Erskine," wears his beloved kilt at a dinner for the Scots of the Birmingham, Alabama, district held at Mountain Brook Country Club. Erskine was born in 1864 in Six Mile Ferry, Pennsylvania, to Robert Ramsay and Janet Erskine, immigrants from Scotland. (Courtesy of the Mount Pleasant Public Library Archives.)

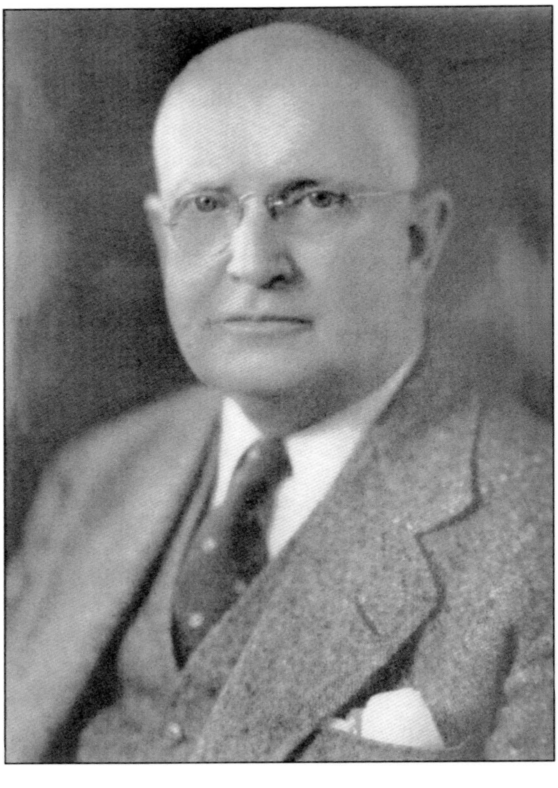

Erskine Ramsay was a mining engineer, inventor, industrialist, and philanthropist. In 1929, he donated money to build the beautifully designed Ramsay High School. His formal schooling was at St. Vincent College, and he spent long days in the machine shop and local coal mines. He was later awarded the William Lawrence Saunders Gold Medal from the American Institute of Mine and Metallurgical Engineers. This affected improvements in coke making that resulted in the establishment of the steel industry in Alabama. (Courtesy of the Mount Pleasant Public Library Archives.)

Frick Memorial Hospital organized a training school for nurses in October 1904. Quarters and classrooms for the student nurses were located on the second floor of the hospital. After three years of training, these nurses are pictured on graduation day. In the early 1900s, nurses were paid $25 per day. (Courtesy of the Mount Pleasant Public Library Archives.)

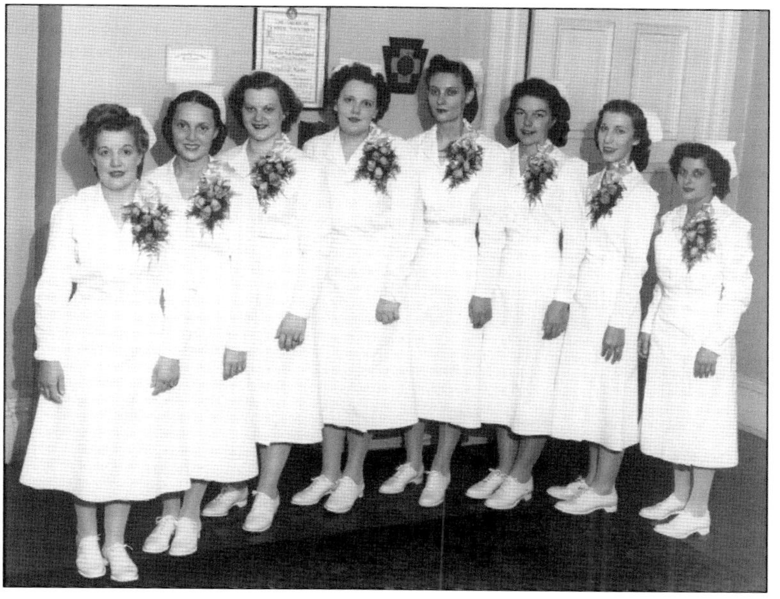

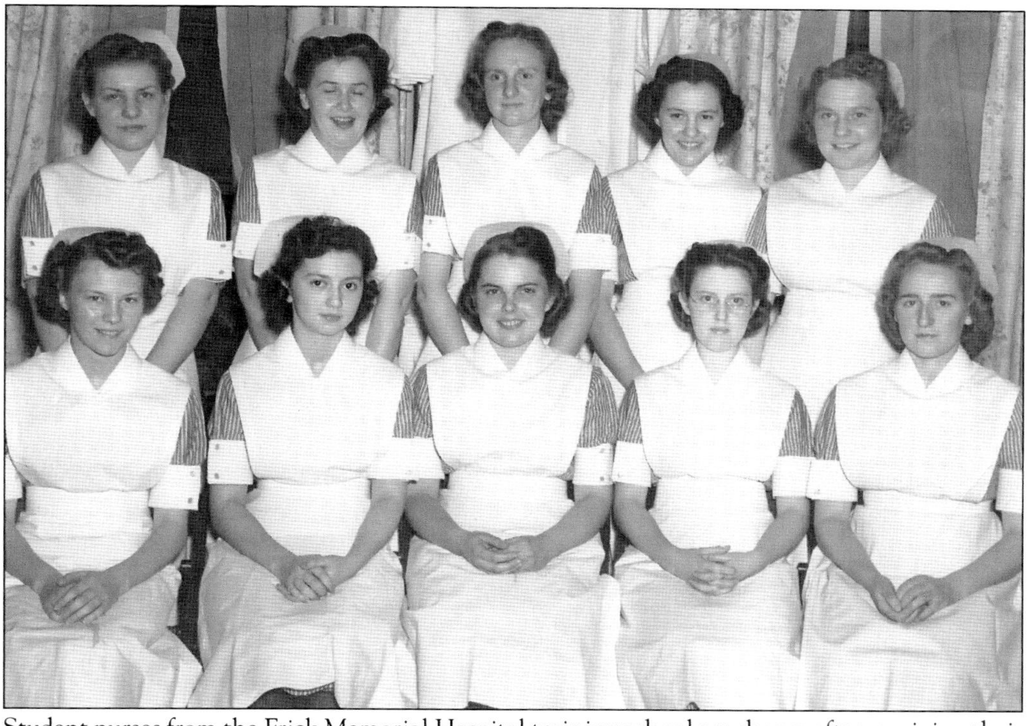

Student nurses from the Frick Memorial Hospital training school are shown after receiving their caps. Dr. W.A. Marsh was the school's founder and teacher. In 1930, using funds bequeathed by Henry Clay Frick, a nurses' residence was built across Stand Pipe Alley behind the hospital. The nursing school closed in 1950. (Courtesy of Karen Stefl.)

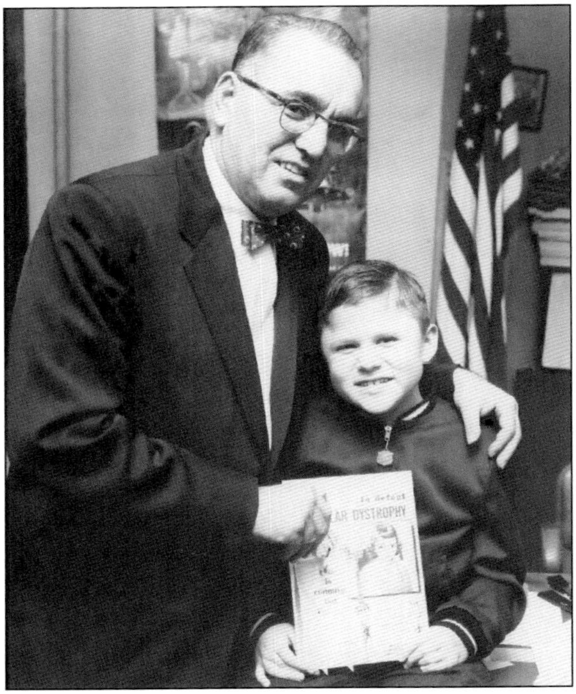

Mayor Sam Etze awards a young boy for his contribution to defeat muscular dystrophy. Sam Etze was mayor from 1954 to 1969. He resided on Washington Street with his wife and three sons, Frank, Sam, and Tony. The Etze brothers served in many leadership roles in Mount Pleasant. (Courtesy of the Mount Pleasant Public Library Archives.)

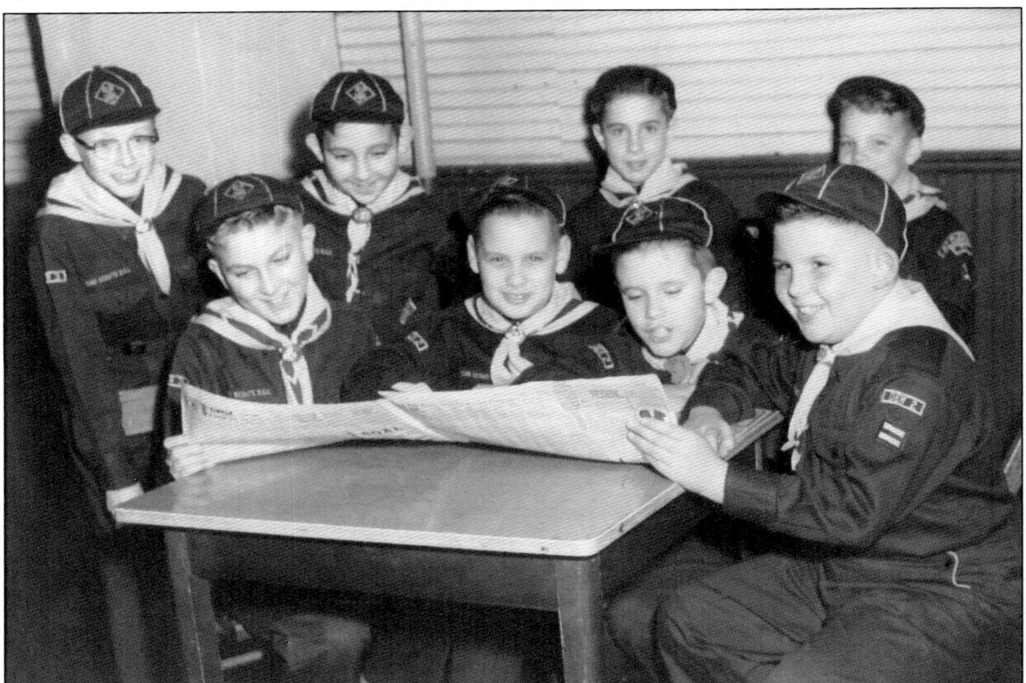

Young men from a local Cub Scout Troop, Den 2, participate in a program called Becoming Critical Consumers of the Media. The Cub Scouts, Boy Scouts, Brownies, and Girl Scouts are still very active in Mount Pleasant. The Pinewood Derby and Girl Scout cookie sales are annual events. (Courtesy of the Mount Pleasant Public Library Archives.)

The First Aid Corps was formed in 1947. Here, a group of Mount Pleasant first aiders learns how to use a portable iron lung in 1952. The truck in the background was purchased in 1949 to carry first aid equipment and to transport injured firefighters and citizens. (Courtesy of the Mount Pleasant Public Library Archives.)

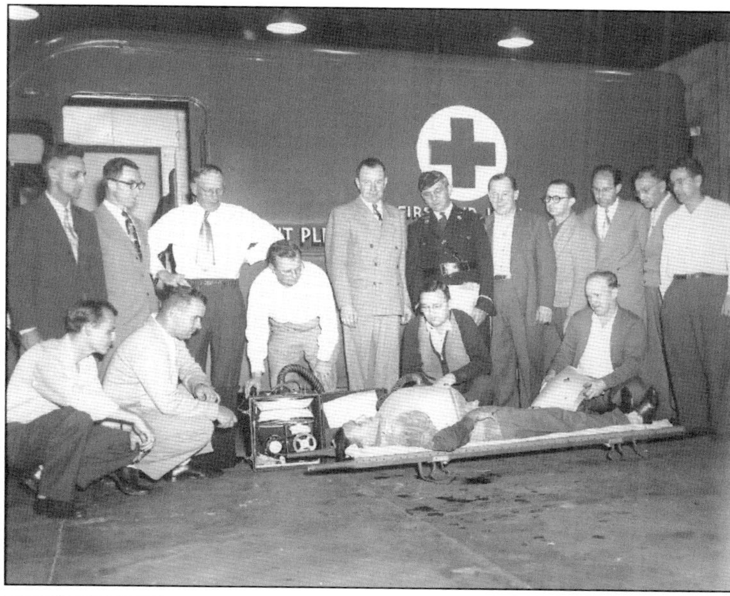

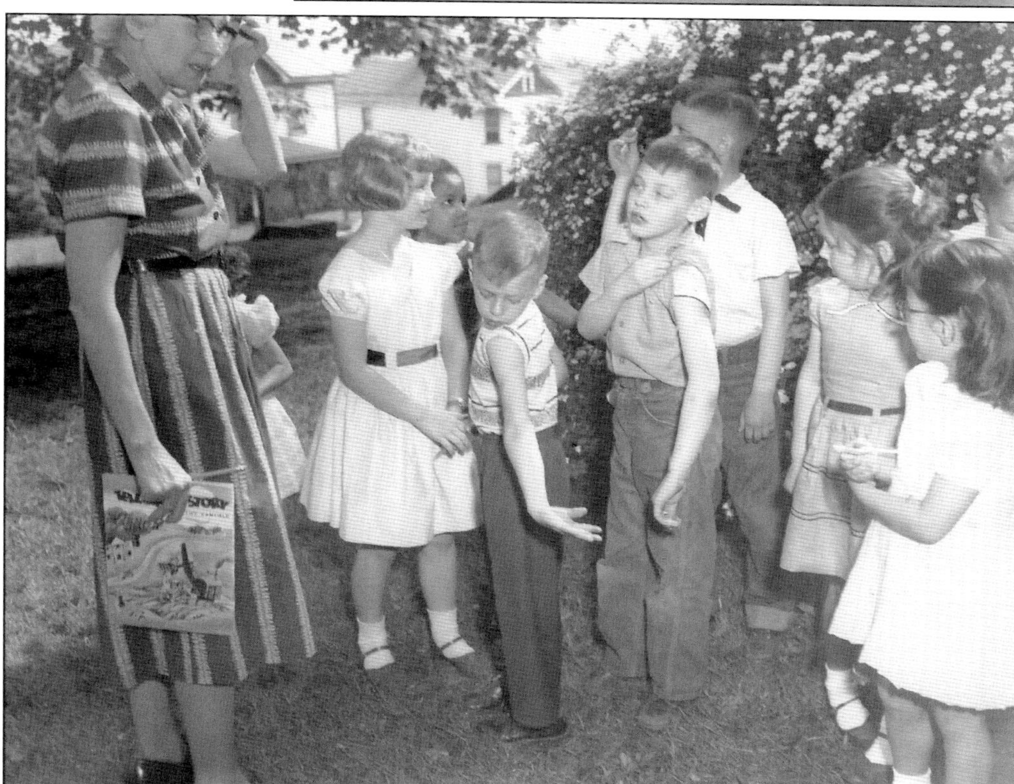

Young children from a local elementary school line up to receive the Salk polio vaccine in 1955. Four million vaccinations were given by August 1955. Salk developed the vaccine at the Virus Research Lab at the University of Pittsburgh. (Courtesy of the Mount Pleasant Public Library Archives.)

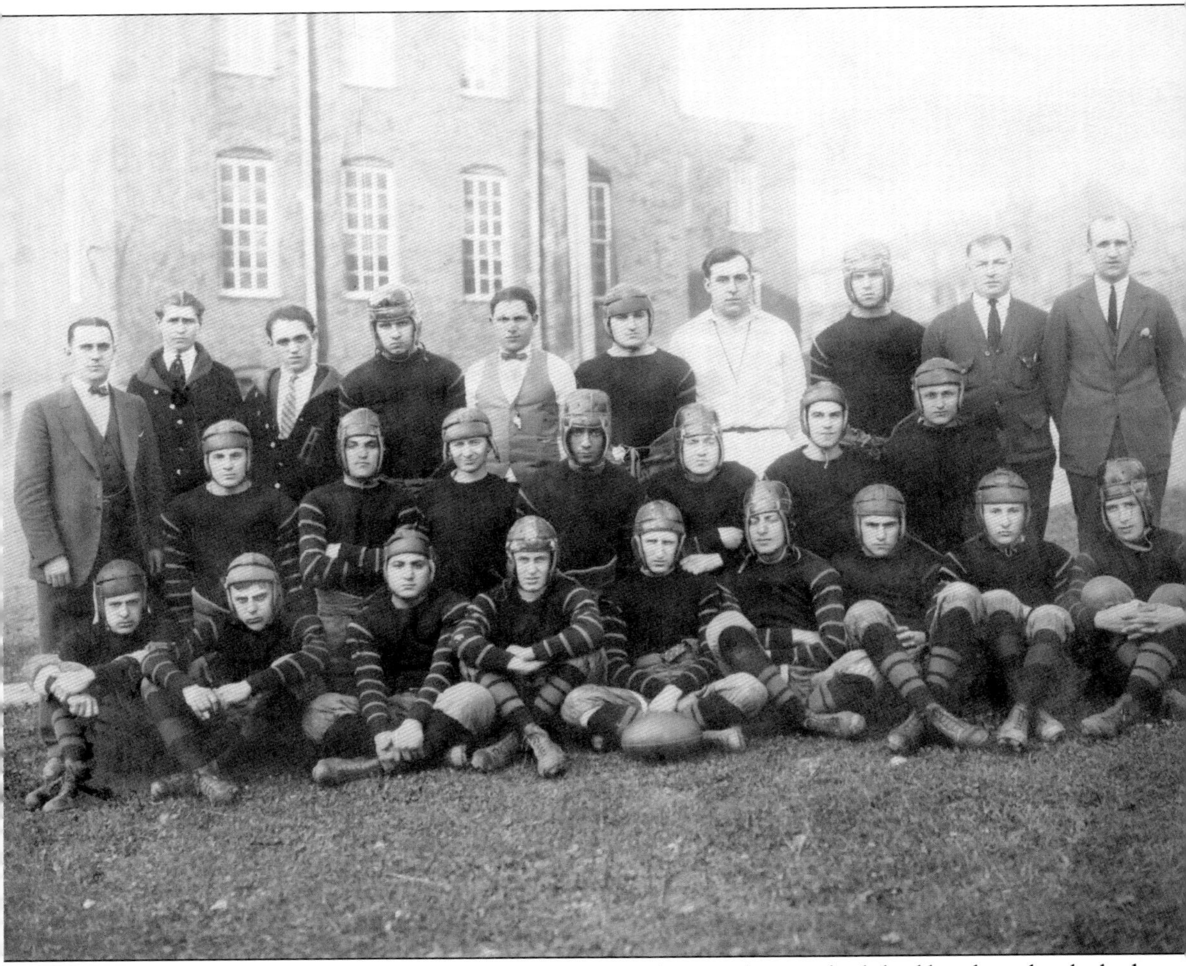

The Bryce Brothers football team of 1929 displays their uniforms, which had headgear but lacked shoulder pads. These uniforms resembled those worn by soccer teams. They are pictured in front of "the institute," which was the site of the Mount Pleasant College, established in 1849. This institute had an 81-year-old history, with ownership changing five times through four different church-affiliated corporations. (Courtesy of Theresa Benedict.)

A young Edward Czekaj, right, of Mount Pleasant practices for the Ramsay Bobcats. He went to Penn State as a student in 1943 and, after his military career, later returned to start as an assistant and worked his way up to become the director of athletics at Penn State University from 1969 to 1980. (Courtesy of the Mount Pleasant Public Library Archives.)

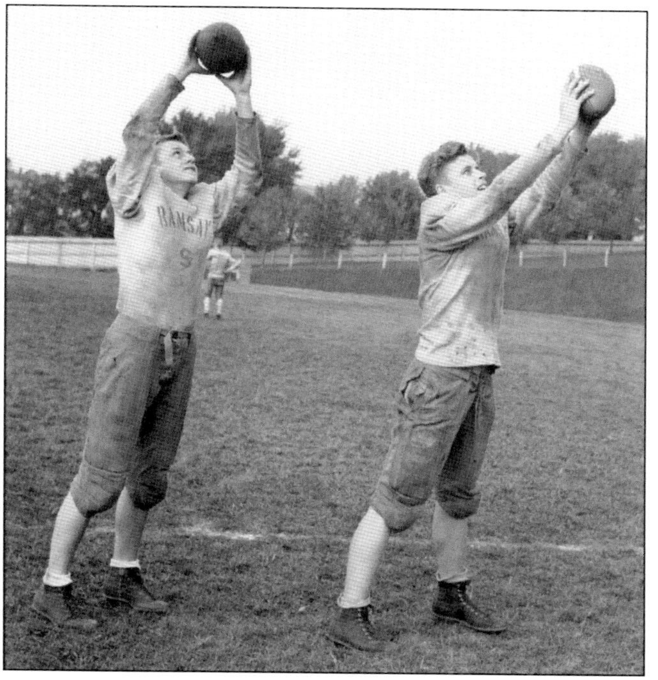

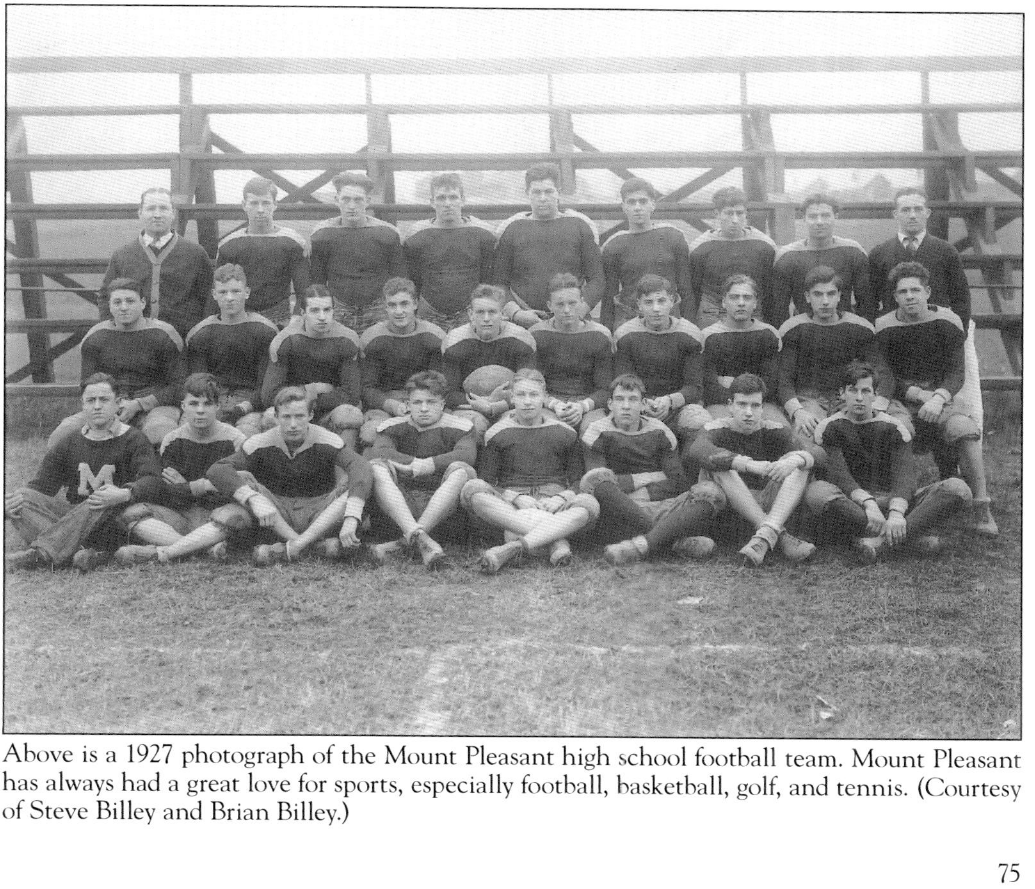

Above is a 1927 photograph of the Mount Pleasant high school football team. Mount Pleasant has always had a great love for sports, especially football, basketball, golf, and tennis. (Courtesy of Steve Billey and Brian Billey.)

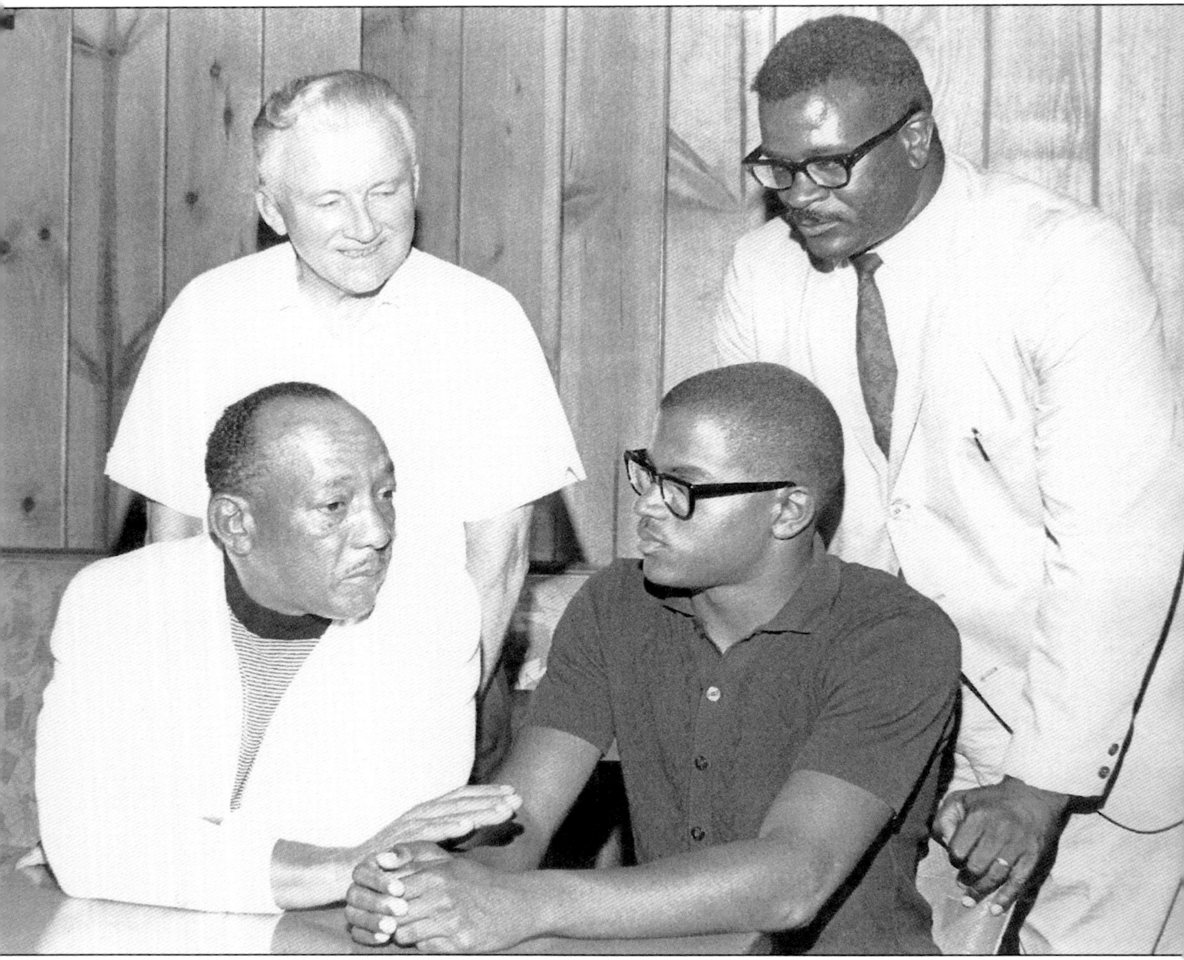

Olympic great Jesse Owens and traveling buddy Eddie Bell visit Mount Pleasant track star LaRoyal Wilson III and James Posta in 1966. Owens had come to Mount Pleasant to speak about his track career. Bell also spoke about his career as a former Philadelphia Eagles football player. LaRoyal broke three records and was a WPIAL champion in track. He placed second in the state's long jump in 1966. (Courtesy of Bonnie and LaRoyal Wilson.)

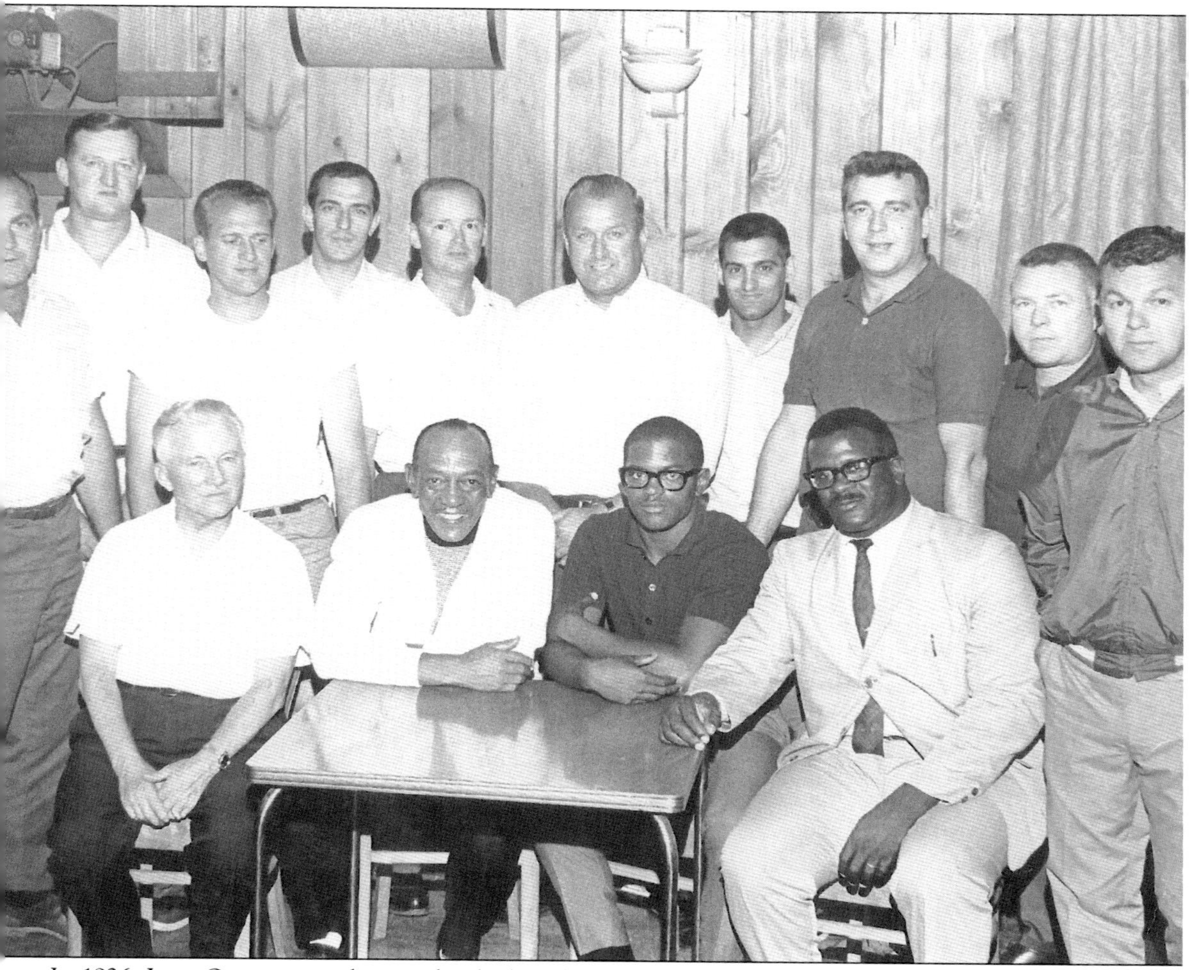

In 1936, Jesse Owens won three individual gold medals in the 100-meter and 200-meter races and the broad jump in the Olympic Games at Berlin, Germany. Owens was a guest speaker at the Elks in 1966. From left to right are (first row) Jim Posta, Jesse Owens, LaRoyal Wilson, and Ron Bell; (second row) Clarence Gorinski, George Hare, Bill Hamacher, Jim Nicolette, Denver Hudec, Ed Wilkins, Coke Yancosky, Ben Malesky, James McKenna, and Tom Miscik. (Courtesy of Bonnie and LaRoyal Wilson.)

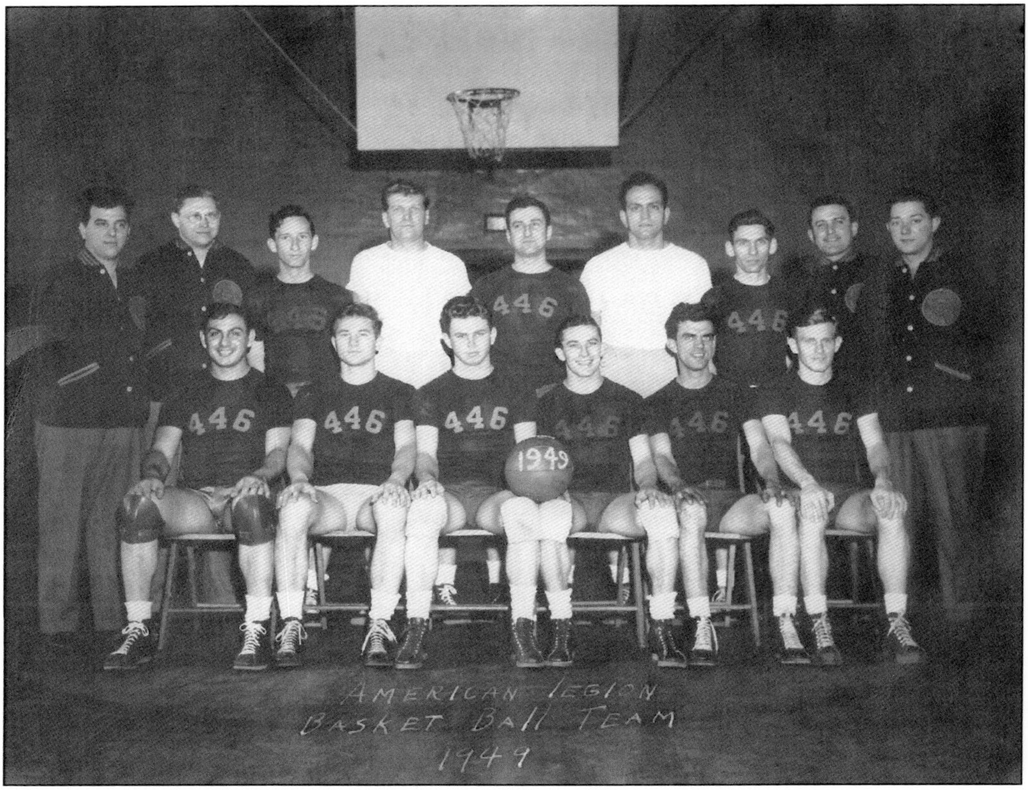

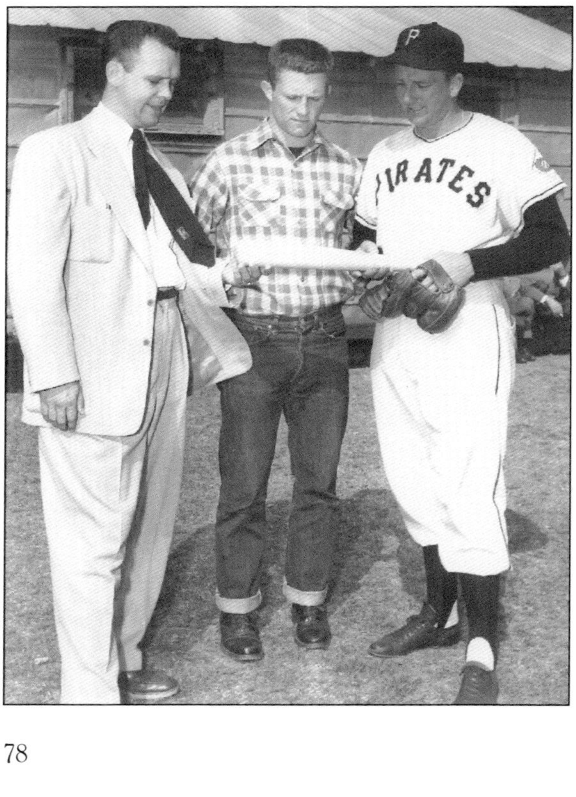

Team members of the American Legion's 1949 basketball team are, from left to right, (sitting) John DePasquale, Eugene Zaucha, Leonard Czekaj, unidentified, Dean Walker, and Louis Czekaj; (standing) unidentified, George Miller, Anthony Garstecki, unidentified, Pete Damico, Nick Etze, Mike Lanzino, Phil Marne, and unidentified. (Courtesy of Joseph Yancosky.)

Cal Metz of Mount Pleasant introduces California high school athlete Marty Keough to Ralph Kiner at spring training camp. Metz, who was connected with the Pirates in California, has aided in signing of quite a few promising athletes for the Pirates. (Courtesy of the Mount Pleasant Public Library Archives.)

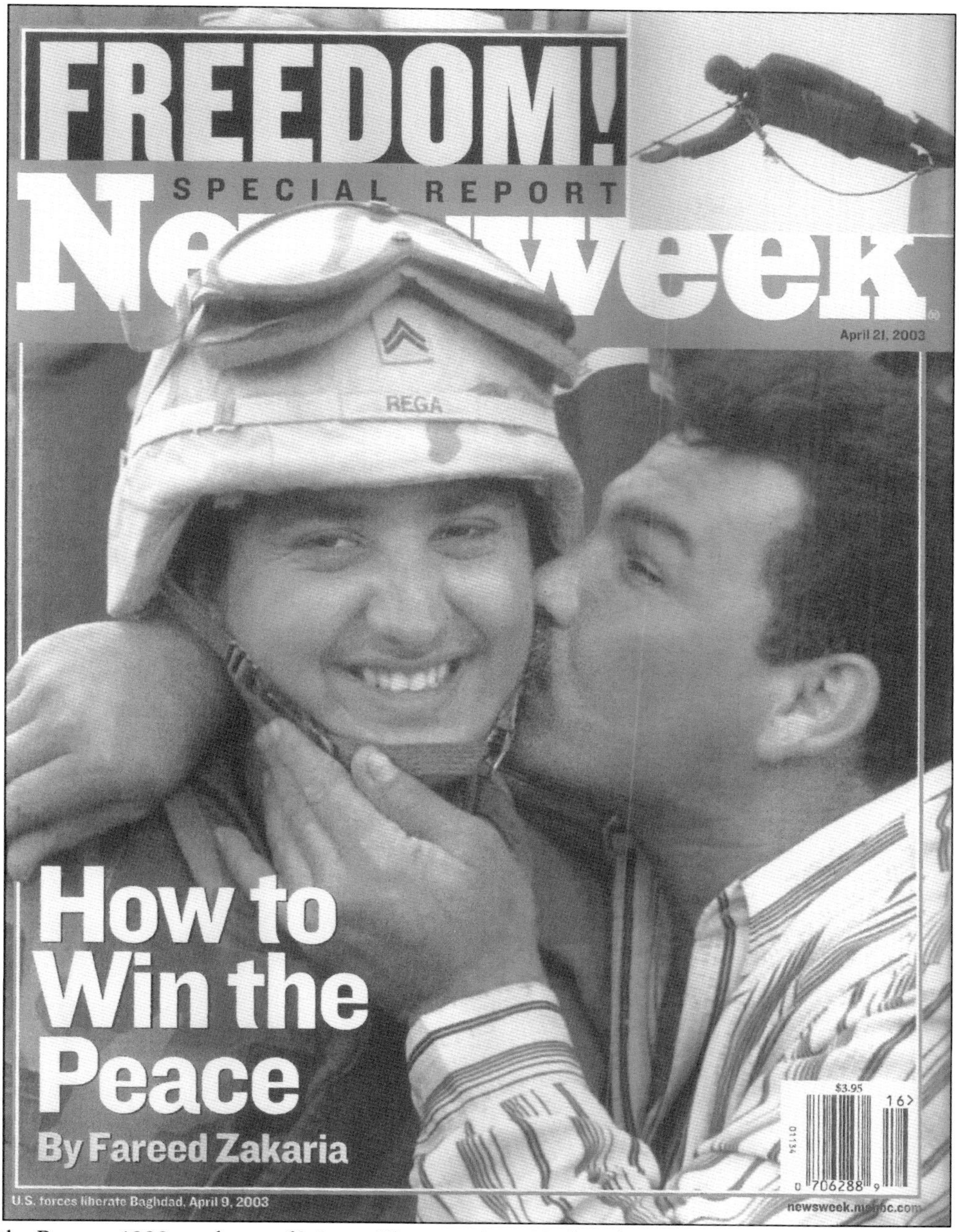

Mike Rega, a 1999 graduate of Mount Pleasant Area High School, joined the Army Reserves in 2000. He was deployed to Bosnia and the Middle East from September 2001 to March 2003. He arrived in Kuwait on March 4, 2003. Army Reserve Cpl. Michael Rega Jr. did anti-drug programs and had his own radio show. Rega was with the 303rd Psychological Operations Company (Tactical) waging the information war and trying to convince the Iraqis that the American presence in their country was a good thing. Mike called his parents to tell them that he had watched Iraqis topple the statue of Saddam Hussein. This image of a thankful kiss from an Iraqi man in downtown Baghdad put Army Reserve corporal Michael Rega Jr. on newspaper front pages around the county in April 2003. (Courtesy of Mike and Cheryl Rega.)

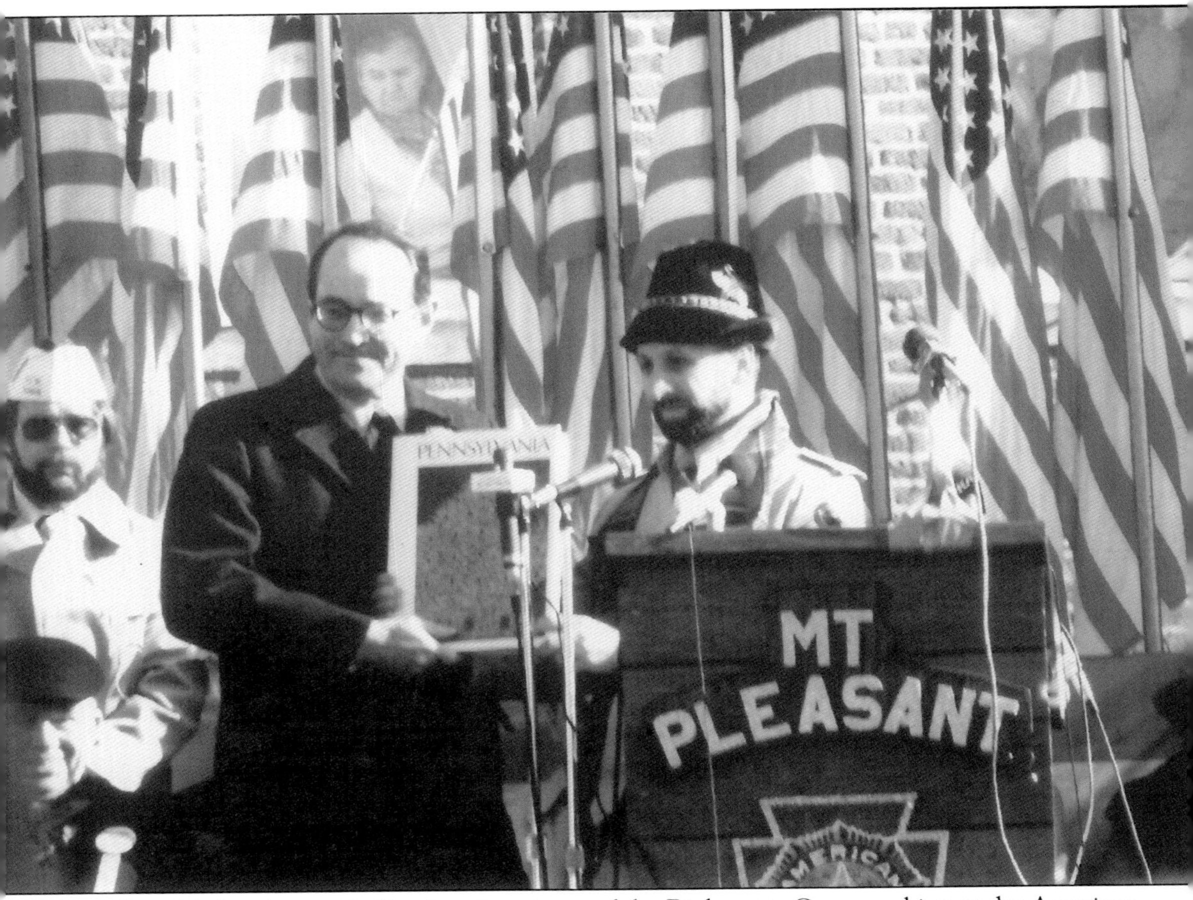

Jerry Miele, along with 51 other Americans of the Diplomatic Corps working at the American Embassy in Tehran, Iran, was taken hostage on November 4, 1979, by Islamic fundamentalist students. They were incarcerated for 444 days and released on January 20, 1981. At the time of the takeover of the American embassy, Jerry worked in the telecommunications portion of the communication's section. His duties included sending out the mission's outgoing processed messages via satellite or high frequency radio and receiving the US government mission's incoming messages. Jerry's service included being in the National Guard Company E in Mount Pleasant, a radioman in the Navy, and 25 years with the US State Department Foreign Service. These lifetime achievements of so many Mount Pleasant natives have given pride to the community and to the country. (Courtesy of Jerry Miele.)

Four

Acknowledging Our Culture

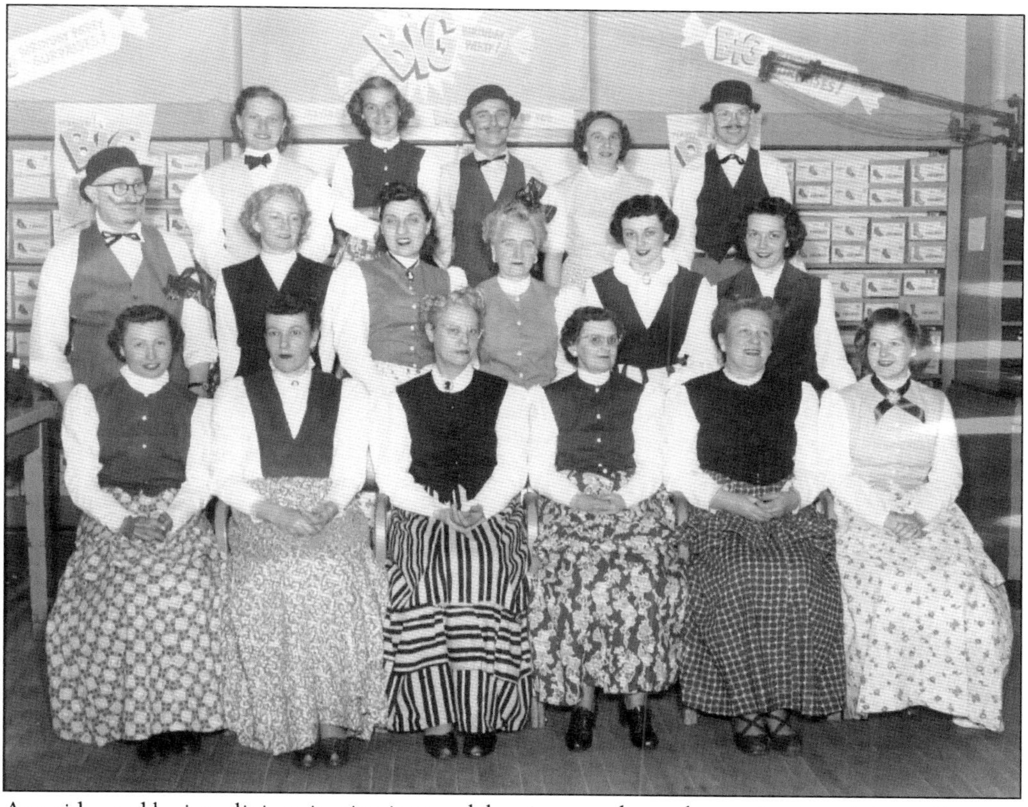

As evidenced by its religious institutions, celebrations, and social organizations, Mount Pleasant culture reflects diverse nationalities and ethnic backgrounds. This chapter is only a sampling of many examples. J.C. Penney employees dressed in ethnic costumes each year. Among those pictured are Julie (Farrell) Keefer, Betty (Krofta) Keller, and Evelyn Melago. (Courtesy of the Mount Pleasant Public Library Archives.)

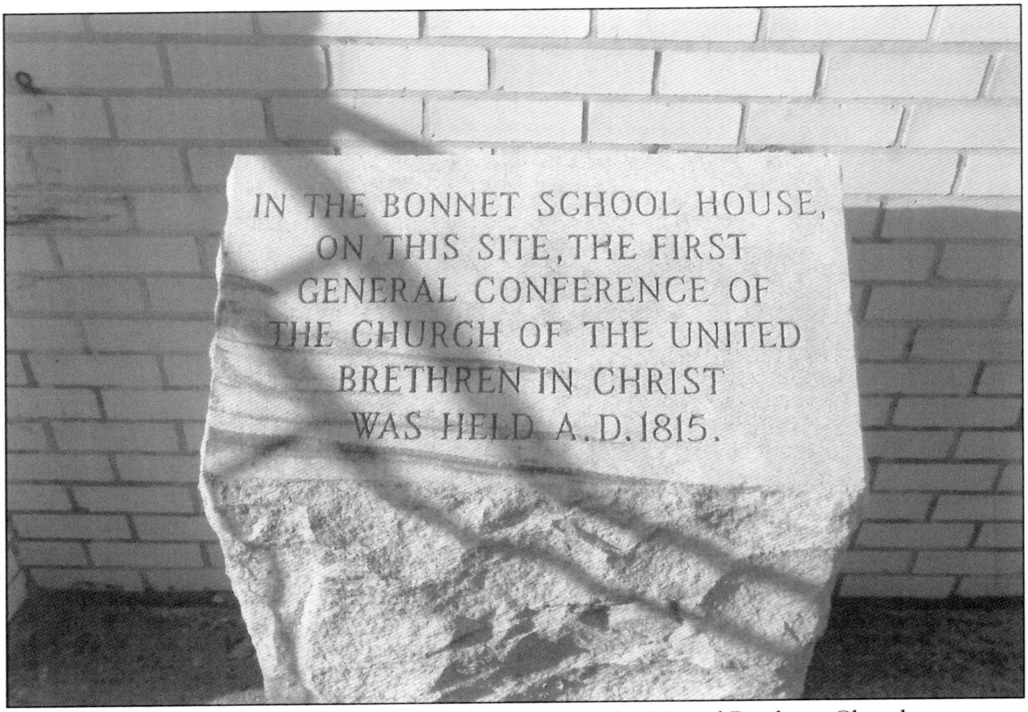

The United Brethren Church congregation did not have a permanent meeting place. They met in homes of the members and at the Bonnet School. The Bonnet School House is remembered on a stone plaque, which commemorates the first General Conference of the Church of the United Brethren in Christ, held in 1815. At this conference, the church formed the Confession of Faith and Discipline. (Courtesy of Nancy Sebek.)

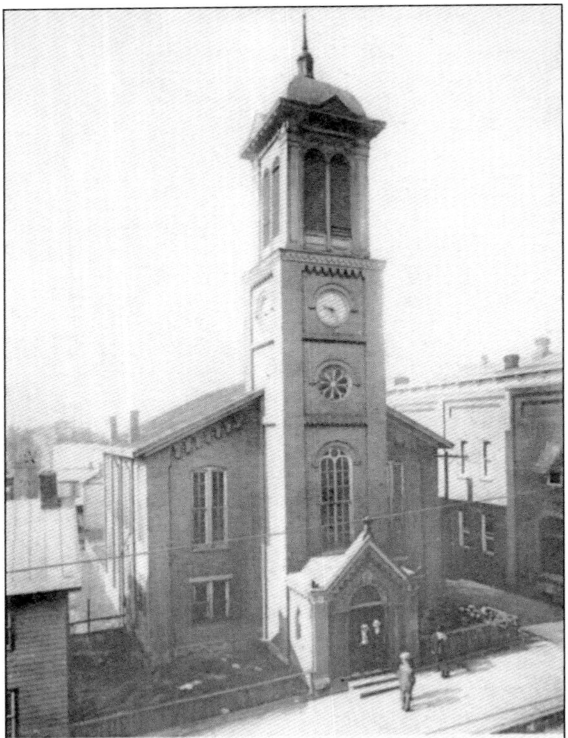

United Brethren Church, Built 1854, Remodeled 1874, Mt. Pleasant, Pa.

The United Brethren Church was built in 1854 and remodeled in 1874. It is located on Main Street and College Avenue. (Courtesy of the Mount Pleasant Area Historical Society.)

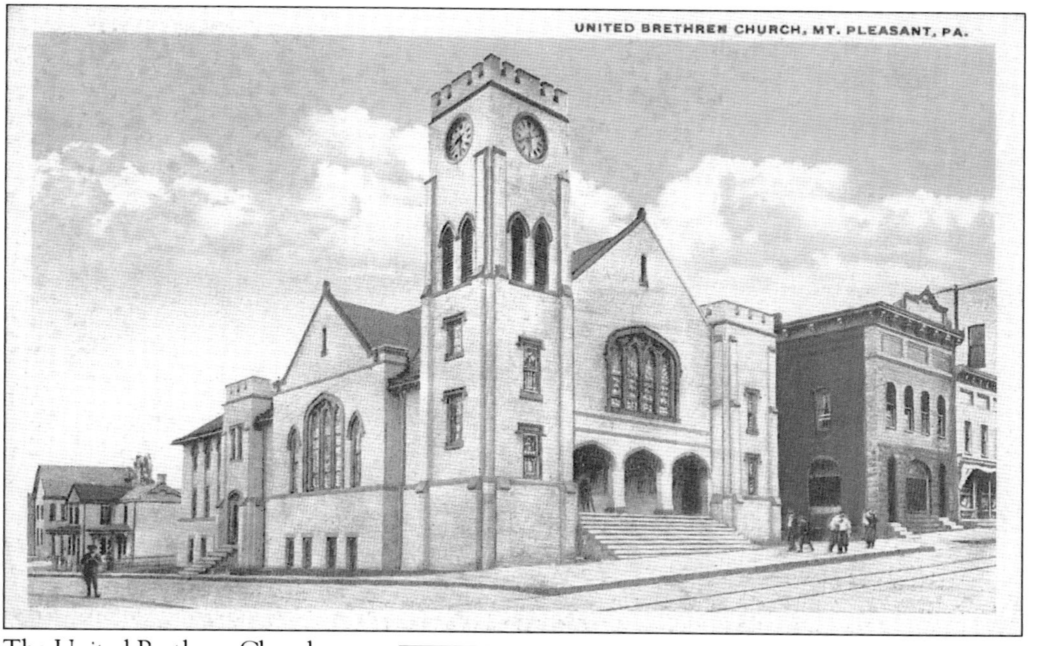

The United Brethren Church was rebuilt in 1912. Now known as the United Methodist Church of Mount Pleasant, "The Town Clock Church" is located on Main Street and College Avenue. (Courtesy of Merl and Fay Pritts.)

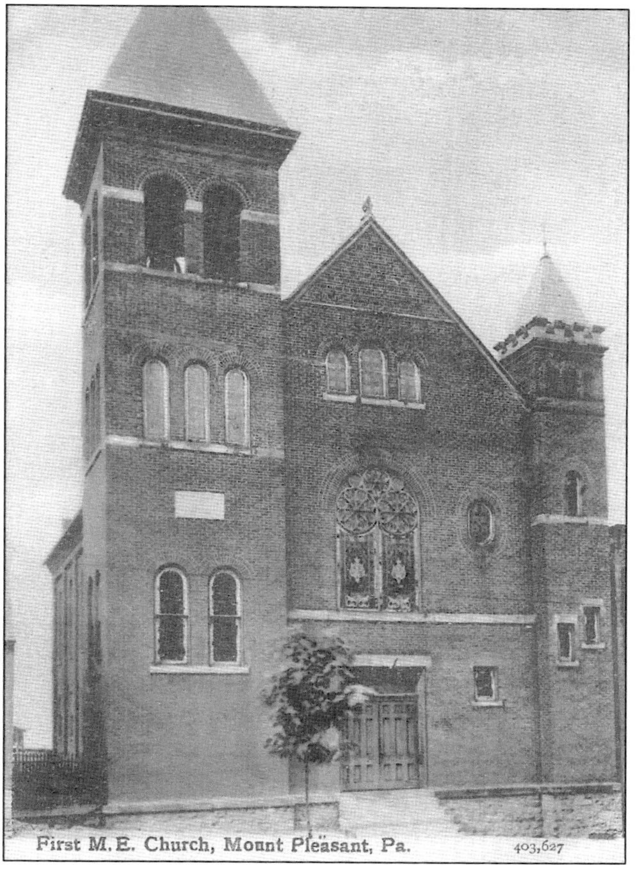

The Wesley Evangelical Church is considered one of the oldest churches in our community. In 1856, Wesley Evangelical Church became the First M.E. Church, which was designed by John R. Harman of Uniontown. It was located at 720 West Main Street. (Courtesy of Merl and Fay Pritts.)

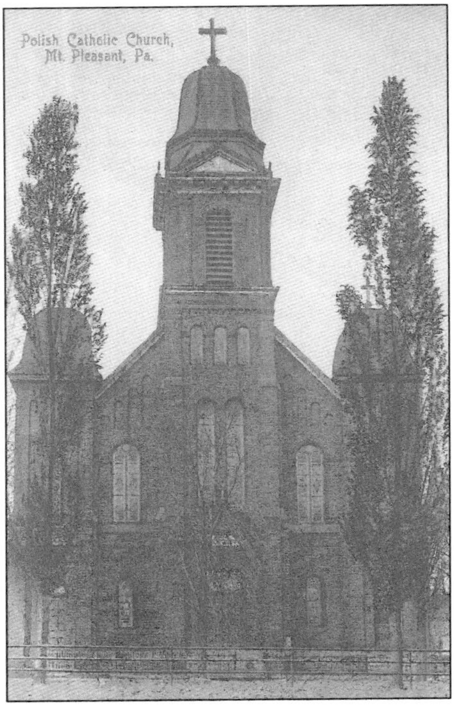

The Transfiguration Church was established by Polish immigrants in 1890. This majestic brick structure had arched windows, a bell-shaped golden roof, and two smaller flanking towers. In the sanctuary, there was a main altar with two smaller altars on each side. On the left there was a statue of St. Therese of Lisieux, the *Little Flower*. The church's elementary school, located across the street, provided a parochial education. This is a graduation photograph of eighth graders. (Both photographs courtesy of Merl and Fay Pritts.)

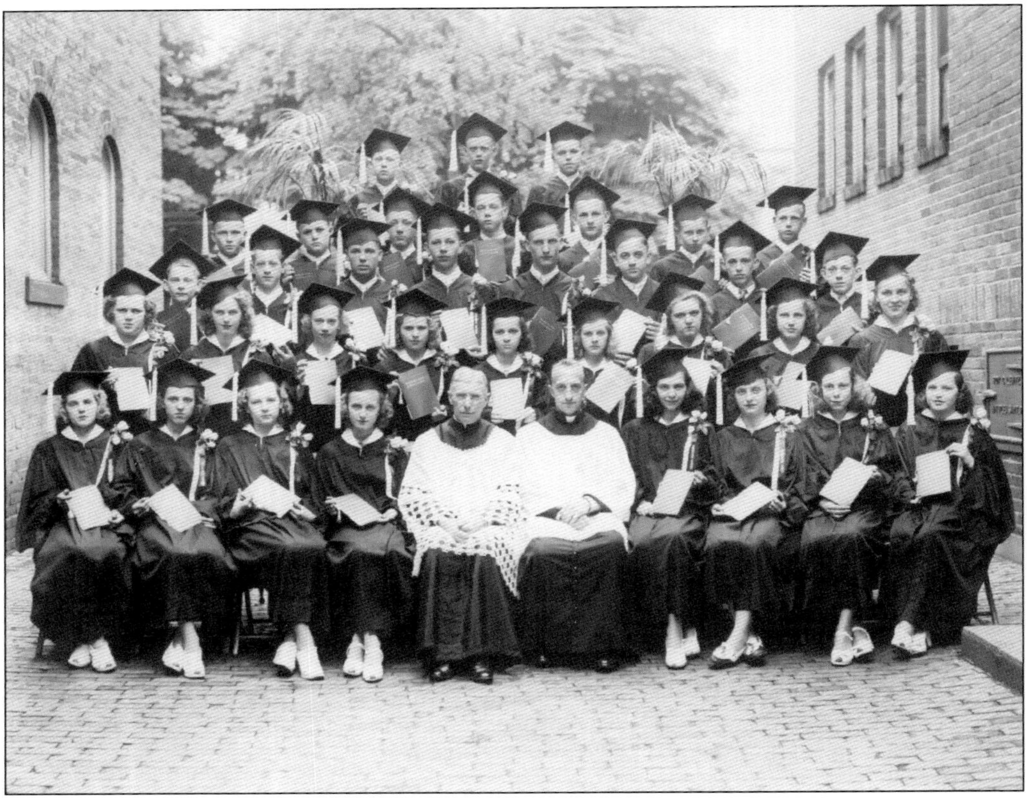

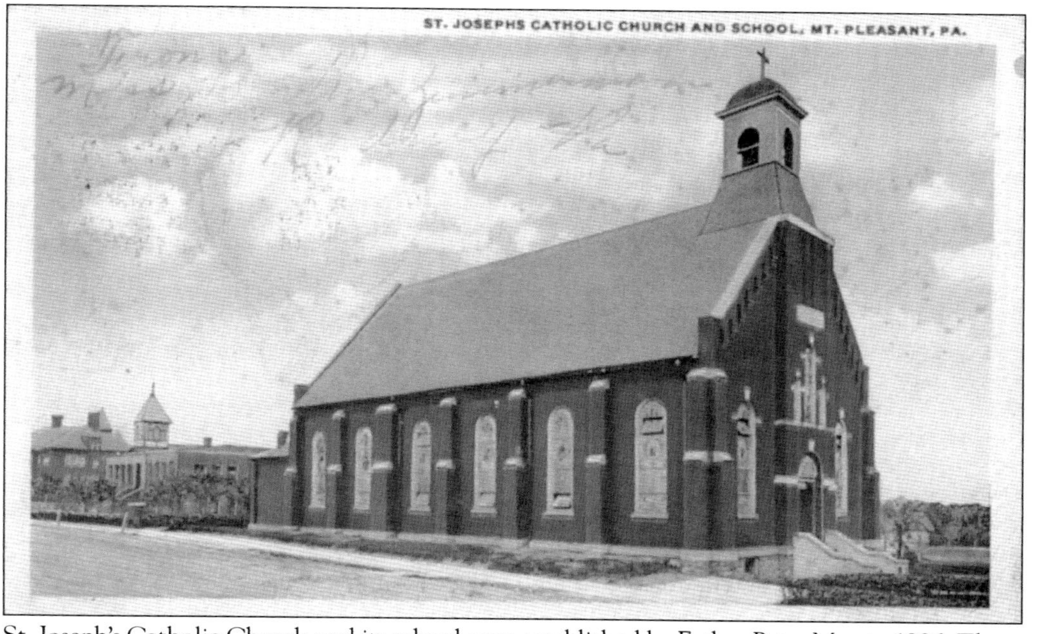

St. Joseph's Catholic Church and its school were established by Father Peter May in 1886. These structures were erected on Summit Street. In June 1963, the Greensburg Diocese recommended the consolidation of St. Joseph's Church and St. Bernadine's Church. St. Joseph's Church was razed, and the new structure, St. Pius X, became the merged parish of these two Catholic communities. (Courtesy of Merl and Fay Pritts.)

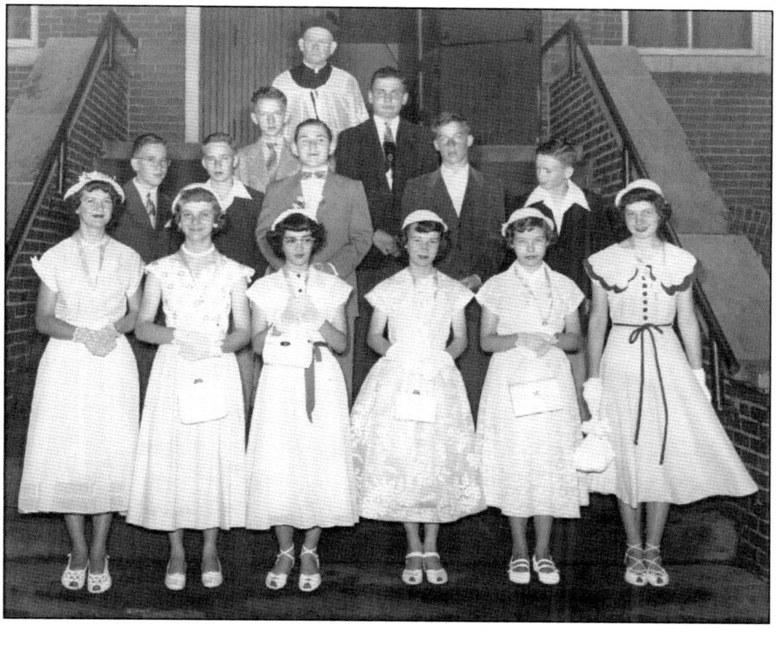

This photograph shows an eighth-grade graduating class at St. Joseph Parochial School. Monsignor Dugan presided at the ceremony. (Courtesy of the Mount Pleasant Public Library Archives.)

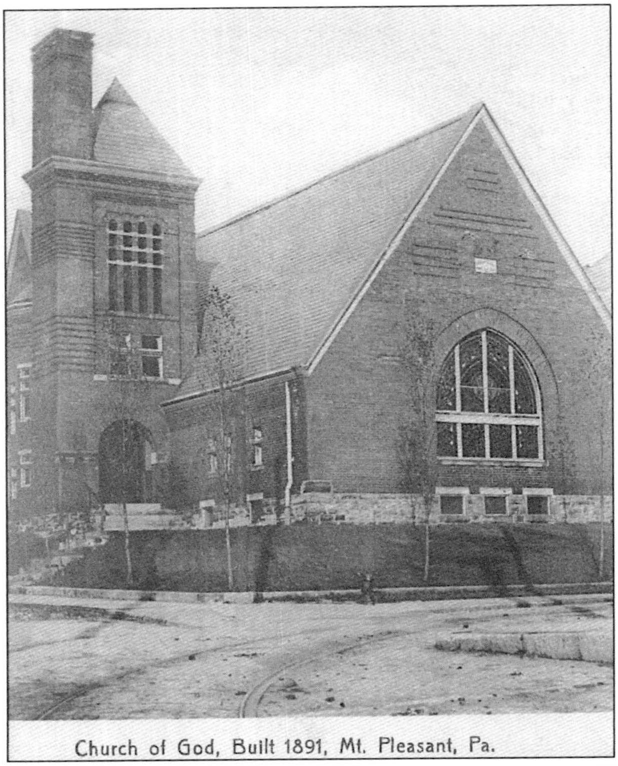

The Mount Pleasant Church of God was established in 1891 and continues to be a thriving community. The church welcomes people from all backgrounds. Following their Sunday morning service, one may read the weekly sermons on the website and a description of their ministries, which include community meals, a youth ministry, a nondenominational grocery relief, and much more. (Courtesy of Merl and Fay Pritts.)

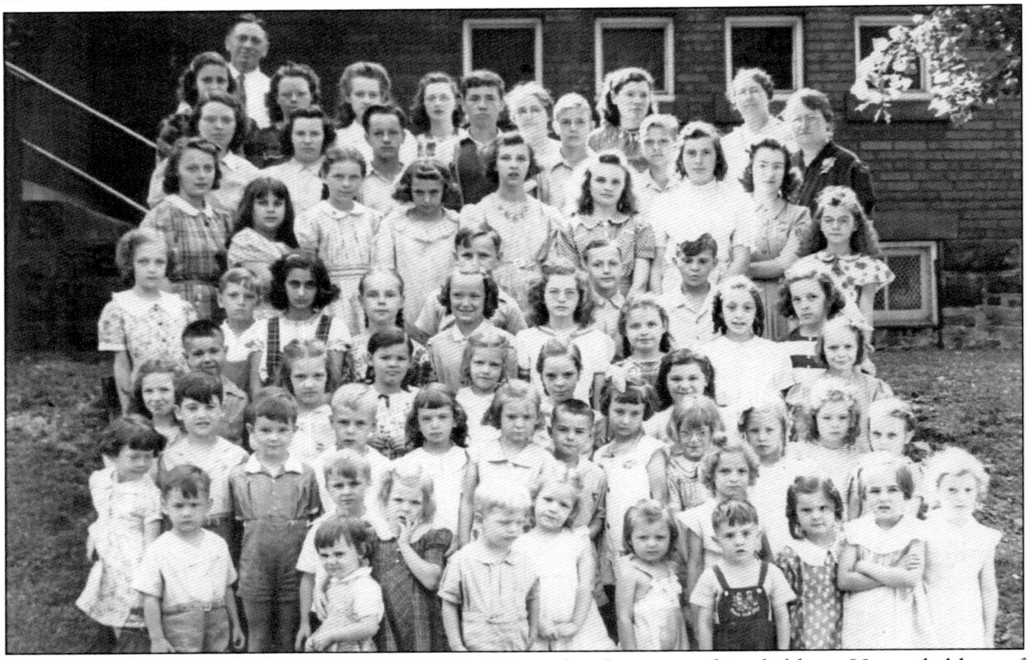

The entire church community promotes the religious development of its children. Here, children of various ages attend a religious camp sponsored by the Church of God. These camps focus on Bible instruction and building friendship. (Courtesy of the Mount Pleasant Public Library Archives.)

Built in 1889, the Reformed Church was located on Main Street in Mount Pleasant. It became the First United Church of Christ, whose ministry is based upon a diverse community of Christians who share faith and action in serving the community at large. This service-oriented religious organization believes in the teachings of Jesus Christ and in providing a connection to the world at large. Their advocacy for living their faith, loving the community, and healing the world is central to their social justice and devotion to the community. (Courtesy of Merl and Fay Pritts.)

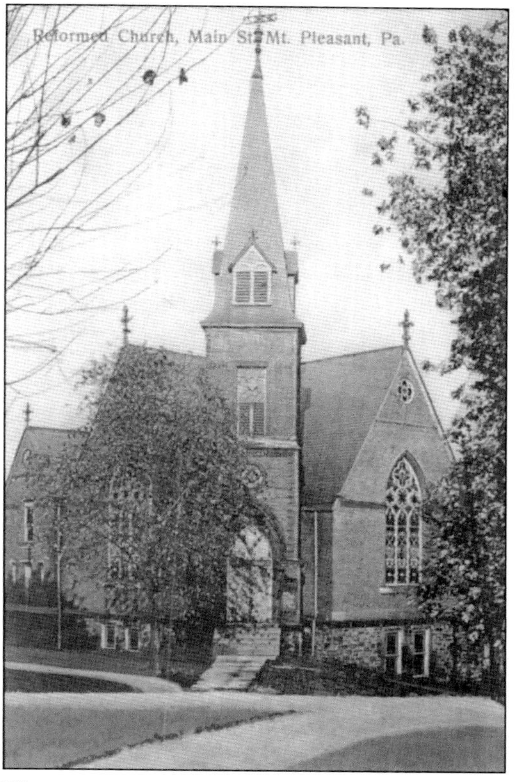

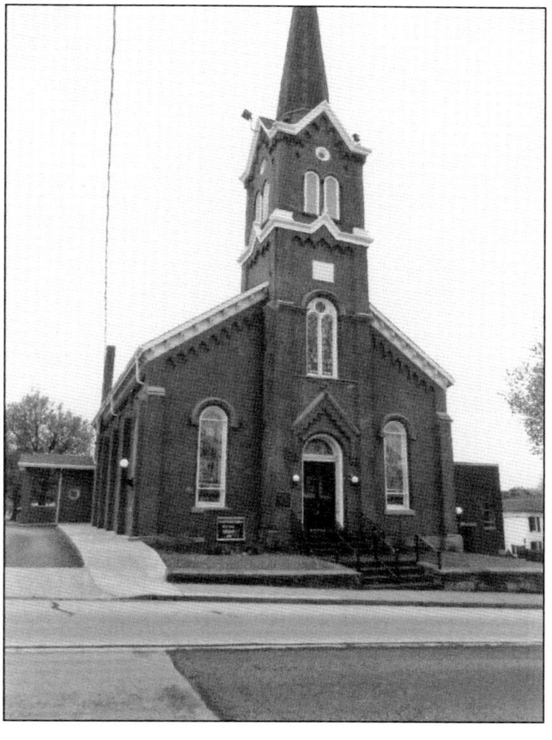

The Reunion Presbyterian Church is located at the corner of Main and Eagle Streets. The cornerstone was placed in 1870. An educational wing was added in 1960, and it is used by the congregation and various organizations in the community. A 1968 expansion included a large parking area. At times, this church combines services with the Middle Presbyterian Church, from which it originated. (Courtesy Nancy Sebek.)

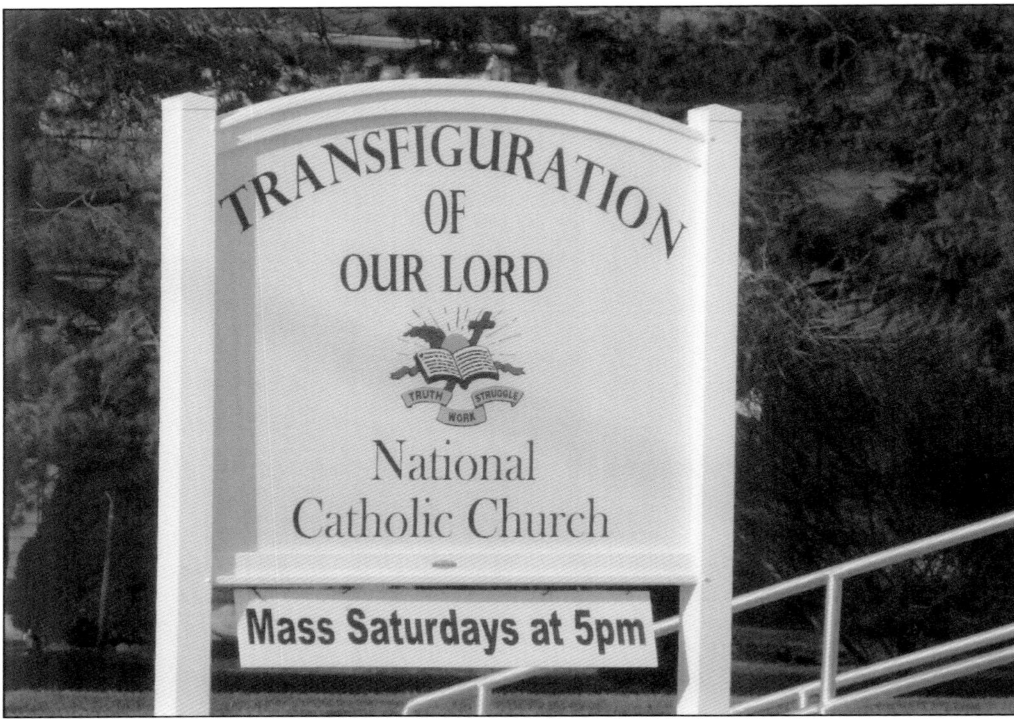

In 2003, the Transfiguration of Our Lord National Catholic Church began as a way to rebuild the former Transfiguration Roman Catholic parish. With passion and conviction, several parishioners decided to rebuild the church and affiliated their church with the Polish National Catholic Church, which was started by Prime Bishop Franciszek Hodur in 1897. Transfiguration of Our Lord Church follows the teachings of unity in God and loyalty to America while maintaining a deep respect for its Polish heritage. The Polish National Church is a Christian denomination that serves the spiritual needs of its members. Transfiguration of Our Lord is located at 353 Bridgeport Street. (Both photographs courtesy of Bonnie Wilson.)

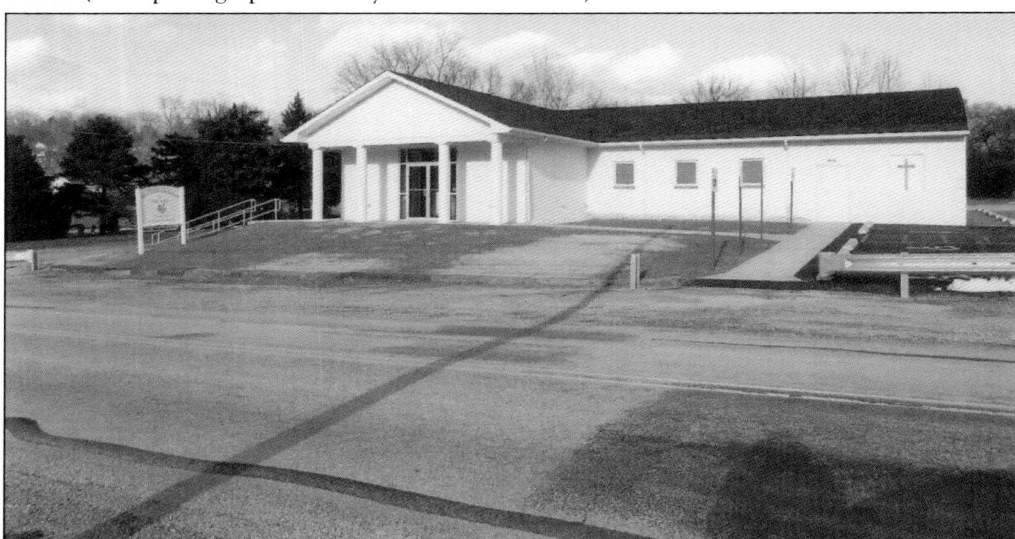

Good Shepherd Lutheran Church was part of the Evangelical Lutheran congregation at Middle Churches. Lutheran German families came west of the Alleghenies prior to the Revolutionary War. At one time, this church had been merged with Zion Lutheran Church in Ruffs Dale, East Huntington Township, and St. John's Lutheran in Middle Churches, Mount Pleasant Township. The church at 822 West Main Street was built in 1884. Based upon Lutheran Christian tradition, it is a place of worship, education, and ministry in the community. (Courtesy of Bonnie Wilson.)

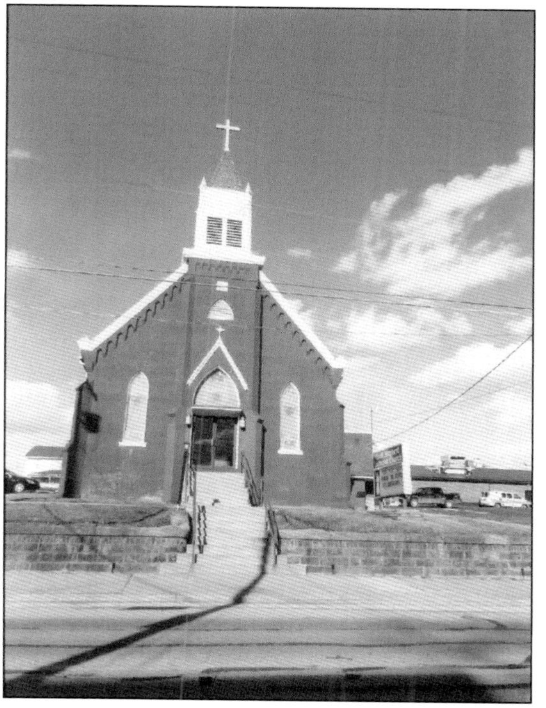

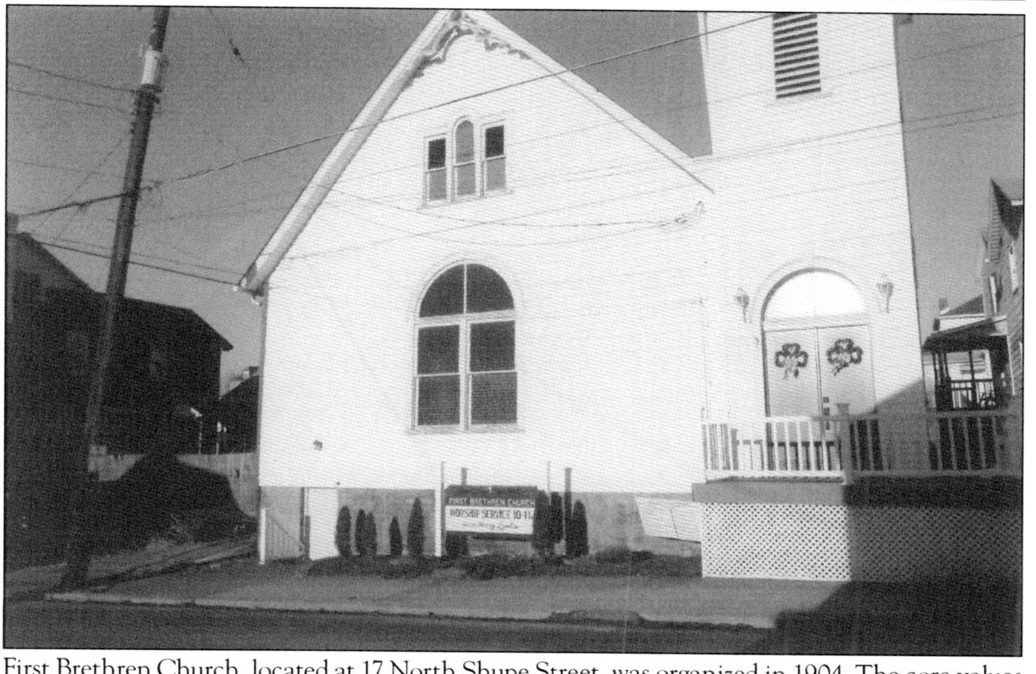

First Brethren Church, located at 17 North Shupe Street, was organized in 1904. The core values of the Brethren Church include building a relationship with a loving God; supporting a mission to showing Christ's love; caring for spiritual, emotional, and financial needs; encouraging new disciplines and leaders; and transforming a global connection in both neighborhoods and the world today. (Courtesy of Nancy Sebek.)

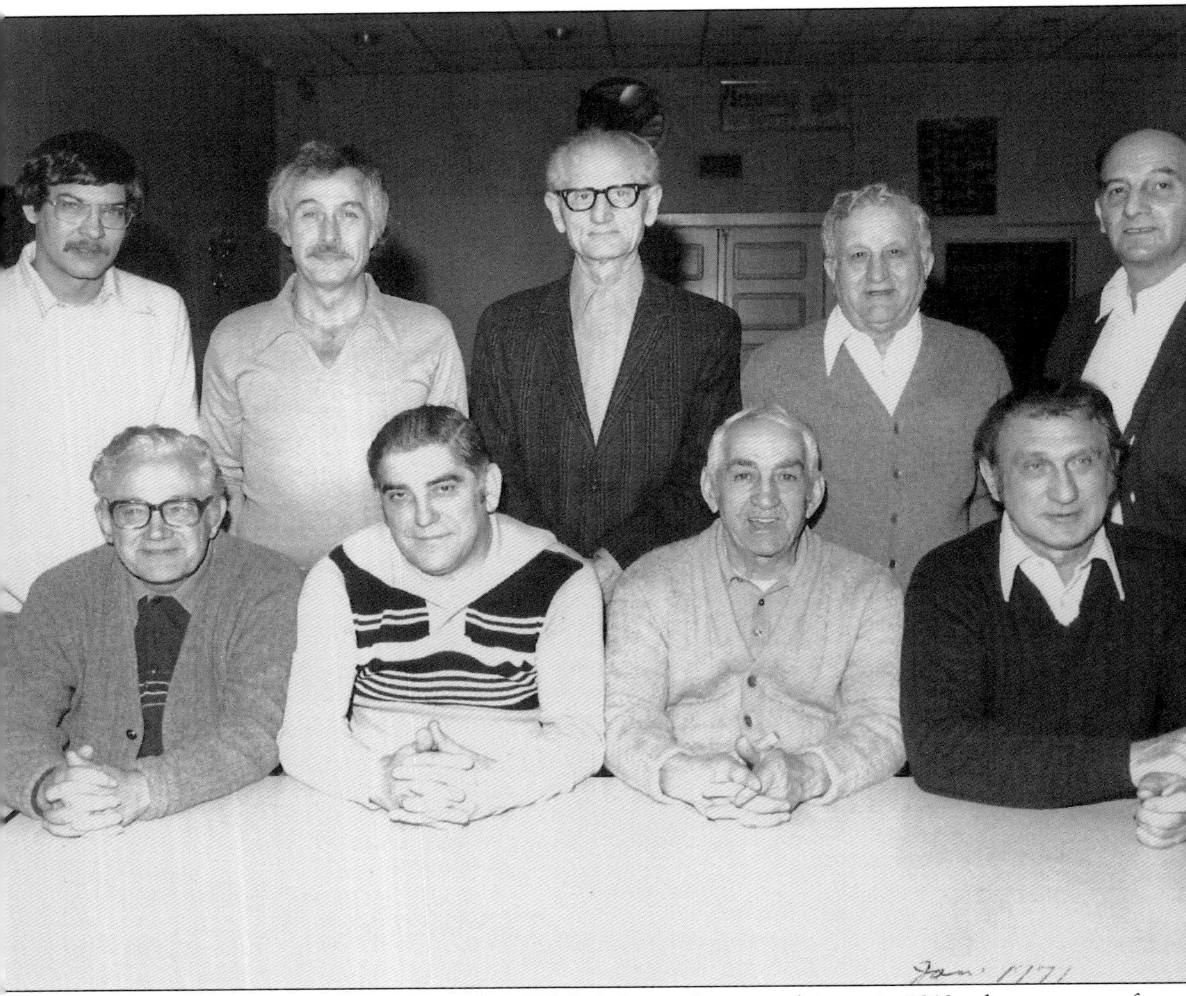

The Italian Assunta Club, located at 205 Oak Street, began its history in 1910, when a group of Italian immigrants wanted to incorporate some of their traditions into their new lives in Mount Pleasant. As active members in St. Bernadine's Church, these Italian men and women formed a vital outreach of service to the community. Some of the community events included a weekly bingo and fundraisers that supported the members and the senior citizens. As a thriving service-oriented association, the women and men became integral to providing many social activities, including games, auctions, and crafts. The former officers featured prominently here are (seated) D. Ciprella, G. Spinella, F. Comfort, and J. Testa; (standing) J. DiPasquale, F. Damico, C. Splendore, S. Visconti, and J. D'Amato. (Courtesy of Mary Agnes Spinella and Gerri Spinella.)

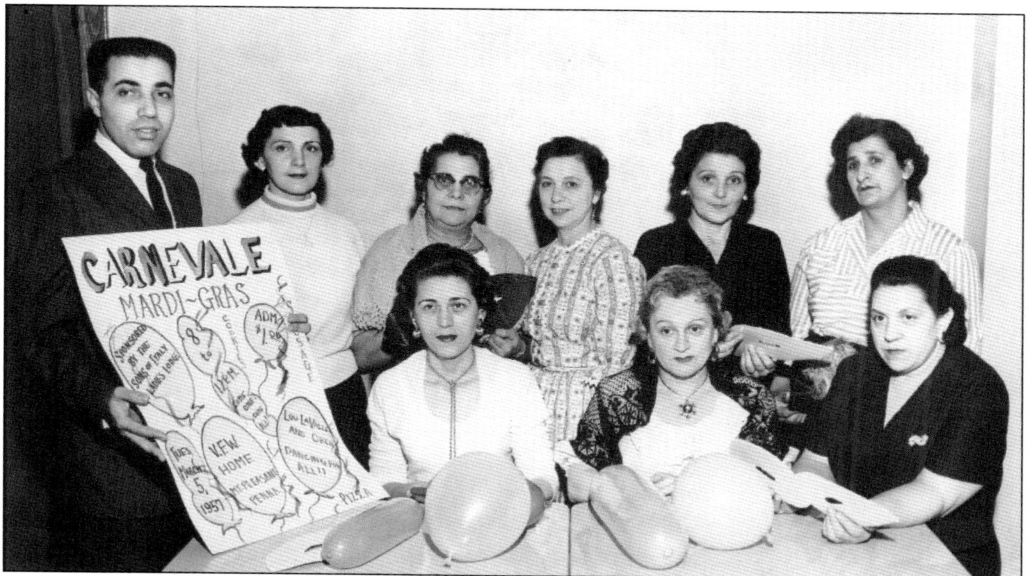

The Italian culture thrived in promoting the traditions and camaraderie for its members and the community at large. For example, the Sons of Italy Ladies Lodge sponsored the Carnevale Mardi-Gras in 1957. Pictured from left to right are (seated) T. Tesauro, E. Antonette, and J. Zeman; (standing) M. Comfort (a former art teacher at Mount Pleasant High School), A. Miele, E. Constabile, J. Coppolino, ? DePalma, and M. Ceroni. They promoted the dancing, food, and entertainment for all to share. (Courtesy of the Mount Pleasant Public Library Archives.)

These women in traditional Italian clothing share artifacts from Italy, including a *carretto siciliano* (Sicilian cart), which is a colorful carved horse-drawn carriage with two wheels that was primarily used to carry produce, wood, wine, or people in Sicily. Pictured here are (seated) R. Rozell and T. Tesauro; (standing) E. Antonette, A. Miele, E. Constabile, J. Zeman, and J. Coppolino. (Courtesy of the Mount Pleasant Public Library Archives.)

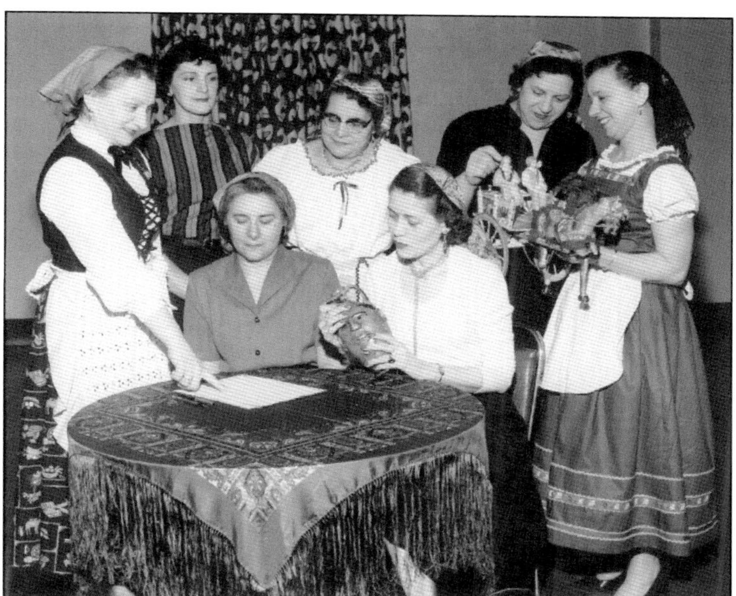

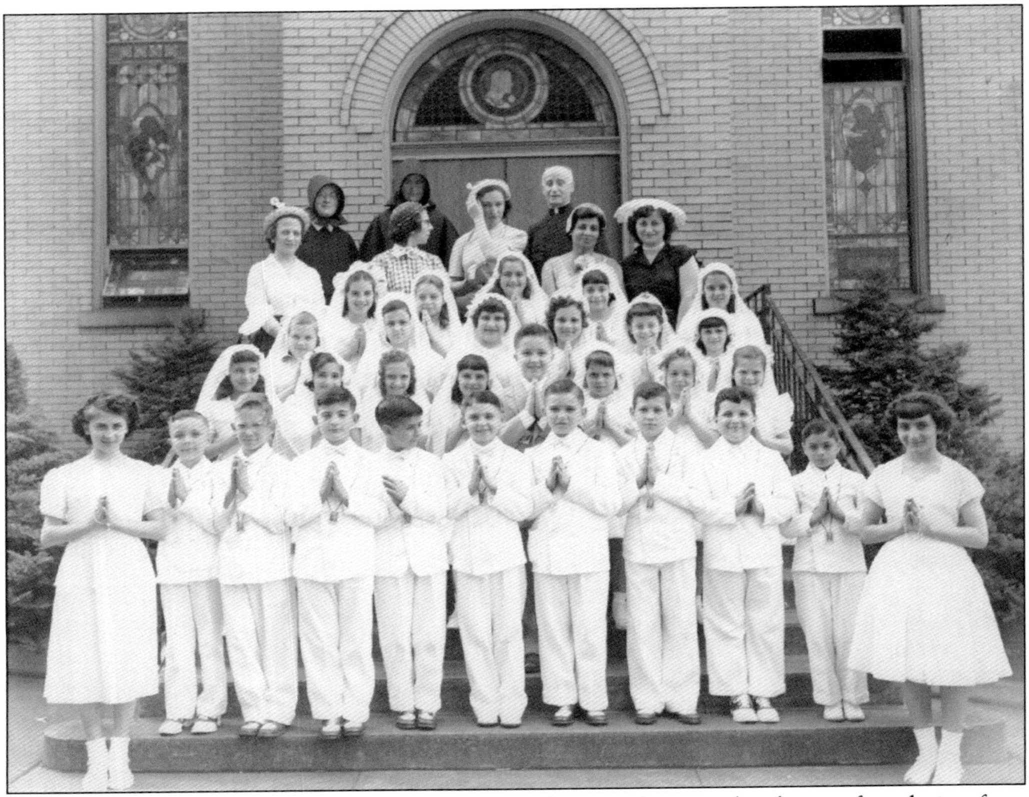

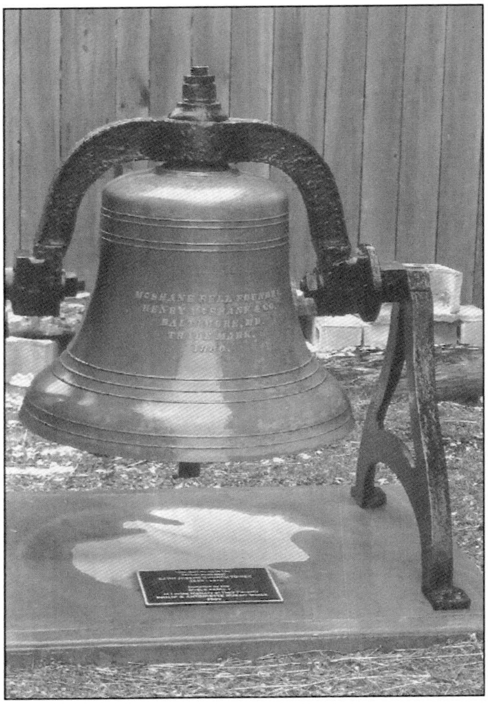

Religious education has been a foundation for youth from many different denominations. Established in 1906, St. Bernadine's Church had a long tradition of educating children. The first communion class of June 15, 1952, is shown on the front steps of the church. Pictured with the children are Reverend DeSantis, two Sisters of Charity, and instructors T. Galone, F. Farrell, C. Miele, R. Farrell, and F. Comfort. These individuals were instrumental in readying these children for this important Catholic sacrament. (Courtesy of Theresa Benedict.)

This bell was obtained from the tower of St. Joseph's Church by the Miele family. In loving memory of their parents, Philip and Antoinette Rosso Miele, the bell was donated to the Mount Pleasant Area Historical Society by the Miele family in 2009. The bell is part of Old Town and takes its place of significance with the two log cabins. (Courtesy of Rose Eckman.)

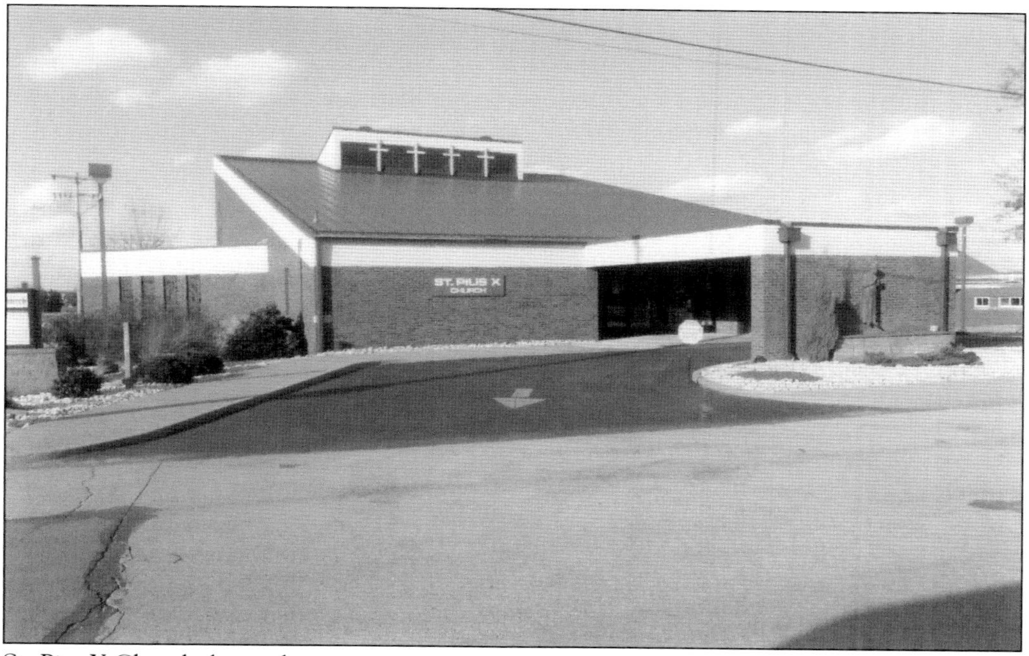

St. Pius X Church, located on Summit Street, serves 1,167 households for a total of 2,077 individuals. This modern-style church was built in 1978. Adjacent to the church is an active community center that provides service activities—including Lenten meals, breakfasts, and bingo games—that benefit the community at large. (Courtesy of Nancy Sebek.)

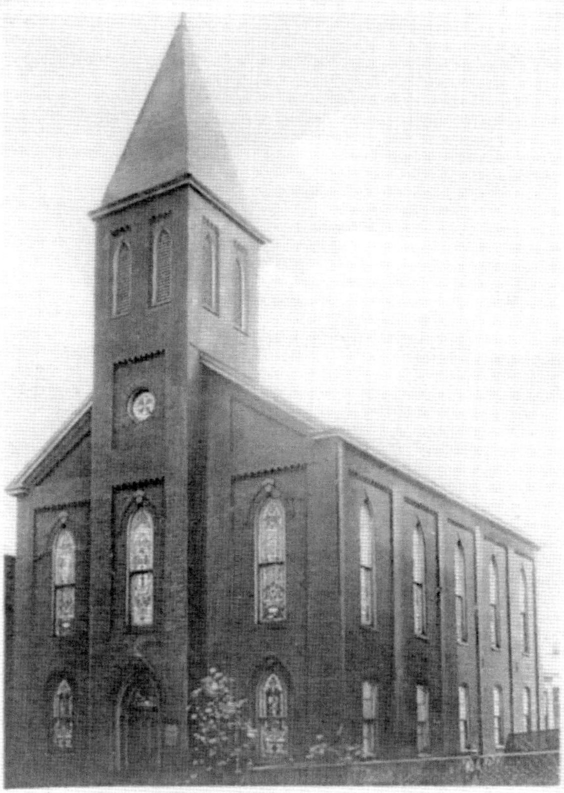

First Baptist Church, Mt. Pleasant, Pa.

In 1803, the First Baptist Church was organized and located at 709 West Main Street. The brick building was constructed in 1869 and was destroyed by fire in 1894. However, due to the perseverance of the church members, the building was quickly restored. A central bell tower and brick pilasters are seen, with pointed, arched stained-glass windows that form the front the building. Following the Christian tradition, the communities of believers share their support through worship, fellowship, and service. (Courtesy Merl and Fay Pritts.)

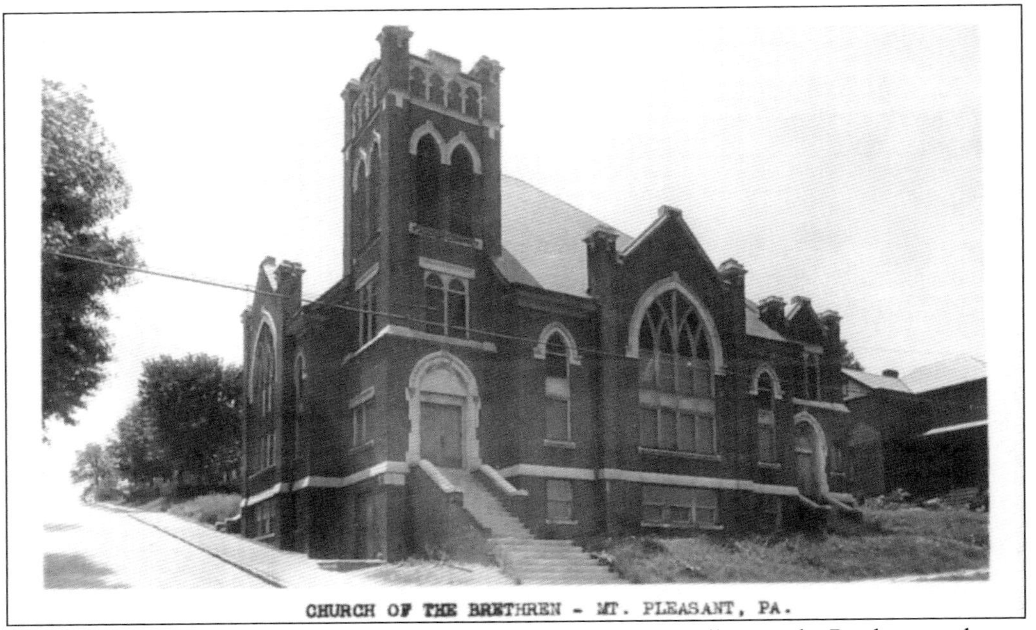

The Church of the Brethren is located at 201 Washington Street. Following the Brethren tradition, this community supports volunteer service in the community and connections to the mission at large. These welcoming communities provide worship, service, and celebrations to all. (Courtesy of the Mount Pleasant Public Library Archives.)

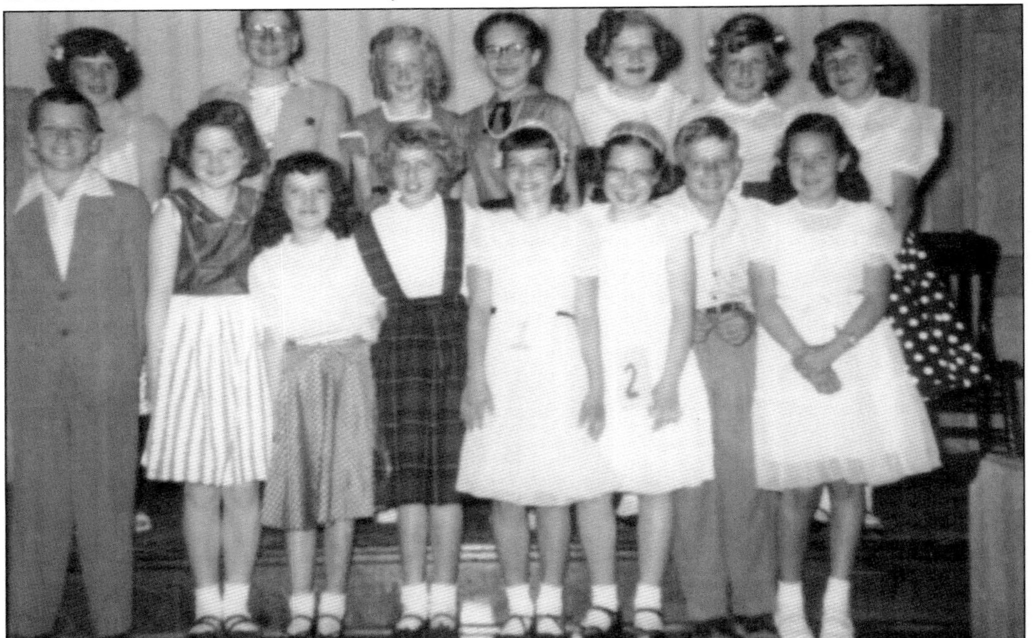

The 1953 Bible class of the Church of the Brethren is pictured here. From left to right are (first row) B. Eutsey, K. Christner, S. Eutsey, V. Overly, K. McIndoe, N. Solomon, V. Bitner, and A. Miller; (second row) N. Eutsey, unidentified , B. Baird, B. Geary, F. Overly, and two unidentified girls. (Courtesy of Nancy Sebek.)

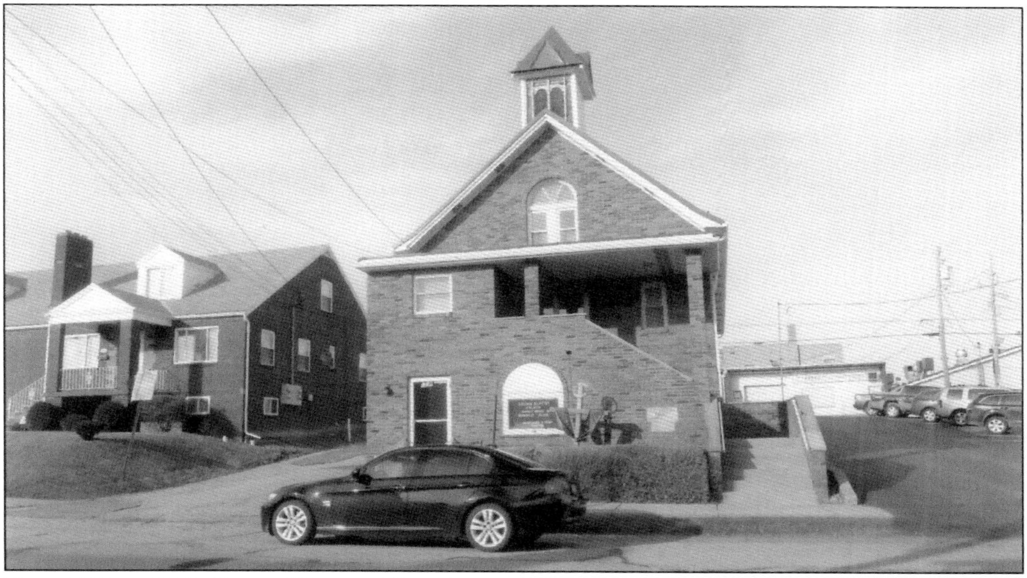

From 1896 to 1900, Second Baptist Church met in the Mud Lane School House on North Shupe Street. In 1915, they built their present church on Washington Street. Over the years, they have made many improvements to the church. In 2014, Second Baptist Church added a vibrant, new red-metal roof. The Second Baptist Church cultivates Christ-centered values that celebrate faith, fellowship, and service to the community and connections to other churches. Rev. Dr. William Terry leads the congregation. (Courtesy of Nancy Sebek.)

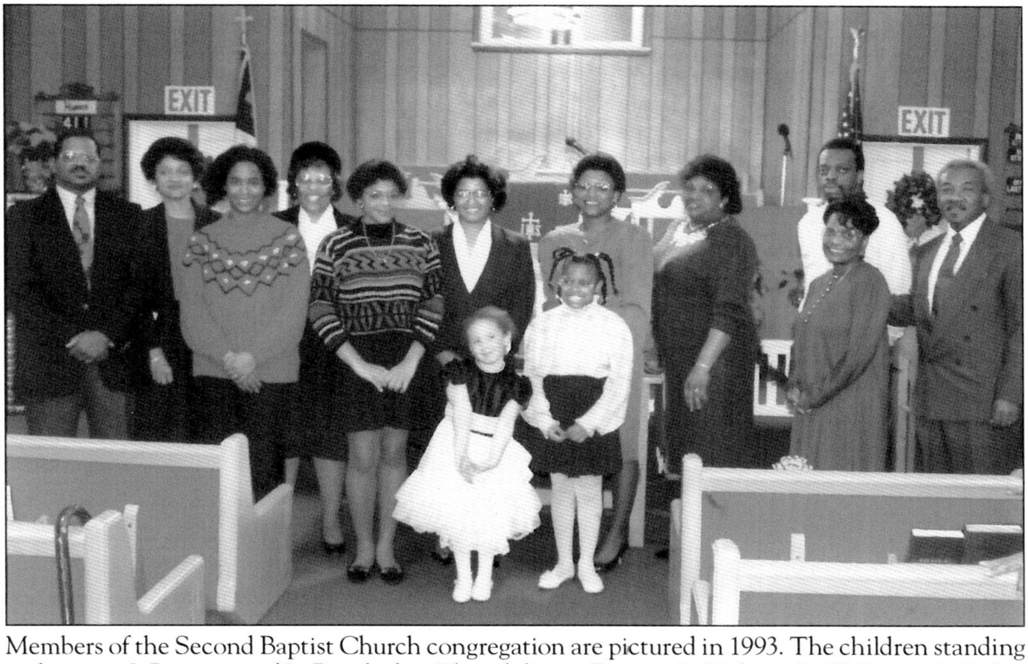

Members of the Second Baptist Church congregation are pictured in 1993. The children standing in front are J. Bryman and L. Bundridge. The adults are Deacon L. Wilson, D. Williams, S. Coles, E. Thomas, N. Williams, P. Brymm, A. Bundridge, S. Rogers, R. Rogers, Rev. J. Whitley-Fields, and Rev. F. Fields. (Courtesy of LaRoyal Wilson.)

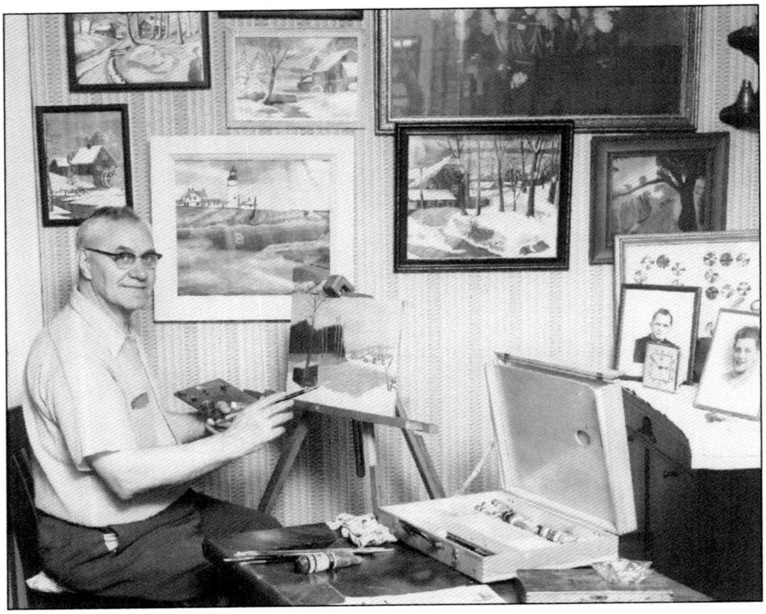

John Jendras was a recognized artist in the community who painted landscapes and portraits. He was the grandfather of Lynn Hebda, who was an art teacher in the Mount Pleasant School District. Although he had a plumbing and heating business, Jendras had a passion as an artist. His first art show was held at the Tree of Life Synagogue. (Courtesy of the Mount Pleasant Public Library Archives.)

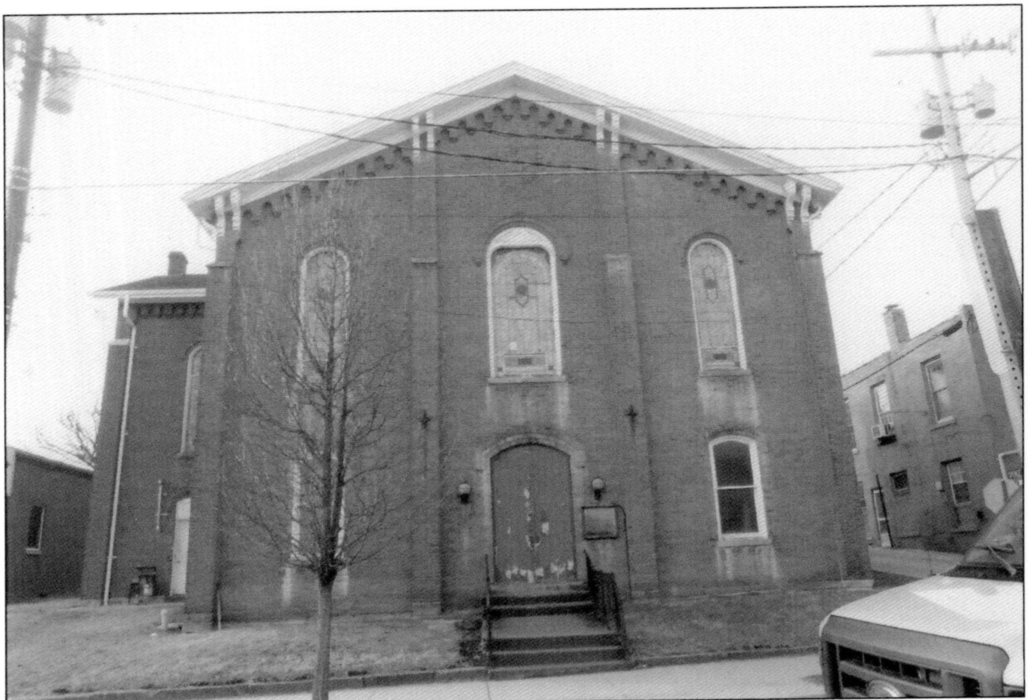

The Tree of Life Synagogue was established to promote the cultural and spiritual needs of the Jewish community. Members of this congregation were prominent in establishing several businesses. When the congregation moved to Greensburg, other religious groups used the building for a time; eventually, it was donated to the community. (Courtesy of the Mount Pleasant Public Library Archives.)

Visitation of the Blessed Virgin Mary Roman Catholic Church, often called the Slavish Roman Catholic Church, is noted for its Eastern European traditions. This yellow-brick, two-tower structure is used by 952 households, a total of 1,570 individuals. Next to the church, the community center is noted for providing activities, including breakfasts and fundraisers that serve the community at large. It is located at 740 Walnut Street and is a partner parish to St. Pius X in Mount Pleasant. (Courtesy of Kathy Stanislaw.)

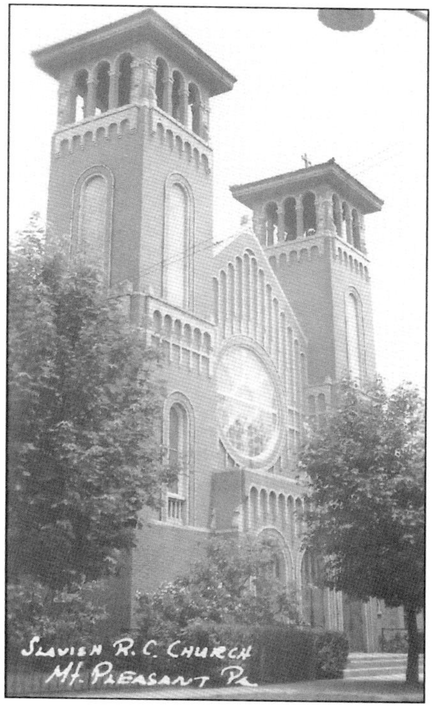

This graduating class of eighth graders holds their diplomas, which are rolled up like scrolls. Taught by the Vincentian Sisters of Charity, the students have met the requirements of their parochial education. Reverend Janda presided over the graduation. (Courtesy of the Mount Pleasant Public Library Archives.)

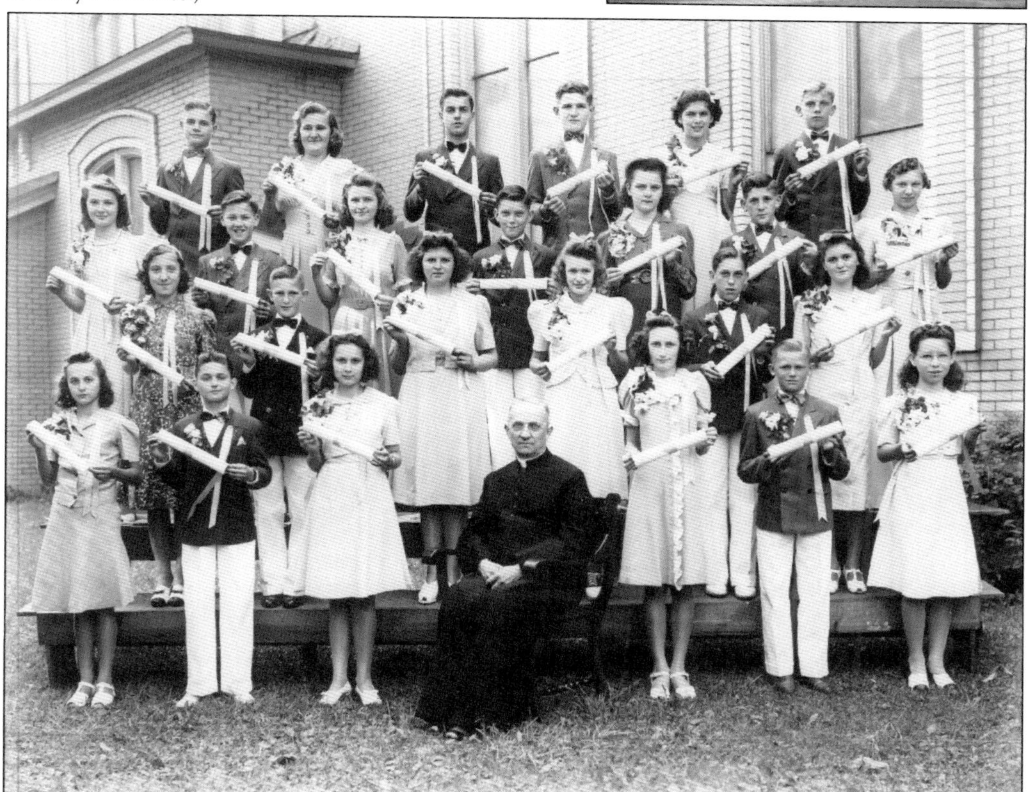

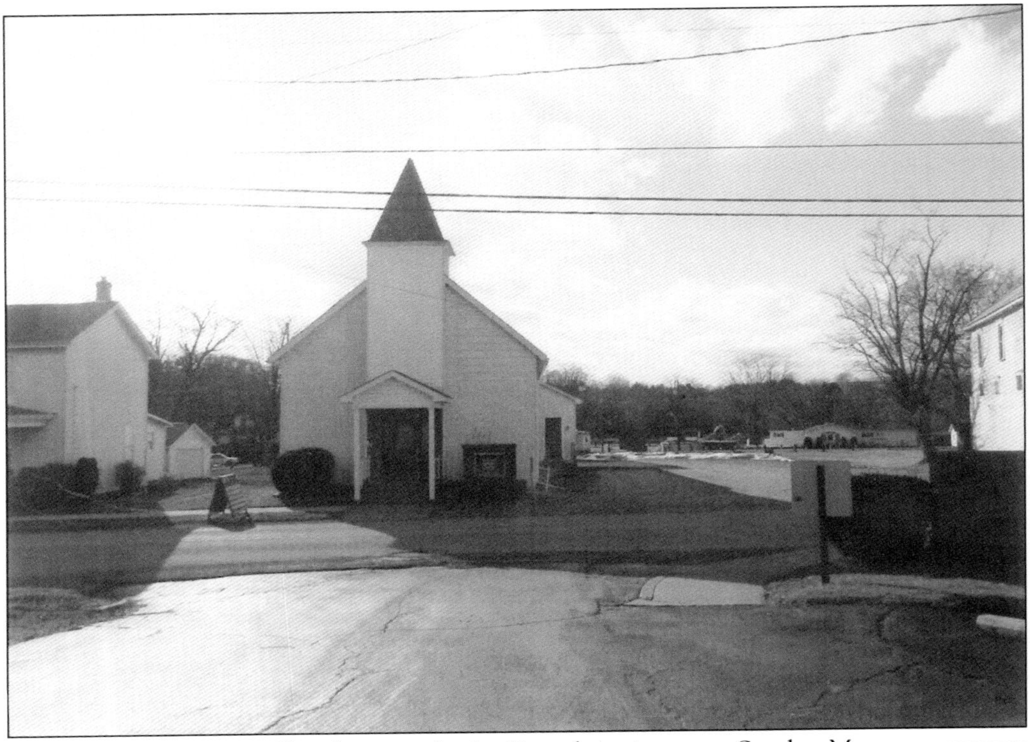

New Hope Community Church is popular for Gospel singing every Sunday. Many congregants attend this celebration. (Courtesy of Bonnie Wilson.)

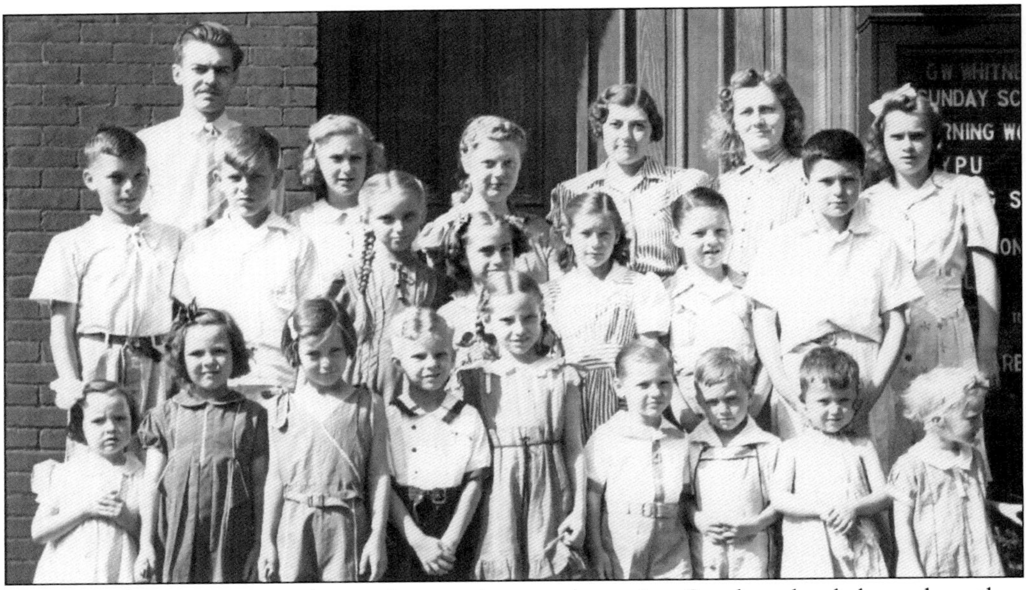

Following the Protestant tradition, these students took part in a Sunday school class, where they learned about their traditions and participated in worship in their churches. In these religious settings, the children were important to the overall development of values and service in their church communities. (Courtesy of the Mount Pleasant Public Library Archives.)

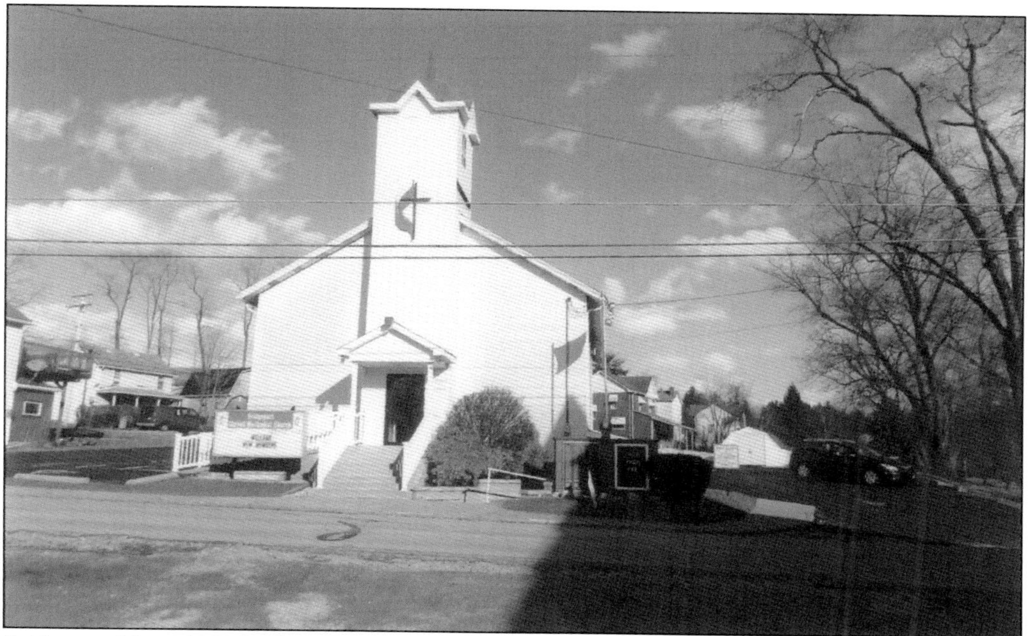

Bridgeport United Methodist Church was established in 1877. This church began with 52 members in the lower level of Jacob Sigwalt's home and stayed there until 1883, when the church building was erected. Bridgeport United Methodist Church was part of Paradise United Methodist Church when it was an Evangelical church. There have been several renovations over the years. They incorporated computer technology and added a pavilion in 2014. (Courtesy of Bonnie Wilson.)

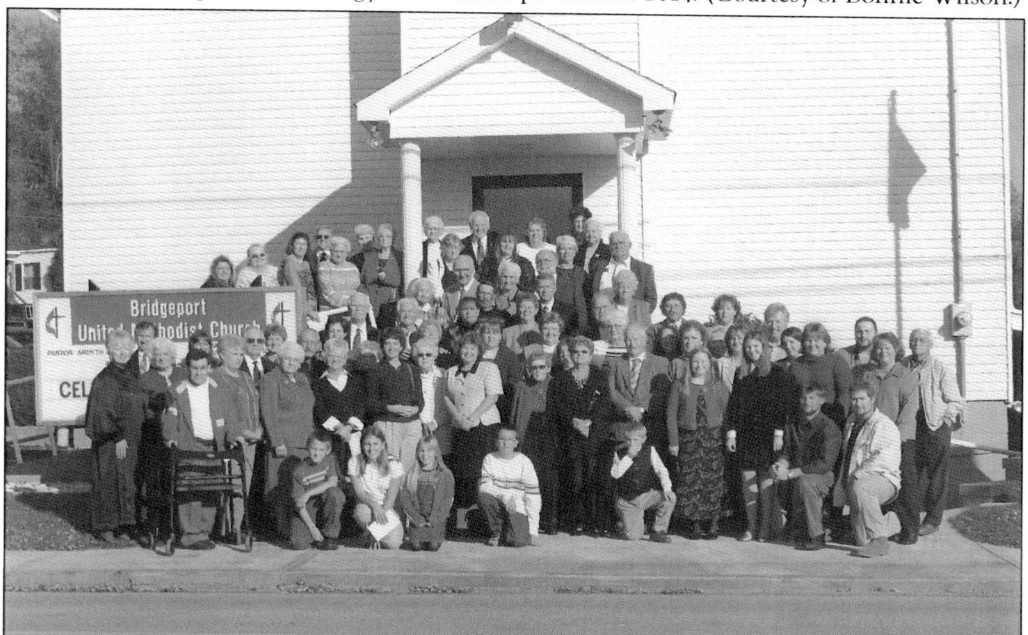

The congregation from Bridgeport United Methodist Church celebrated their 125th anniversary. Some of the pastors who attended this celebration include Rev. K. Lashen, J. Schmidt, Ardyth Hill, and R. Trudgen. (Courtesy of Bonnie Wilson.)

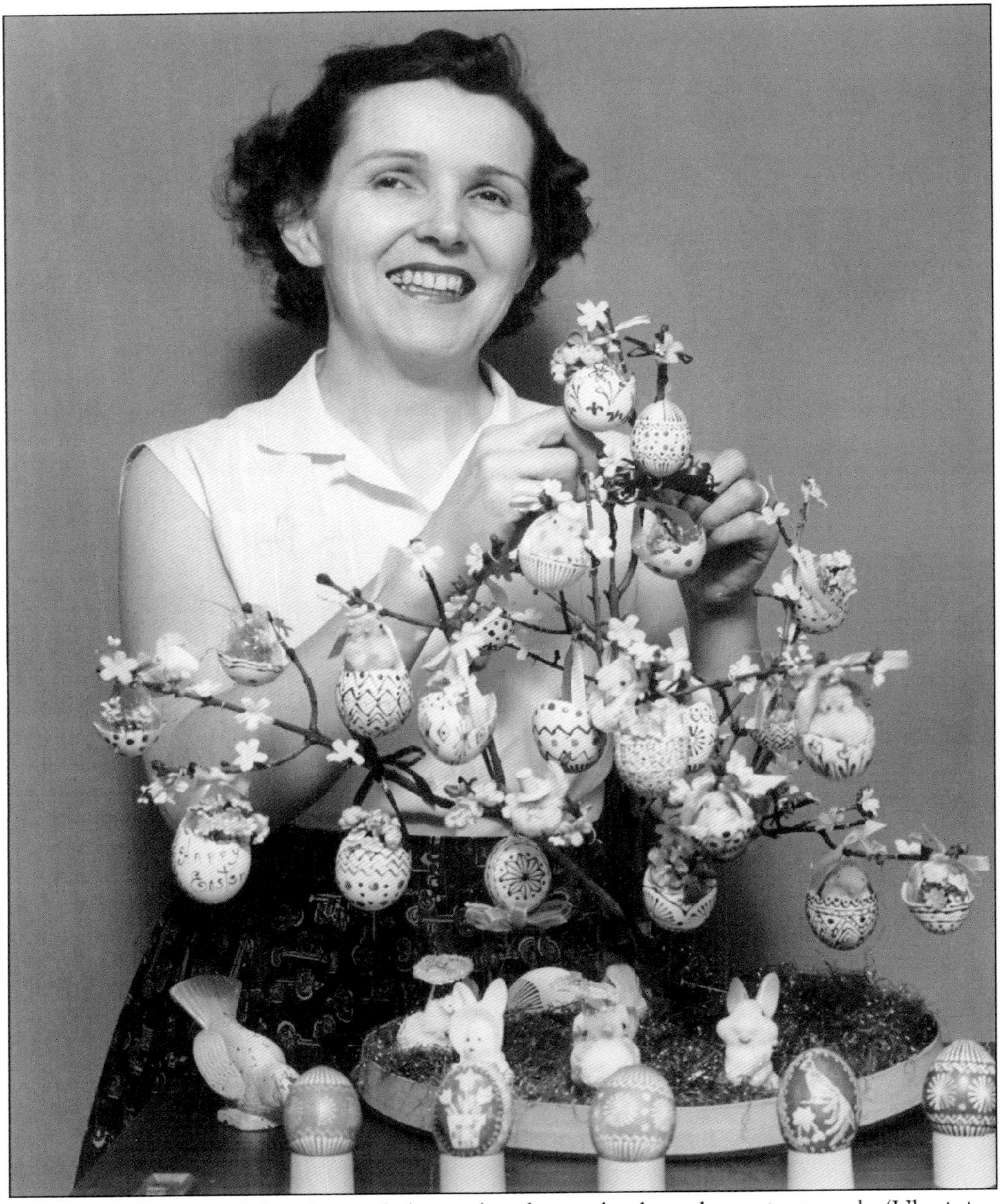

Nancy Macaluso—a well-loved artist, baker, and gardener—has been decorating *pysanky* (Ukrainian Easter egg) for over 75 years. She mastered the art from her mother, who lived in the village of Lemoko, near the Ukrainian Border. During the Easter season, Nancy would continue this folk-art custom, which began in Central Europe. Nancy was noted for baking delicious pies, quiches, and special-order desserts for Nino's Restaurant. For over 25 years, Nancy made pizzas weekly with J. Caletri, J. Visconti, and many more at the Monday-night bingo of St. Pius X Church. Nancy's generous spirit will be remembered for her sharing and giving to the community. (Courtesy of Maria Macaluso.)

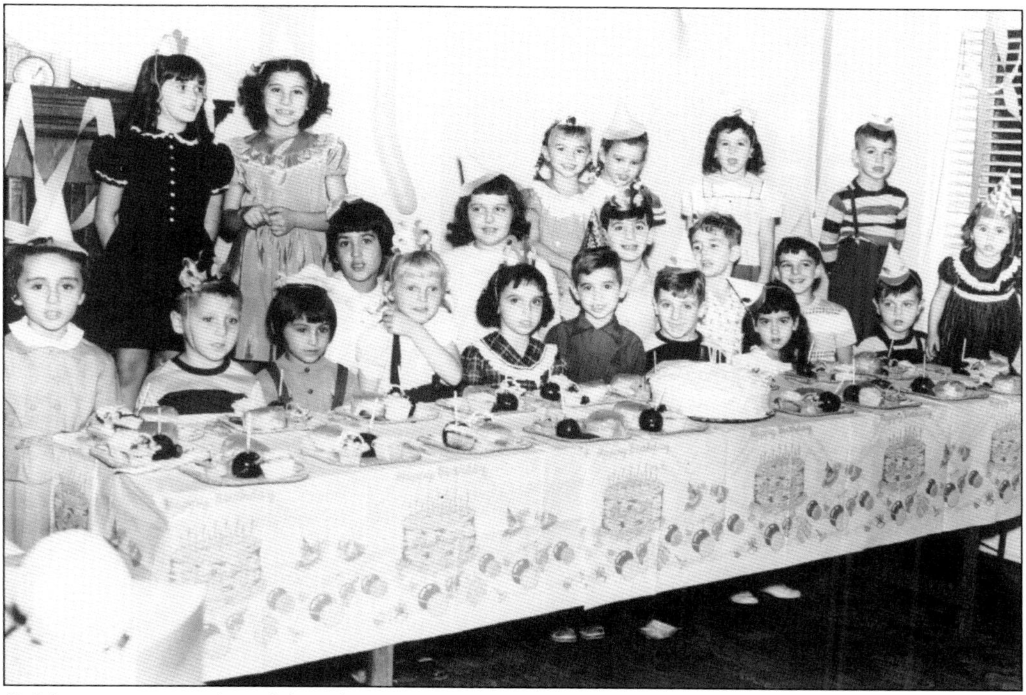

Celebrations were plentiful in the community, such as this birthday party for Anthony Caletri. Food was abundant, and each child wore a colorful birthday hat. (Courtesy of the Mount Pleasant Public Library Archives.)

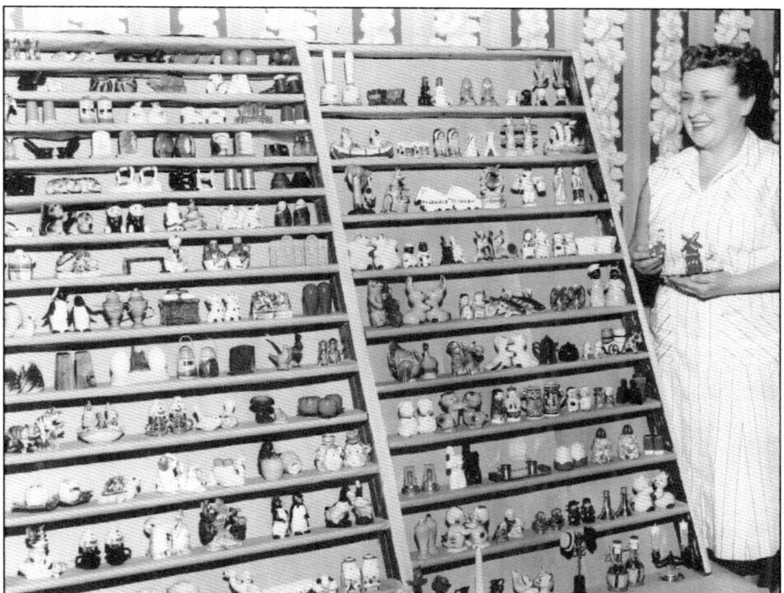

Mrs. Dolan displays her one-of-a-kind collection of salt-and-pepper shakers. This visual display included many varieties of shakers, including animals and other familiar objects for all to appreciate. (Courtesy of the Mount Pleasant Public Library Archives.)

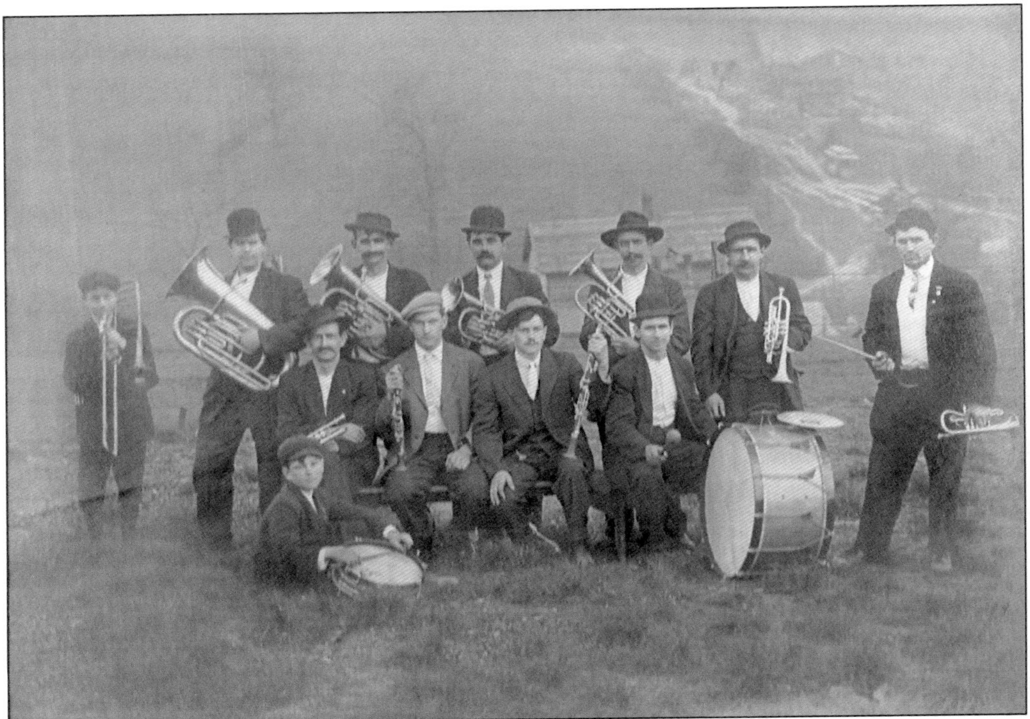

The oompah-type band was prominent in the Mount Pleasant community because it represented a distinct blending of sounds from the tuba, clarinet, trombone, and drums. Previously associated with popular German music, this band played the polka or the waltz. The Mount Pleasant City Band expanded by including more players, who were also part of the community's parades and festivities. One can see that the clarinet was added to the band, and there is a prominent drum major in the front. Mount Pleasant is noted for its bands, whose versatility in playing melodies from different ethnic groups added to their popularity. (Both photographs courtesy of Kathy Stanislaw.)

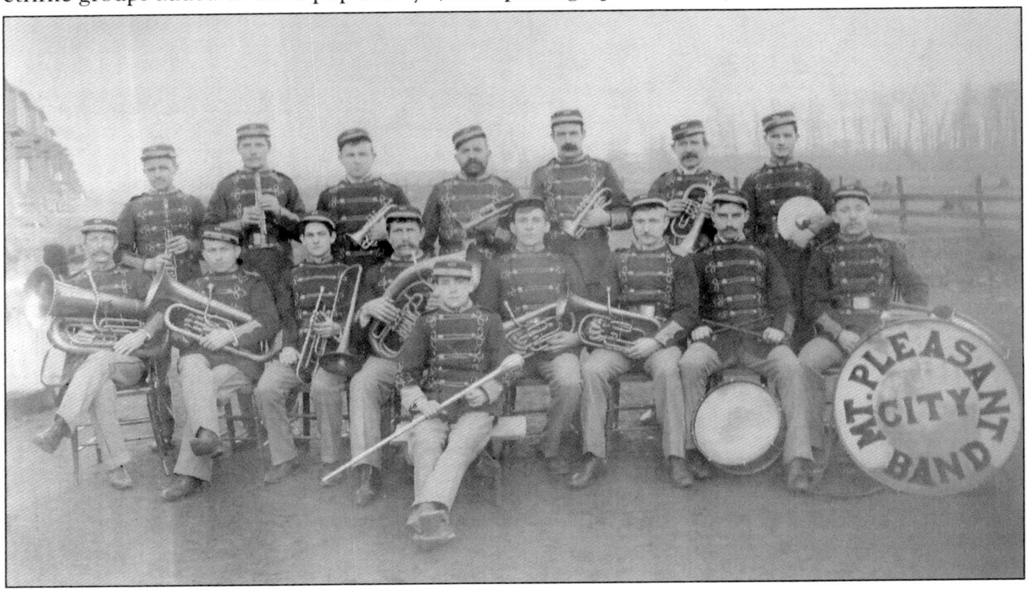

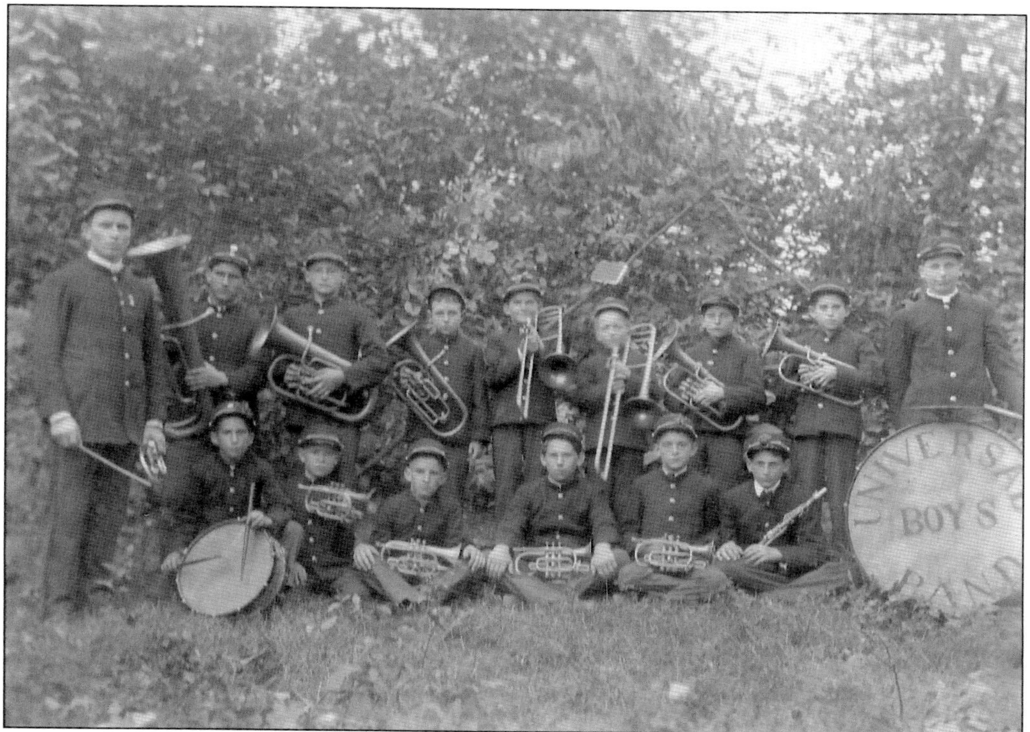

In early 1900s, The Universal Boys Band was established to train boys to play the trombone, tuba, horn, and drums. Its vibrant tone and melodies could be heard at local parades and festivities. Each boy is dressed in a uniform that includes a hat, a tailored one-button down coat, and white pants, which were popular during this time. (Courtesy of Kathy Stanislaw.)

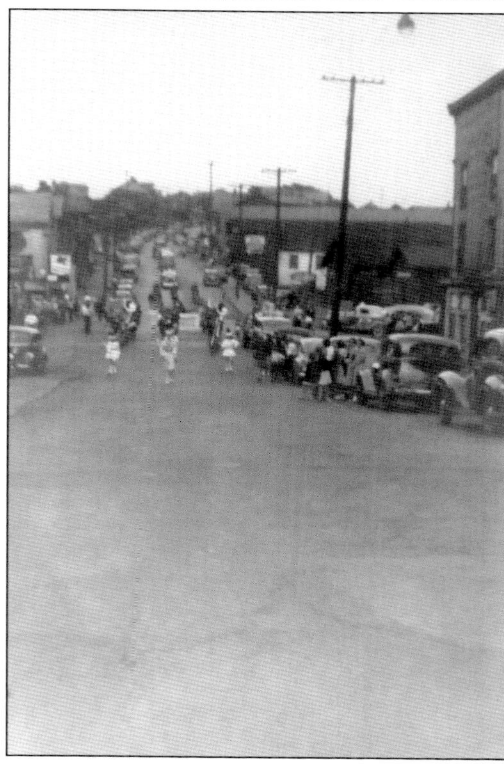

Parades were an integral part of holiday celebrations in Mount Pleasant. In this photograph looking east on Main Street, the Mount Pleasant High School band performs in a parade, following the tradition of making music part of the community's culture. (Courtesy of the Mount Pleasant Public Library Archives.)

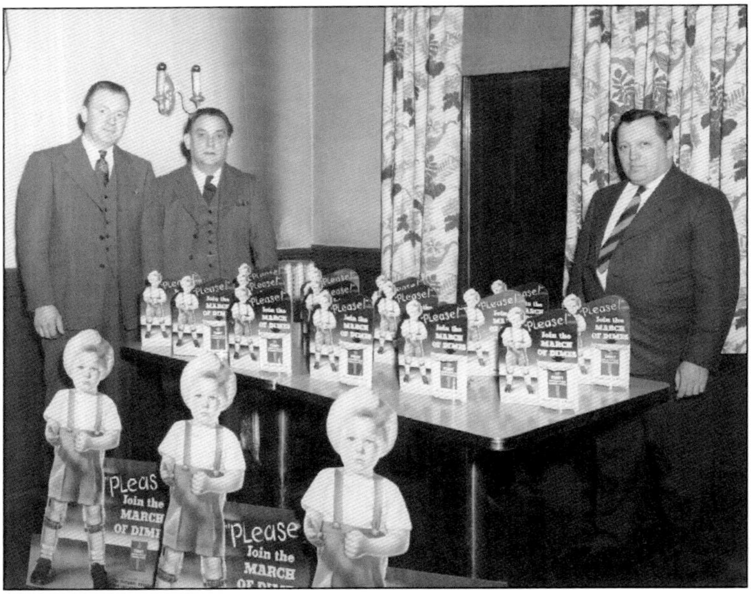

Outreach to others is essential to building community values. Mount Pleasant promoted this service through many different fundraisers, thereby connecting the community to the world at large. Here, village officials, including R.C. Bingaman and H. Lentz, request that residents contribute to the March of Dimes. (Courtesy of the Mount Pleasant Public Library Archives.)

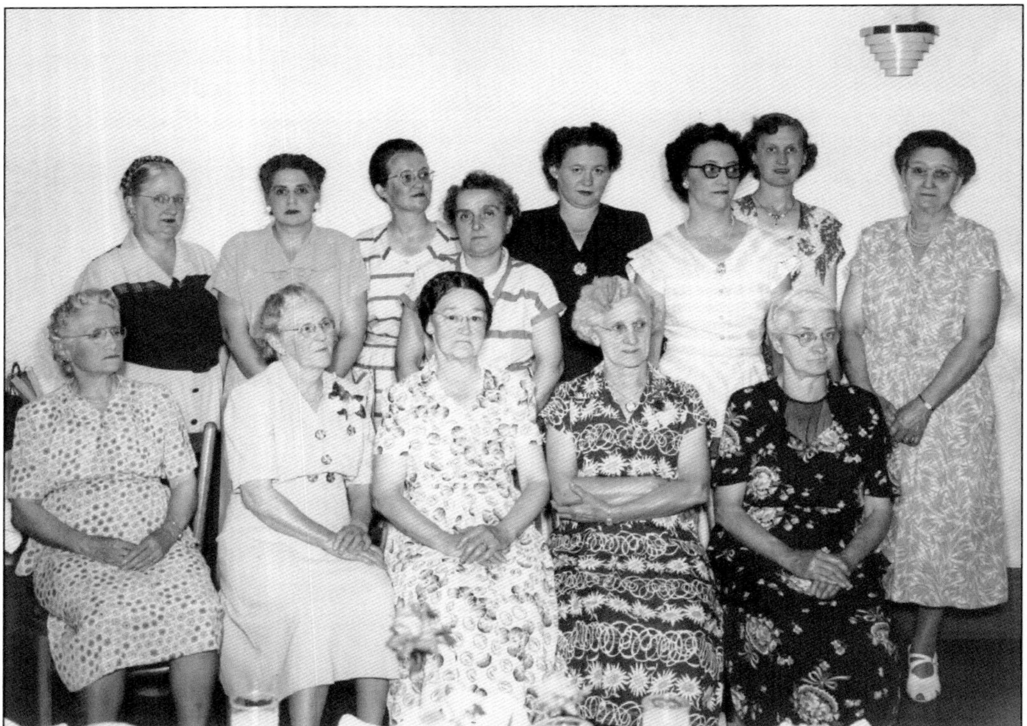

The Ladies Firemen's Auxiliary was a strong group of women leaders who supported one another in promoting service to others. They offered their talents to several fundraisers and community-oriented ventures. Among those in this 1950 photograph are M.J. Noss, R. Martorella, A. Lentz, R. Benedict, F. Benedict, G. Sargent, and ? Hudek. (Courtesy of the Mount Pleasant Public Library Archives.)

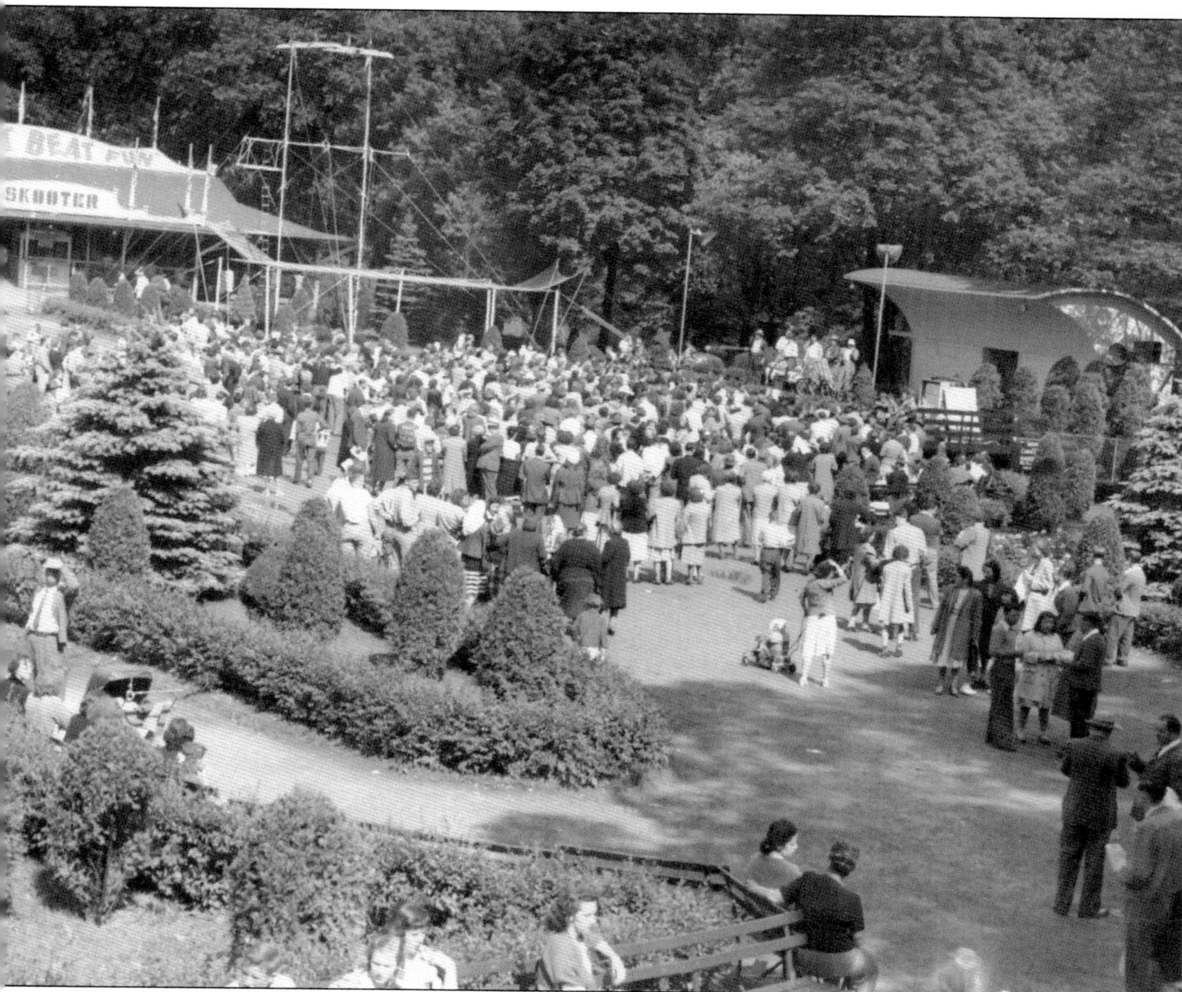

Civic pride was also promoted through annual community days, which were held at Idlewild Park in Ligonier, near Mount Pleasant. Many residents gathered to socialize with one another and enjoy the rides and entertainment available during this special day. (Courtesy of the Mount Pleasant Library Archives.)

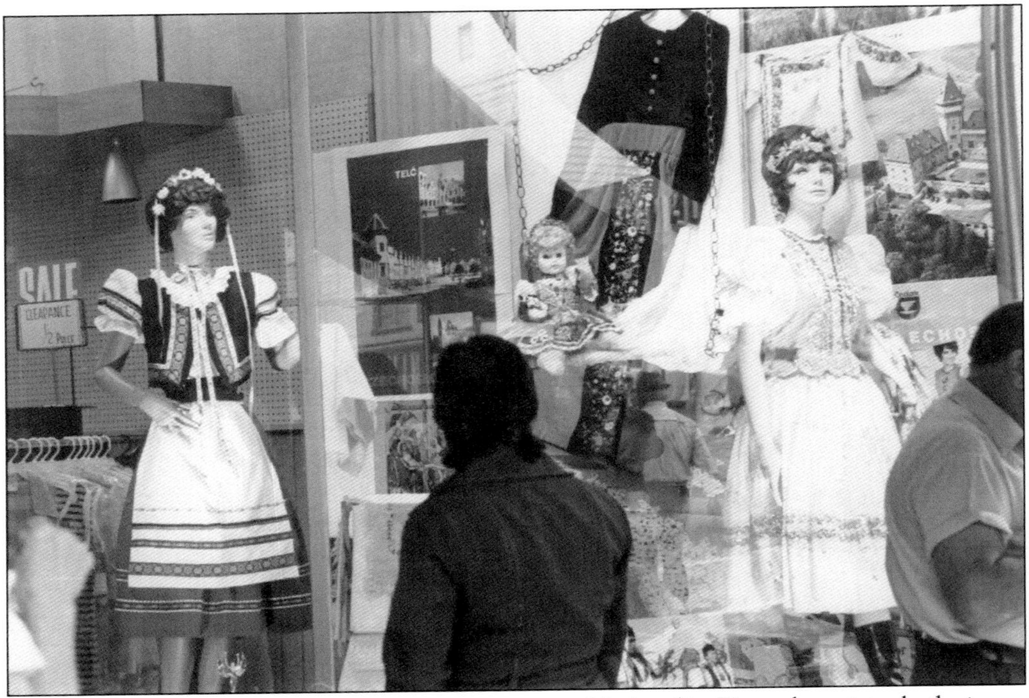

Nationality Days, the original ethnic celebration on Main Street, became the Ethnic Festival, which was later moved to Washington Street. Ethnic dress was displayed on mannequins, and there were dolls from different counties. (Courtesy of Maria Macaluso.)

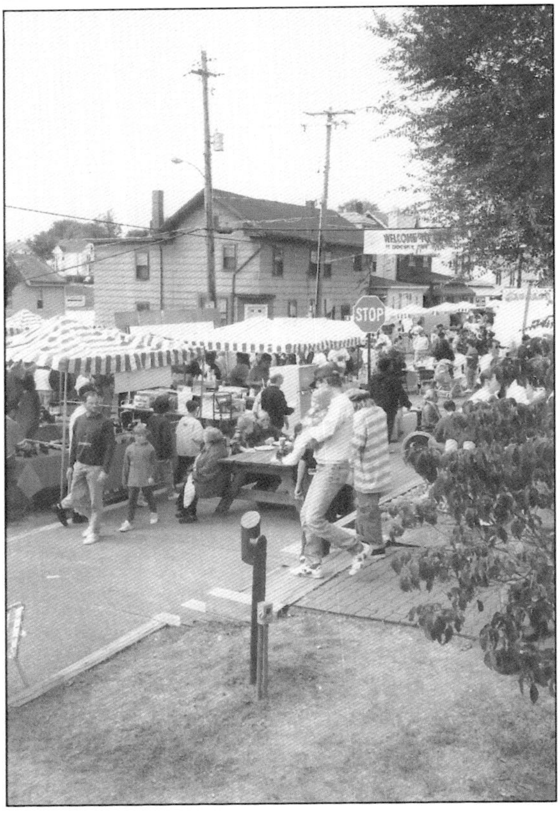

Volunteers under red-and-white tents supply food and crafts to visitors. People from near and far came to enjoy the different ethnic food and music, which was performed by local entertainers. (Courtesy of Maria Macaluso.)

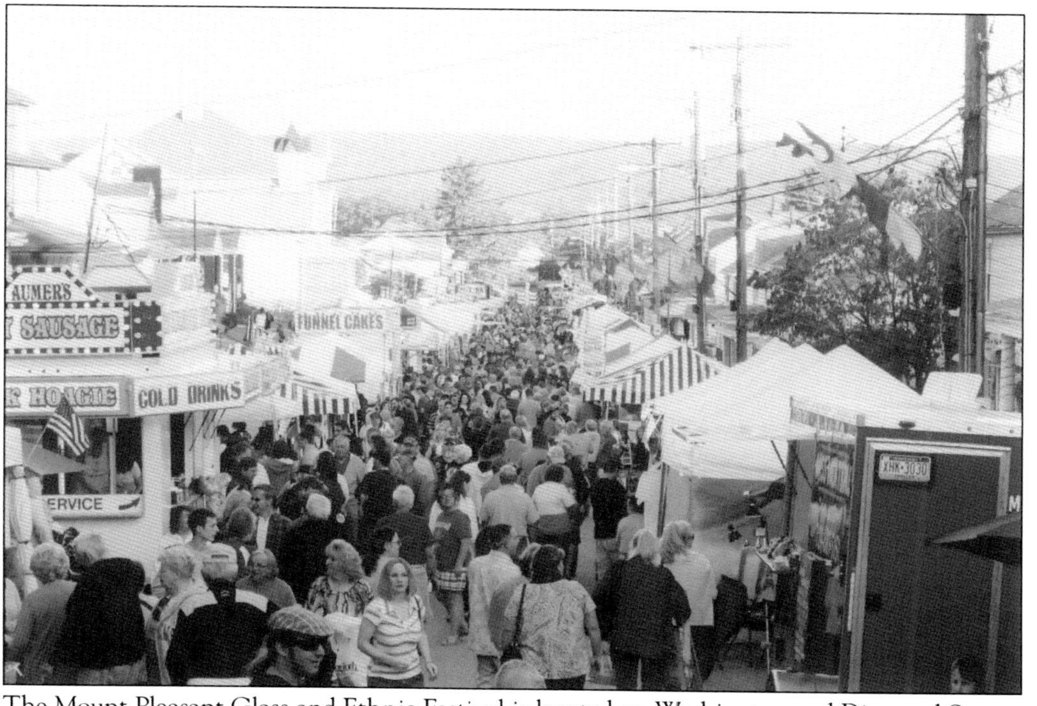

The Mount Pleasant Glass and Ethnic Festival is located on Washington and Diamond Streets and in Veterans Park. The three-day festival in September celebrates the town's industrial glass heritage and ethnic diversity. Over 100 vendor booths, entertainment, a sparkle spectacular light show, an illumination launch, a parade, and fireworks attract over 40,000 guests. The festival received its highest honor by being selected as an addition to the Library of Congress's Local Legacies project in 2000. (Courtesy the Mount Pleasant Glass and Ethnic Festival.)

Gerald Lucia, the present mayor of Mount Pleasant, has served for over 28 years. His leadership has encouraged growth and prosperity, including the establishment of the Veterans Wall and the Veterans Digital Wall. He also promotes the Ethnic Festival each September. Lucia and Mr. Landy, the borough manager, have a radio show that discusses current topics in the community. (Courtesy of Maria Macaluso.)

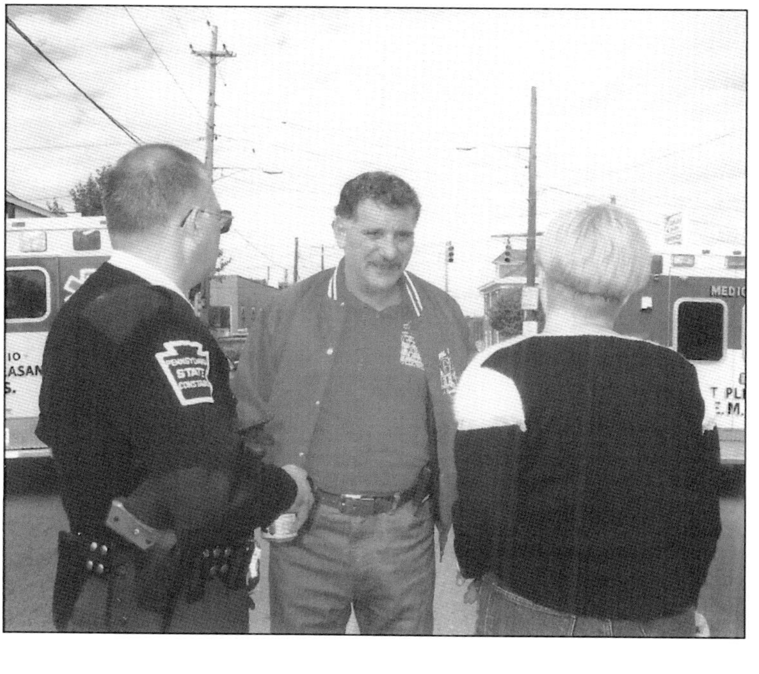

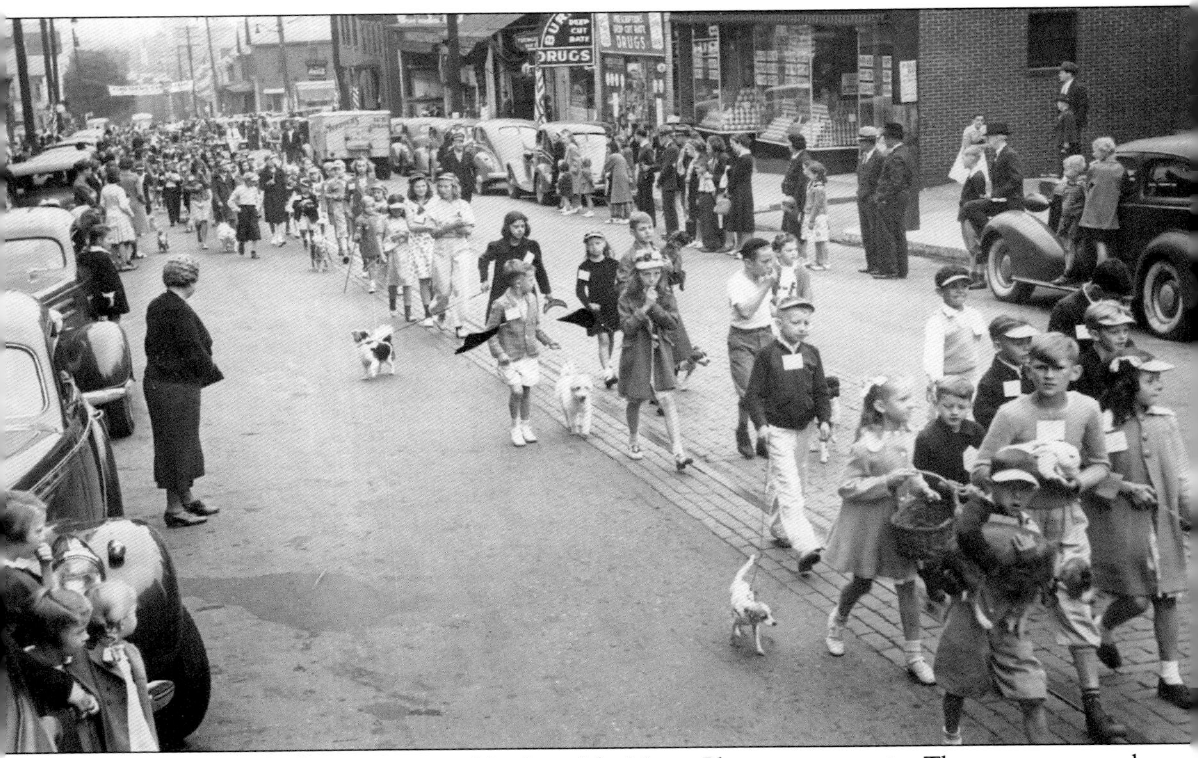

Children are the future citizens and leaders of the Mount Pleasant community. They are encouraged to show their patriotism in many ways. During this c. 1940 Fourth of July parade, children of different ages walked with their favorite pets down Main Street. Spectators were able to admire the children and their companions, which included dogs, rabbits, and other friends, too. The community continues to promote and encourage its children to be part of activities that enrich both their heritage and appreciation of all that is held dear in Mount Pleasant. (Courtesy of the Mount Pleasant Public Library Archives.)

Five

Progressing with Education

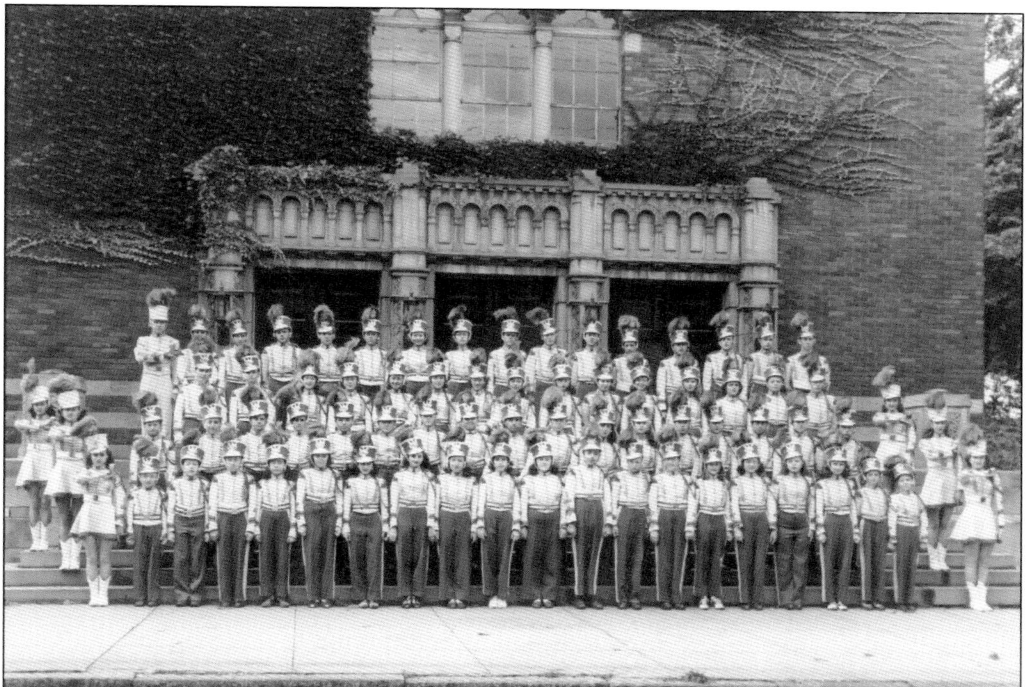

Mount Pleasant promotes the importance of extracurricular activities for students. Under the direction of Fred Houseman, the Ramsay High School band had a large student participation. Wearing their blue-and-white uniforms, the band's synchronized marching delighted spectators when they played at football games, parades, and in concerts. Pictured on the steps of the ivy-covered Ramsay High School, these students were proud to be part of this tradition. (Courtesy of the Mount Pleasant Public Library Archives.)

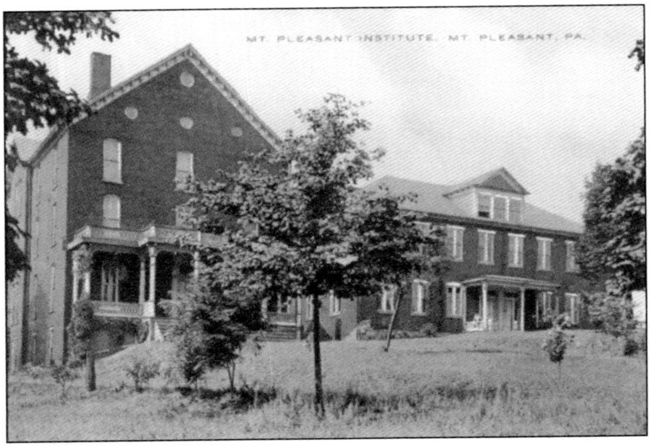

In 1849, Mount Pleasant became the site of one of the first colleges in the county. The college changed names five times before it closed in 1931. In 1936, a monetary endowment fund, buildings, and four acres of land were transferred to Bucknell University. Although the borough wanted the property for educational purposes, Bucknell sold it to Evertt Leadingham in 1941. (Courtesy of the Mount Pleasant Public Library Archives.)

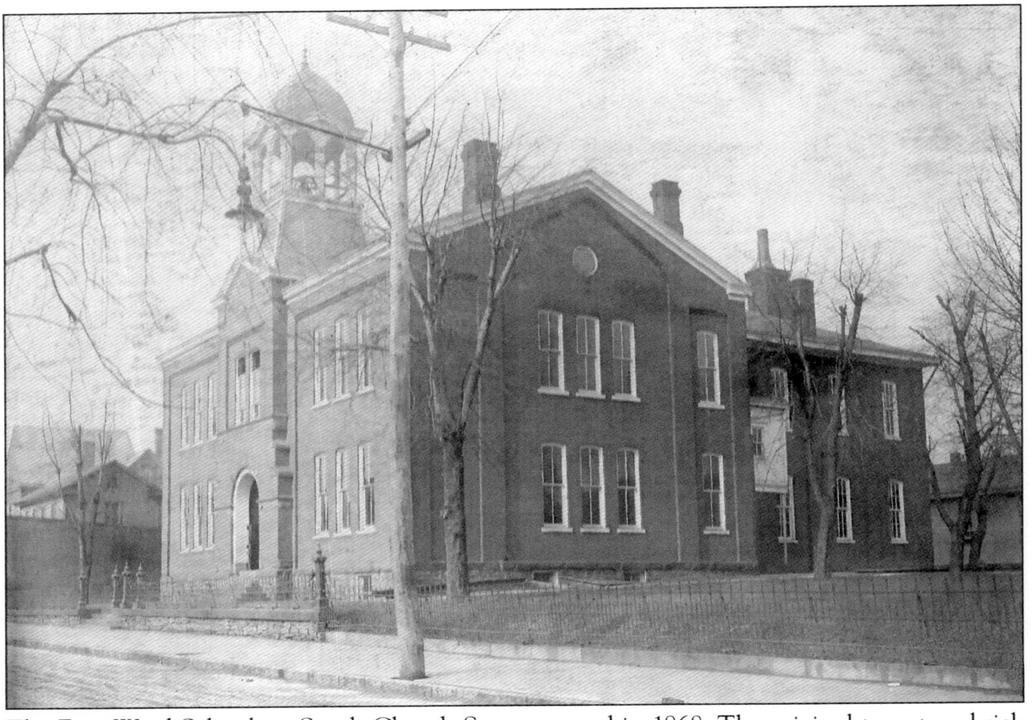

The First Ward School on South Church Street opened in 1868. The original two-story brick building had four rooms, and five additional rooms were added in 1885. It was a two-year high school with a curriculum that included algebra, bookkeeping, history, literature, and physiology. As enrollment increased over the years, a two-room building was built behind the school. In 1939, this building became the site of the Mount Pleasant Public Library. (Courtesy of the Mount Pleasant Public Library Archives.)

Sixth graders pose for a class picture on the lawn of the First Ward School in 1937–1938. Later, this school was used for industrial arts classes and as the headquarters of the turnpike commission while the Pennsylvania Turnpike was being built. (Courtesy of the Anthony and Jean Gaudiano family.)

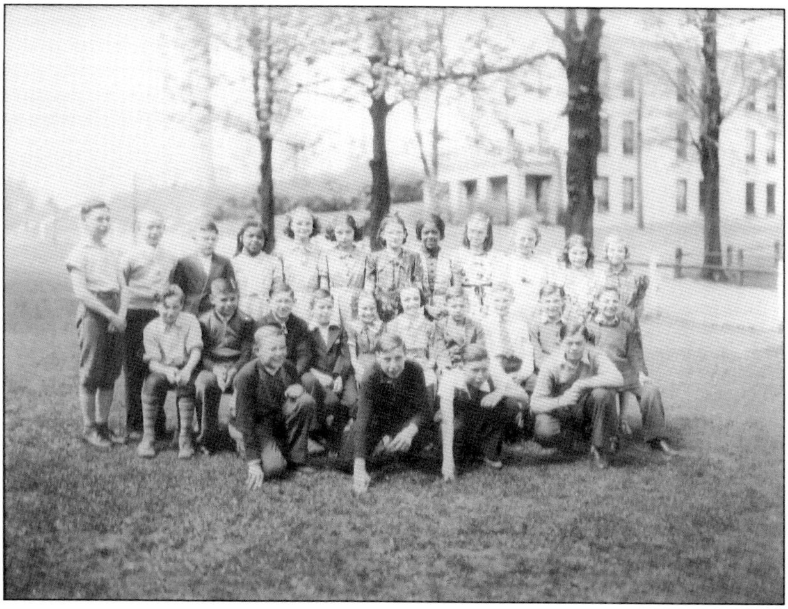

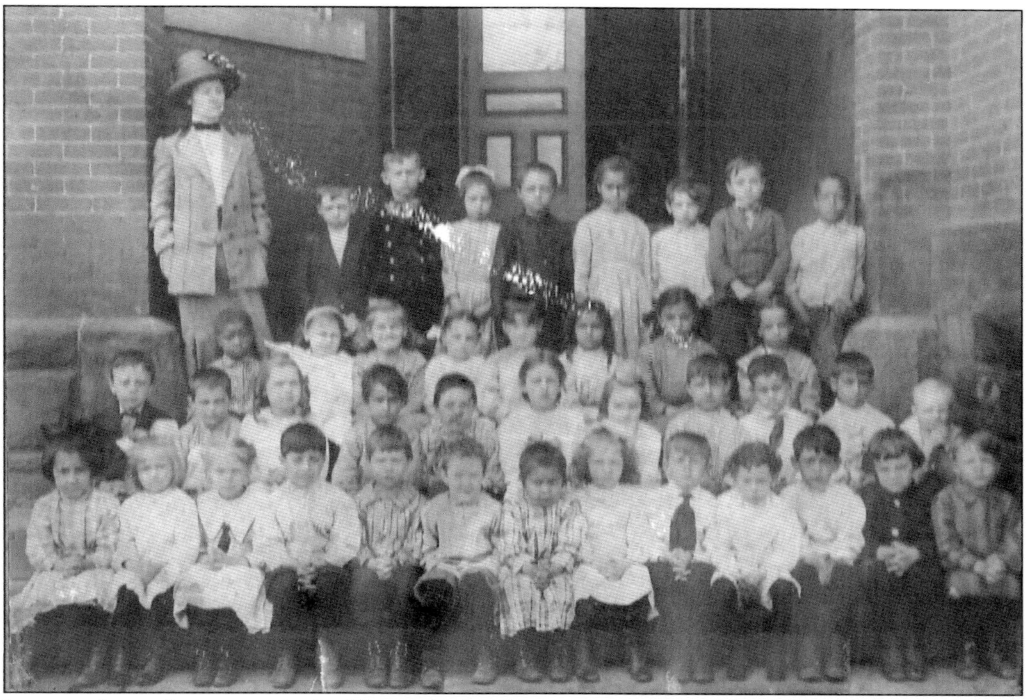

Increased population required additional school construction, and Third Ward School was built at the corner of Oak and Washington Streets in 1896. It had 13 rooms and was constructed of red brick. At the present time, Third Ward is a child-care facility. (Courtesy of the Anthony and Jean Gaudiano family.)

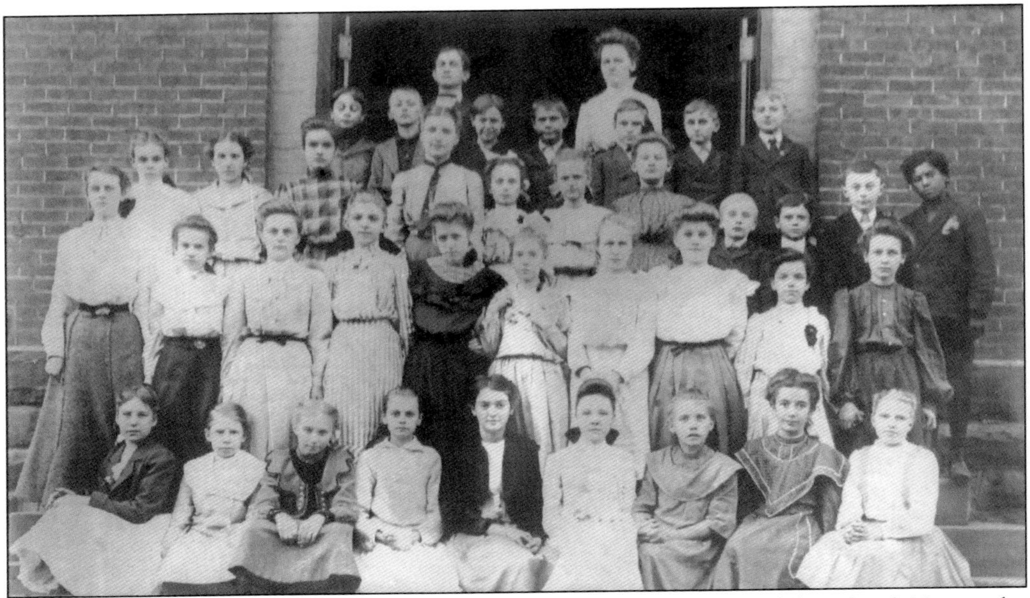

Third Ward students pose for a class picture in 1930 on the side steps of the school. Notice the girls' long dresses with sashes and the boys' suits with ties. The school housed grades one through six. In the back row are the two teachers, one male and one female. Students had a traditional education and were taught by one teacher, who taught all the subjects and often had more than one class in a room. (Courtesy of the Anthony and Jean Gaudiano family.)

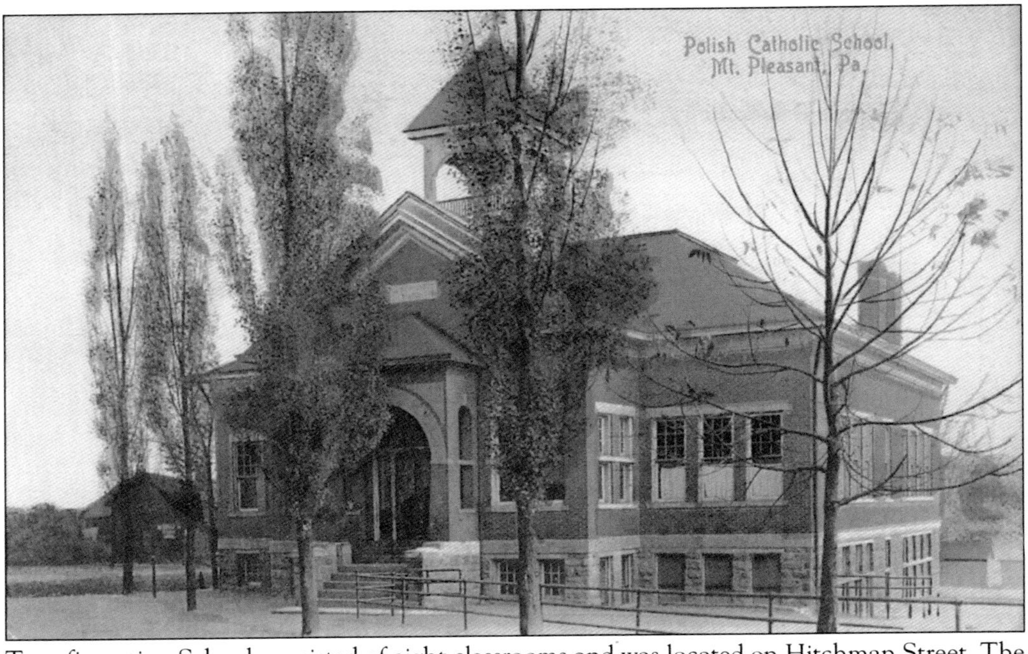

Transfiguration School consisted of eight classrooms and was located on Hitchman Street. The Felician Sisters gave instruction in all subjects, including religious education. Students attended Mass each day at the Transfiguration Church located across the street. (Courtesy of Merl and Fay Pritts.)

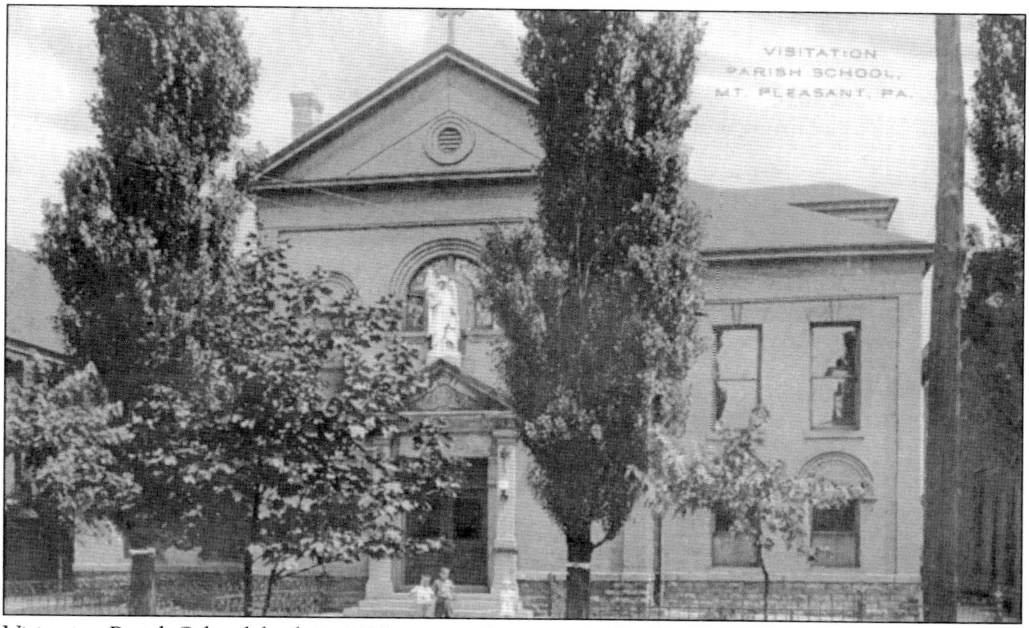

Visitation Parish School, built in 1908, was an elementary school on Walnut Street. The Vincentian Sisters of Charity taught the students in this 2.5-story building that included an apartment complex above the classrooms and an auditorium. The Catholic Diocese of Greensburg closed the school due to insufficient enrollment. (Courtesy of Merl and Fay Pritts.)

Second Ward School, a large buff-brick building, was built in 1908 at Washington and Diamond Streets. It originally housed the high school. It later became a junior high school, and then kindergarten through second grade was housed there. After serving as a junior high school and elementary school for 45 years, it became the Multi-Service Center for Senior Citizens. (Courtesy of Rose Eckman.)

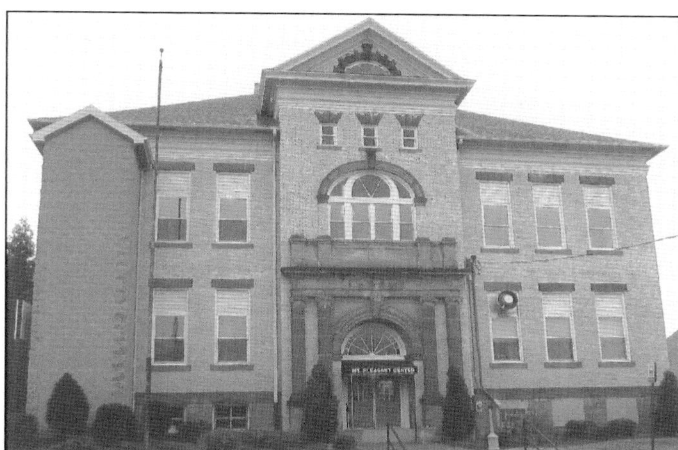

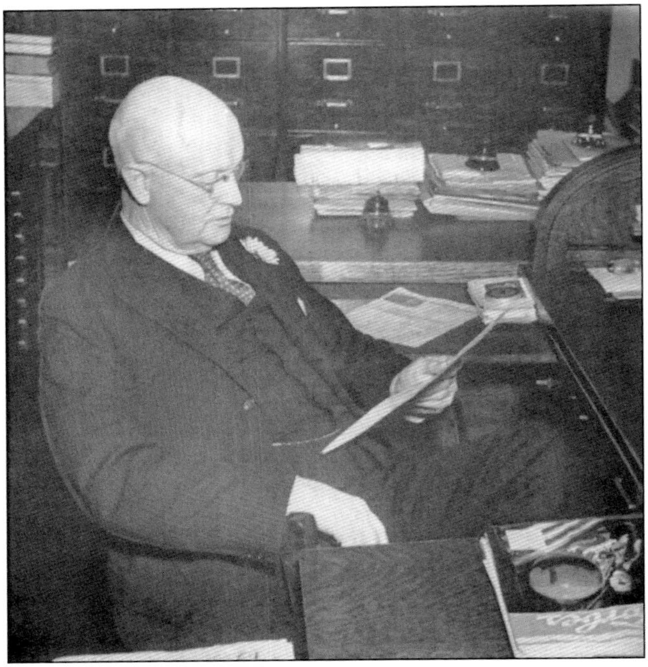

Erskine Ramsay, age 77, is shown at his desk. In 1942, James Saxon Childers authored the biography *Erskine Ramsay: His Life and Achievements.* Ramsay, who made his fortune in the steel industry in Alabama, donated the money for the high school named for him, which was built in 1929 (Courtesy of the Mount Pleasant Public Library Archives.)

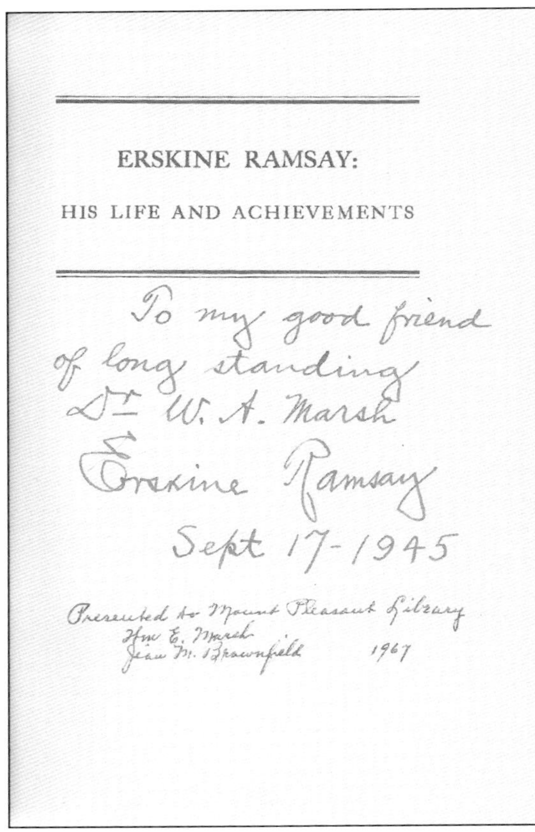

ERSKINE RAMSAY:

HIS LIFE AND ACHIEVEMENTS

To my good friend
of long standing
Dr W. A. Marsh
Erskine Ramsay
Sept 17-1945

Presented to Mount Pleasant Library
Wm E. Marsh
Jean M. Brownfield 1967

In 1945, Erskine Ramsay autographed the book about his life for Dr. W.A. Marsh, a good friend of long standing. William E. Marsh and Jean M. Brownfield presented this book to the Mount Pleasant Public Library in 1967. (Courtesy of the Mount Pleasant Public Library Archives.)

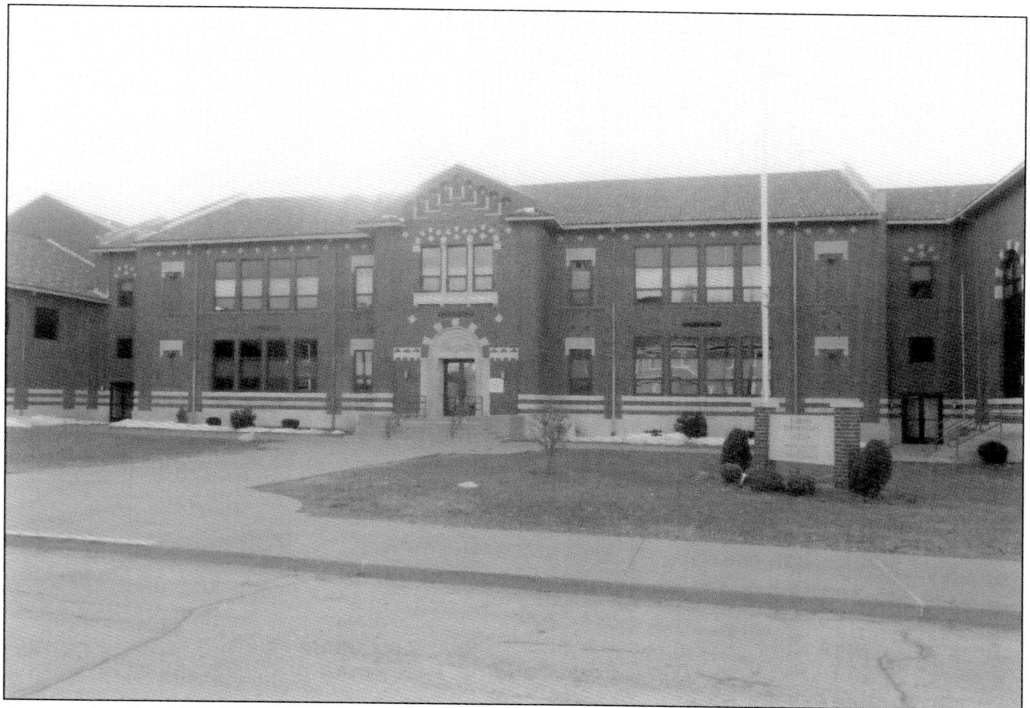

Ramsay High School was built in 1929. The ivy-covered redbrick walls made it one of the most beautiful schools in Westmoreland County. This school was used as a high school until 1965 and then as a junior high school. Mount Pleasant Borough and Donegal students attended this school. Currently, the building houses Ramsay Elementary School, pictured here, in which second through sixth grades are taught. (Courtesy of the Mount Pleasant Public Library Archives.)

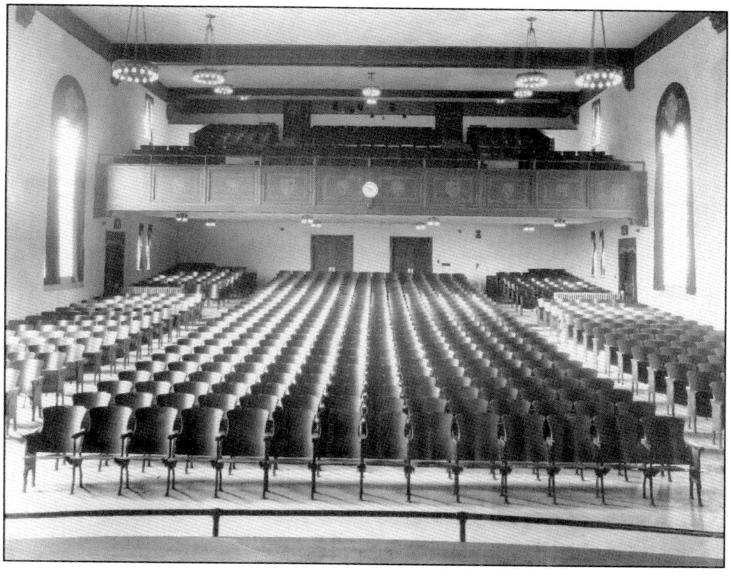

Mount Pleasant is dedicated to providing a comprehensive education to its students. This view of the Ramsay High School auditorium, as seen from the stage, depicts the arch-shaped windows, the round chandeliers, and the balcony. Due to the seating arrangement, all were able to view the stage easily. (Courtesy of the Mount Pleasant Public Library Archives.)

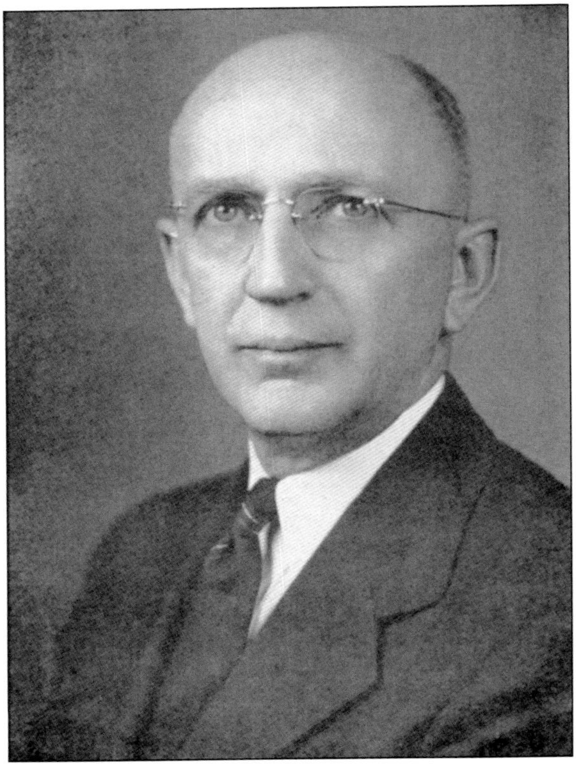

Dr. John C. Haberlen was superintendent of schools from 1921 to 1958. He was an educator in Mount Pleasant schools for 37 years. In 1957, he was designated "Man of the Year" by the chamber of commerce. Even after retirement, he continued to be active in his service to people of the community. (Courtesy of the Mount Pleasant Public Library Archives.)

Lloyd F. Rumbaugh Elementary School houses kindergarten through first grade. The school was rebuilt after it was destroyed by a fire in 1958. It was named to honor Rumbaugh, who was a superintendent of schools during the 1950s. It replaced Fairview Elementary School, which was a two-room schoolhouse. (Courtesy of Bonnie Wilson.)

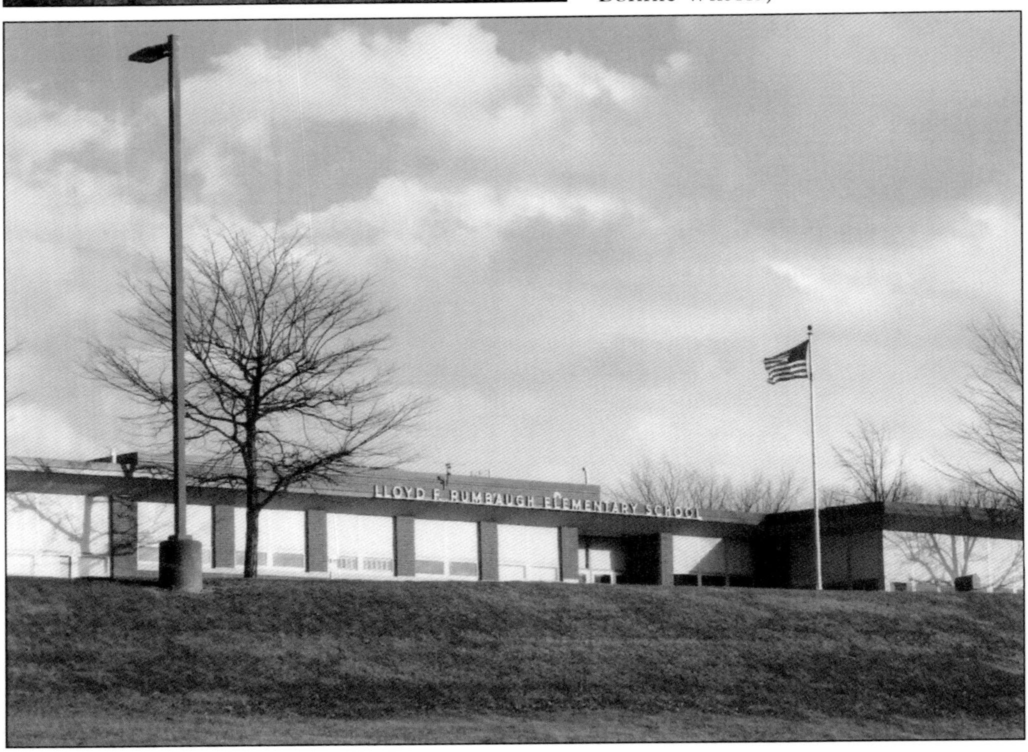

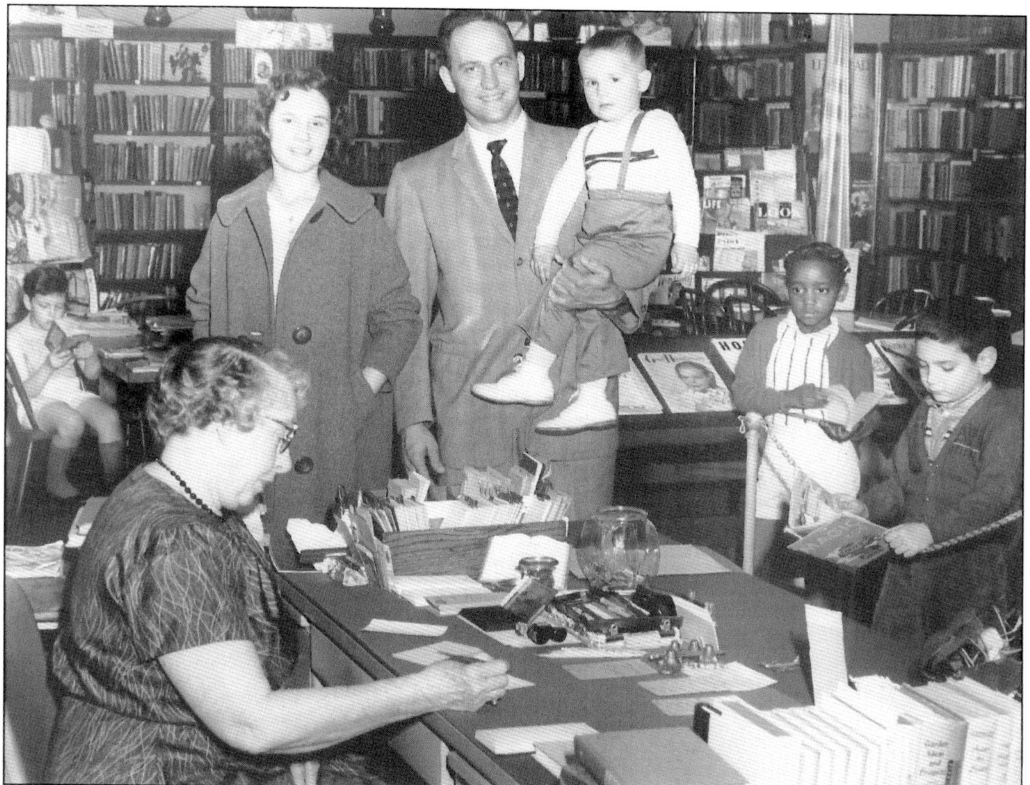

A mainstay of the Mount Pleasant Public Library was Opal Berthel, who was the head librarian for many years. Patrons remembered her as an advocate of orderly conduct in the library. She is shown signing new members Rev. James Morris (of Bunker Hill Church of God) and his son Richie. Some children are seen reading quietly while others wait to check out books. Libraries were a meeting center for citizens in small towns. (Courtesy of the Mount Pleasant Public Library Archives.)

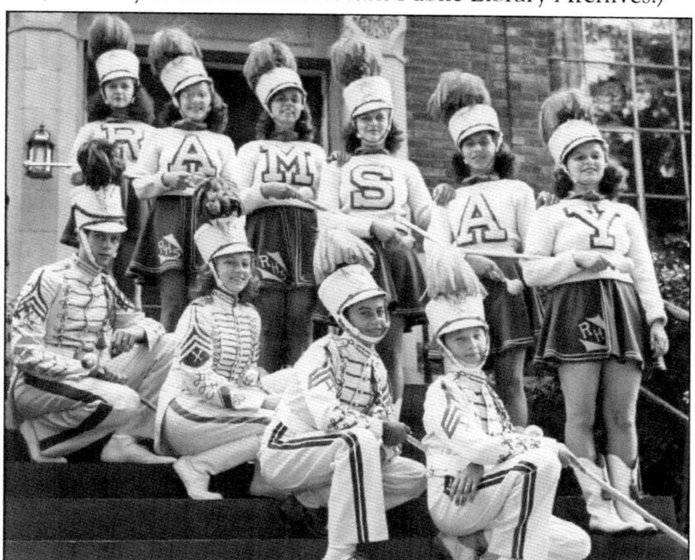

The majorettes had a distinctive presence with "RAMSAY" prominently displayed on their blue-and-white uniforms. The drum majors in the front row sport plumed hats. These student performers demonstrated pride for their school. (Courtesy of the Mount Pleasant Public Library Archives.)

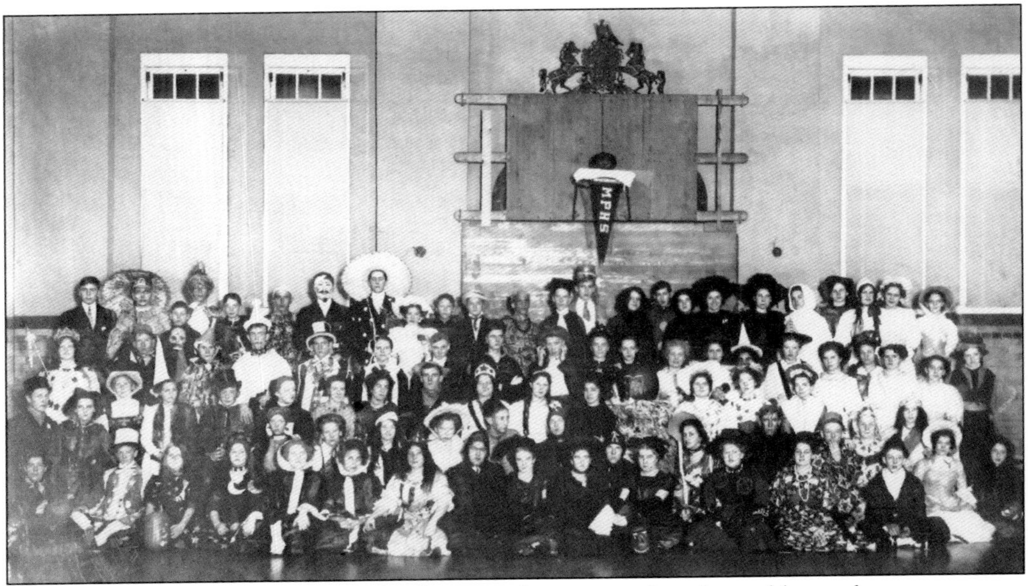

Cultivating the dramatic arts in schools is a tradition passed on from older students to younger students. Note the large array of participation in the elementary school production pictured above. For over 30 years, Robert W. Myers (pictured in the photograph below, at far right) directed the high school plays, which enabled budding actors and actresses to provide memorable and meaningful experiences for parents and the community at large. Students eagerly auditioned for parts in the plays, and others were able to work on set design, props, and lighting. The students involved in the plays developed a camaraderie between one another under the supportive, caring, and authentic direction of Myers, who directed 50 plays in his 25-year career as an English teacher. All who participated will long remember him in the English classroom and on the stage. (Both photographs courtesy of the Mount Pleasant Public Library Archives.)

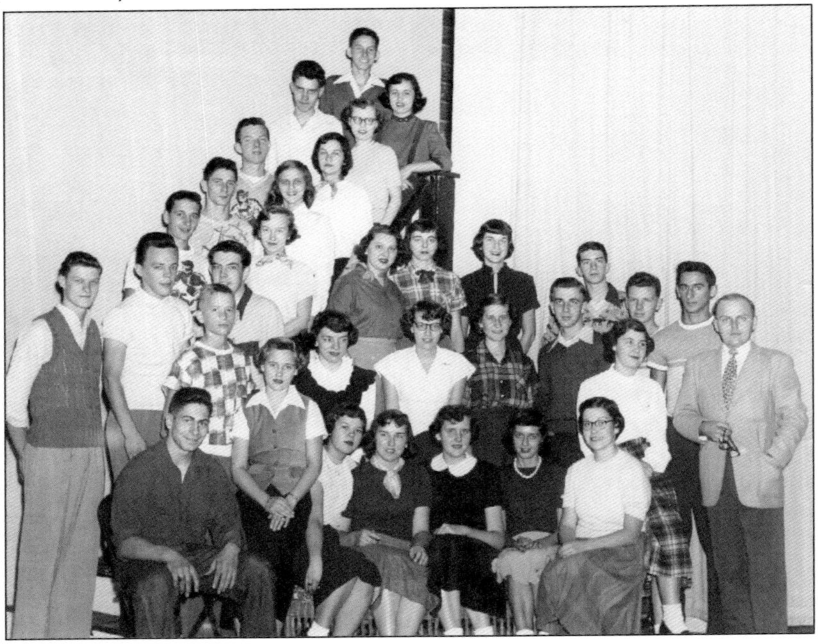

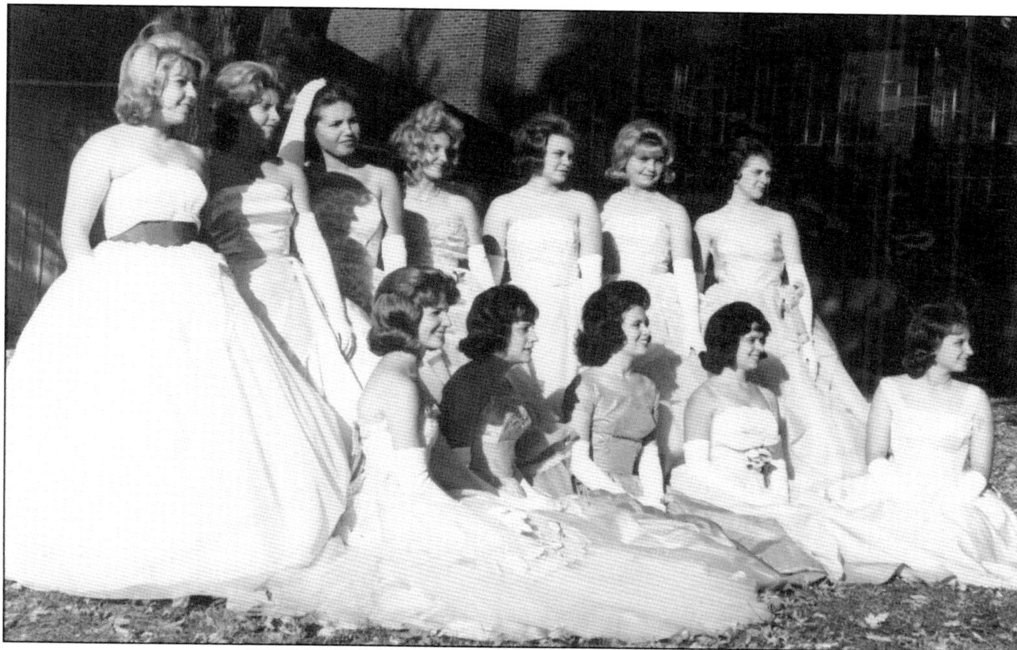

A proud group of students elected to represent their class presides over the 1964 Ramsay High School homecoming court. Each year, the seniors elected several candidates for the court, who were honored at one of the football games. The 1964 candidates are Judy Hyde, Allyn Joyce Chalfant, Marlene Coppula, Gayle Kuhn, Patty Cronin, Beverly Kolacinski, Linda Ahlborn, Patti Kadylak, Janet Cramer, Pauline Hoover, Donna Myers, and Eva-Marie Rossfeld. (Courtesy of the Mount Pleasant Public Library Archives.)

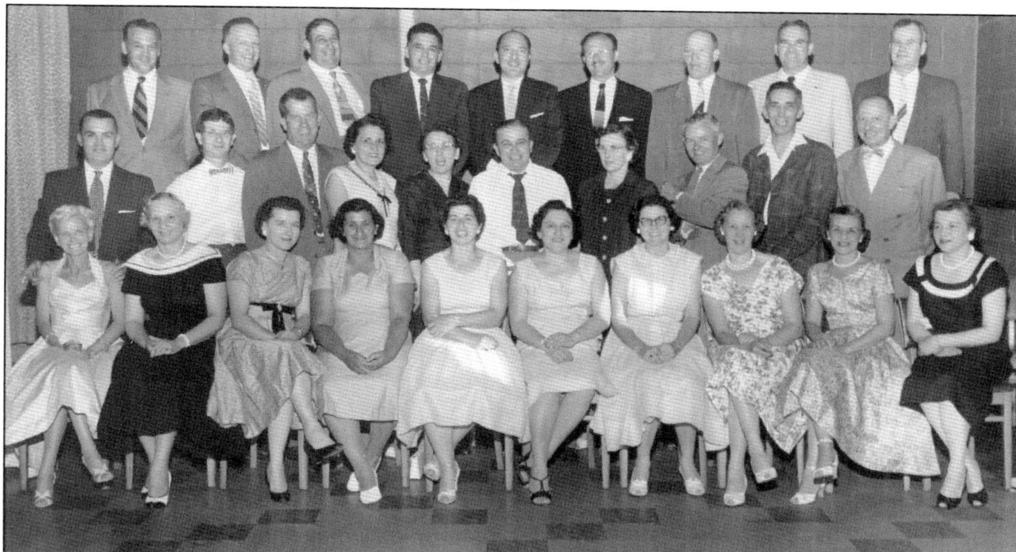

The Ramsay High School class of 1931 is shown at one of their reunions. Among those who attended are Benny Palidino, Joe Valiante, Harry Grosser, ? Copeland, ? Farrah, Margaret Ceroni, Anne Karaffa, Margarite Houseman, and ? Damico. (Courtesy of the Mount Pleasant Public Library Archives.)

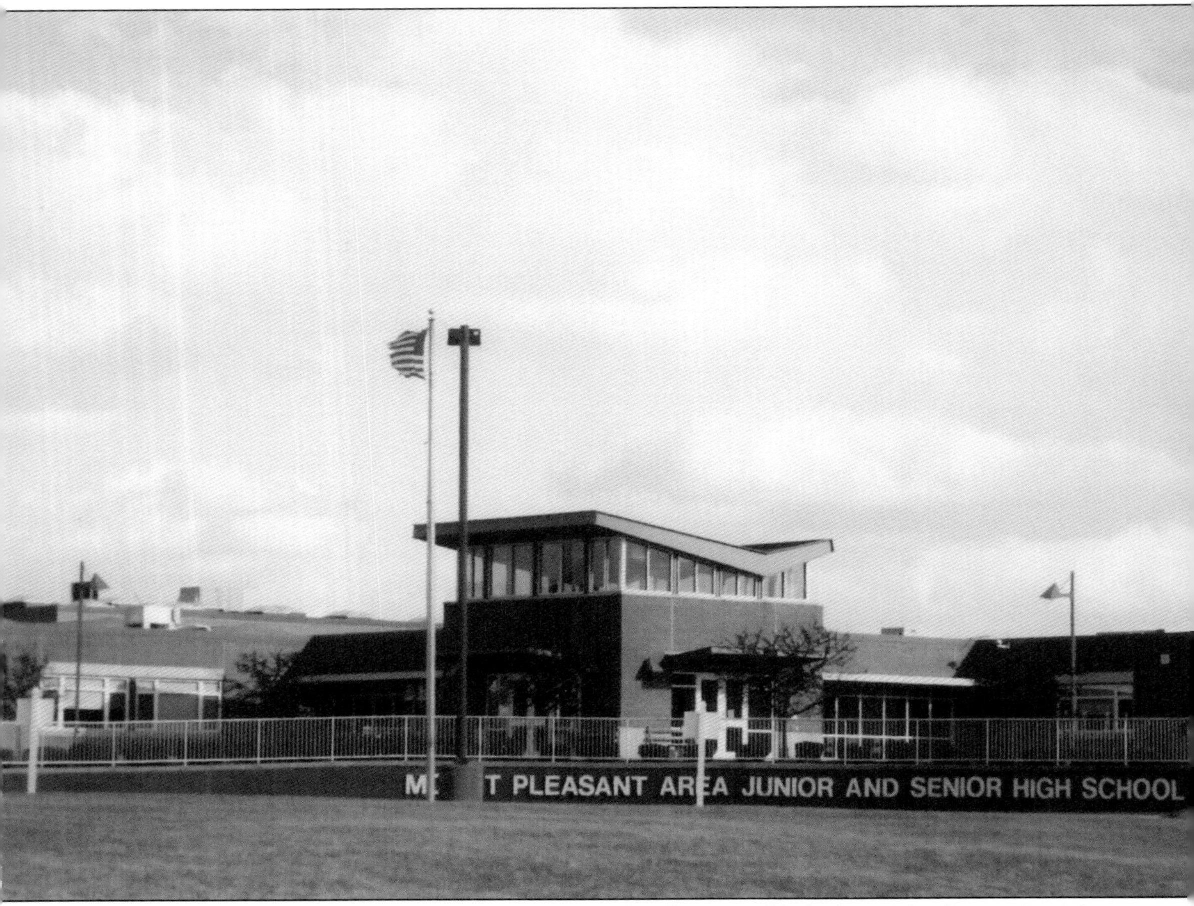

Mount Pleasant Area Junior and Senior High School was established in 1964. Situated in Mount Pleasant Township, the school offers a challenging academic education. Grades 7 through 12 are housed here. In 2010, there were 1,100 students. (Courtesy of Bonnie Wilson.)

Six

Living the Good Life

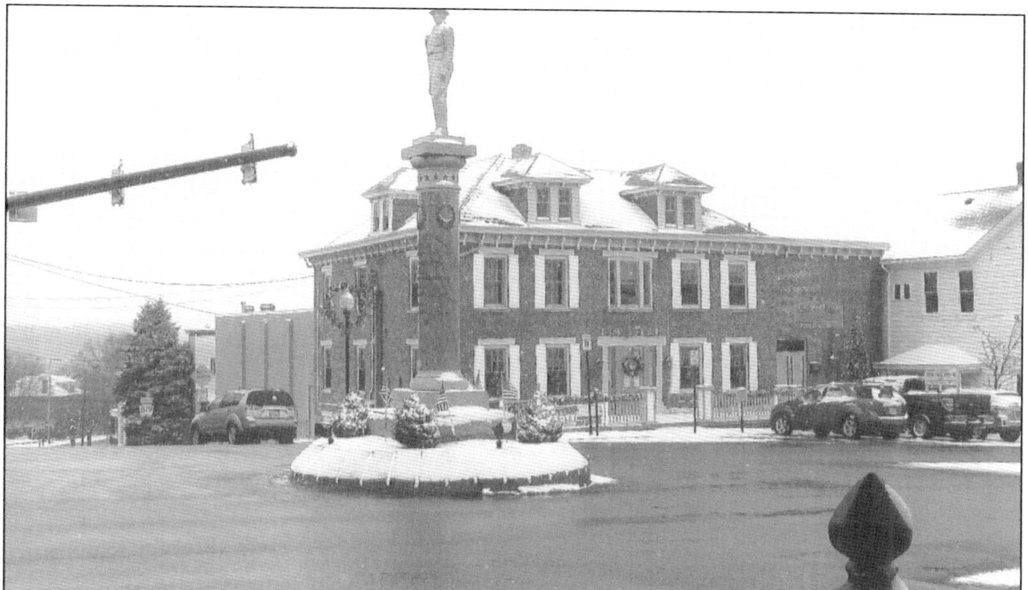

A winter scene on the "Diamond" shows *The Doughboy*, a tall, angled statue of a World War I soldier. In the background is McCali Manor, which originally was the home of Dr. Myers W. Horner. When his family sold the home, it became the Elks Lodge. Throughout the seasons, *The Doughboy* stands as a majestic symbol to honor the area's military servicemen and women. (Courtesy of Rose Eckman and Nancy Sebek.)

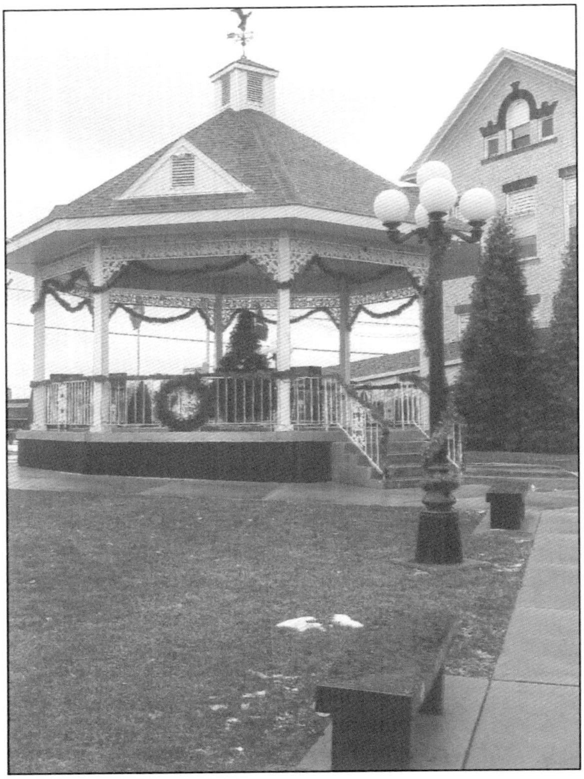

In the center of town is the gazebo, a hexagonal structure framed with white filigree around the roof. A weathervane graces the small cupola. Granite benches dedicated to loved ones surround the structure. (Courtesy of Rose Eckman.)

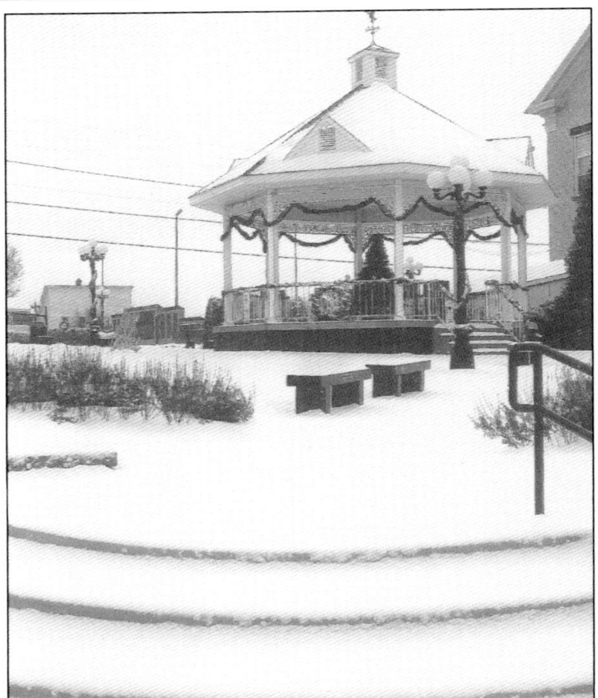

Even in the winter, the gazebo is an essential part of the beauty of Veterans Park. Residents and visitors enjoy the many events held throughout the seasons. It is the site of musical events in the summer and the Glass and Ethnic Festival in September. (Courtesy of Rose Eckman.)

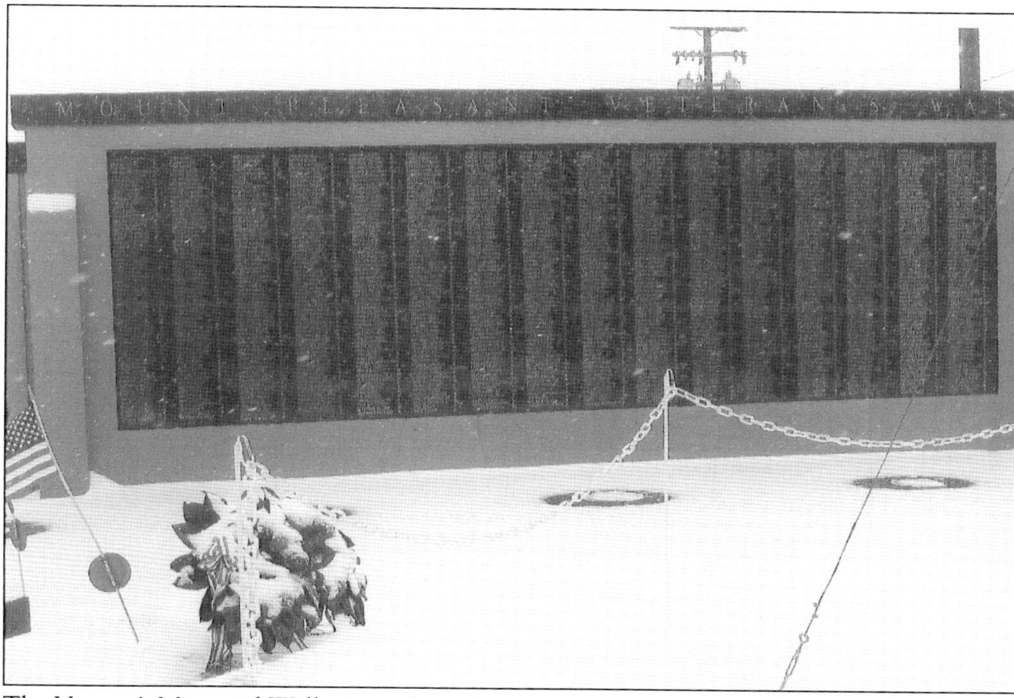

The Veteran's Memorial Wall, situated left of the gazebo, is a perpetual tribute to soldiers, airmen, and sailors whose names, ranks, and branches of service are etched in black granite slabs. Granite markers commemorate the different wars and military leaders. A fountain serves as an ongoing living salute to the heroes. A recent addition is a digital wall that provides histories of past veterans. Military personnel can be added to the digital wall in the future. (Above, courtesy of Rose Eckman; right, courtesy of Bonnie Wilson.)

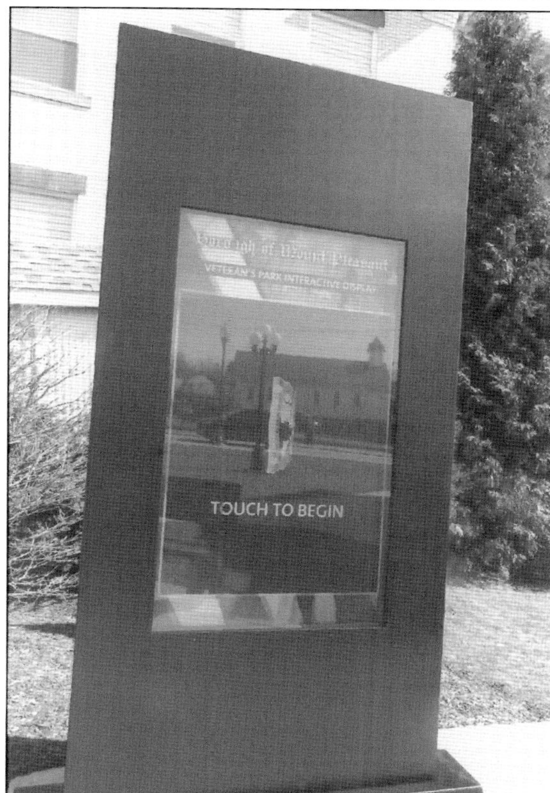

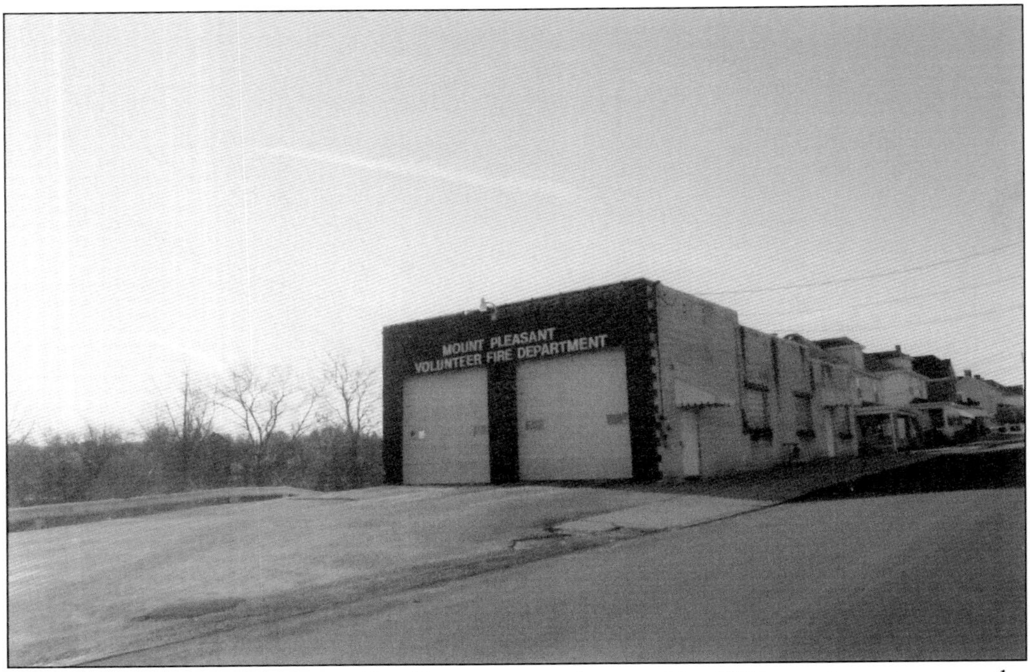

The Mount Pleasant Volunteer Fire Department, chartered in 1899, continues to serve the community and has a membership of 29 men. These two photographs show the buildings located on South Church Street and Center Avenue, which house the equipment. The Mount Pleasant Fireman's Band, organized in 1935, is the oldest fireman's band in the state of Pennsylvania. The volunteer firemen and the ladies auxiliary are highly respected members of the community. (Above, courtesy of Nancy Sebek; below, courtesy of Rose Eckman.)

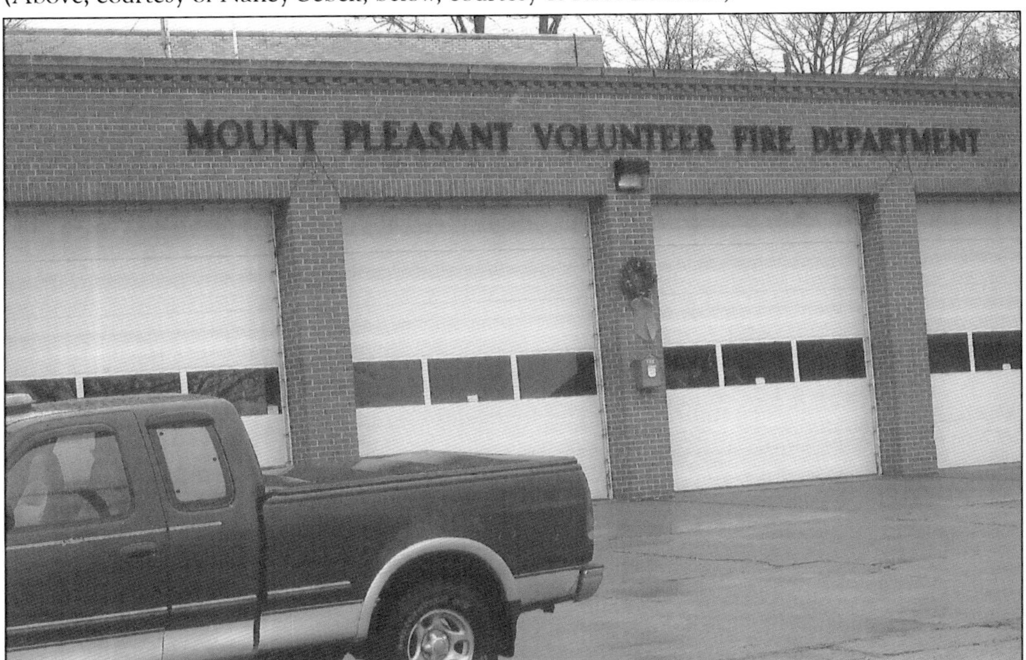

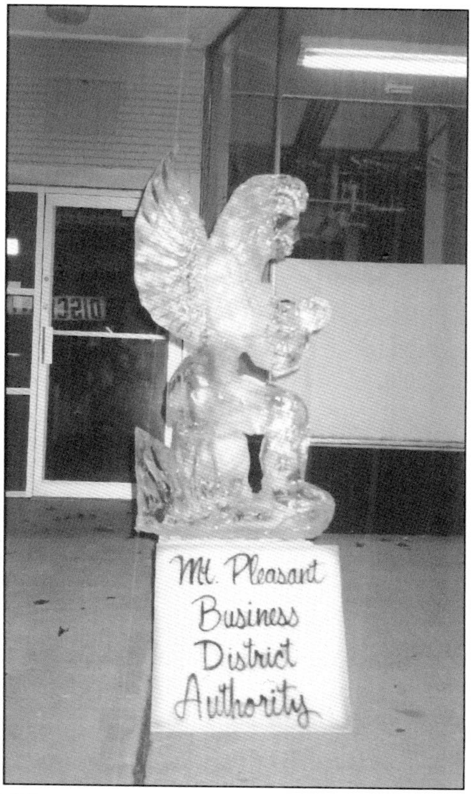

The Mount Pleasant Business District Authority (MPBDA) continues to advance the economic and commercial activities of the community. This ice sculpture, sponsored by the MPBDA, was on display during the holiday season. Located across the street from Veterans Park is the popular restaurant Leo & Son's Grill 31. On the walls of this establishment are numerous original photographs of veterans from all branches of the military. (Right, courtesy of the Mount Pleasant Area Historical Society; below, courtesy of Nancy Sebek.)

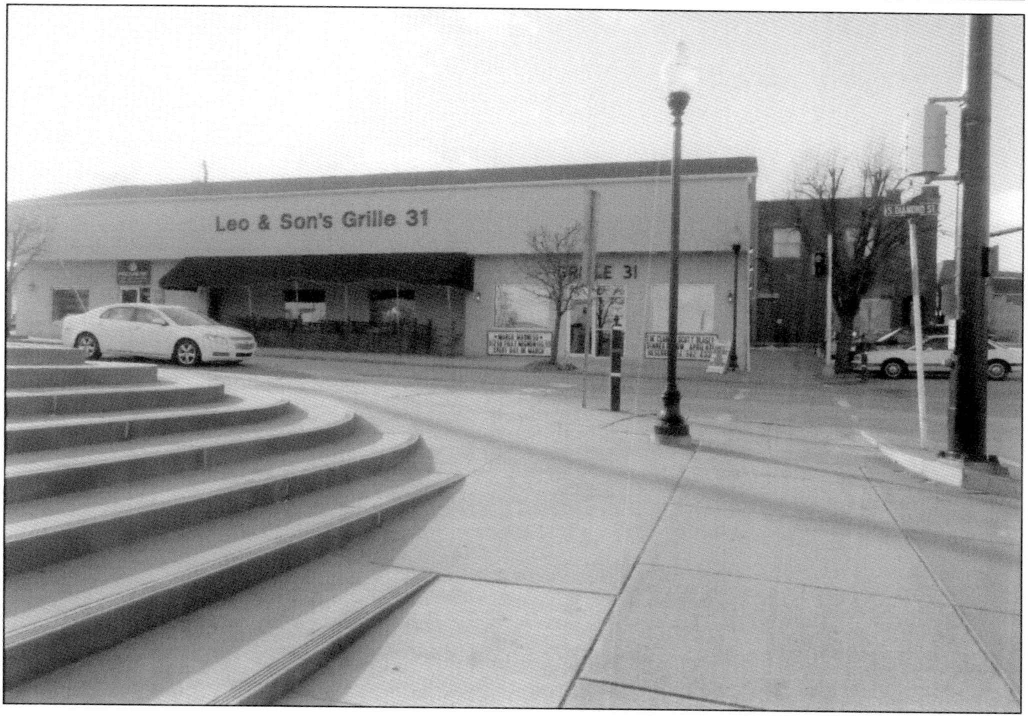

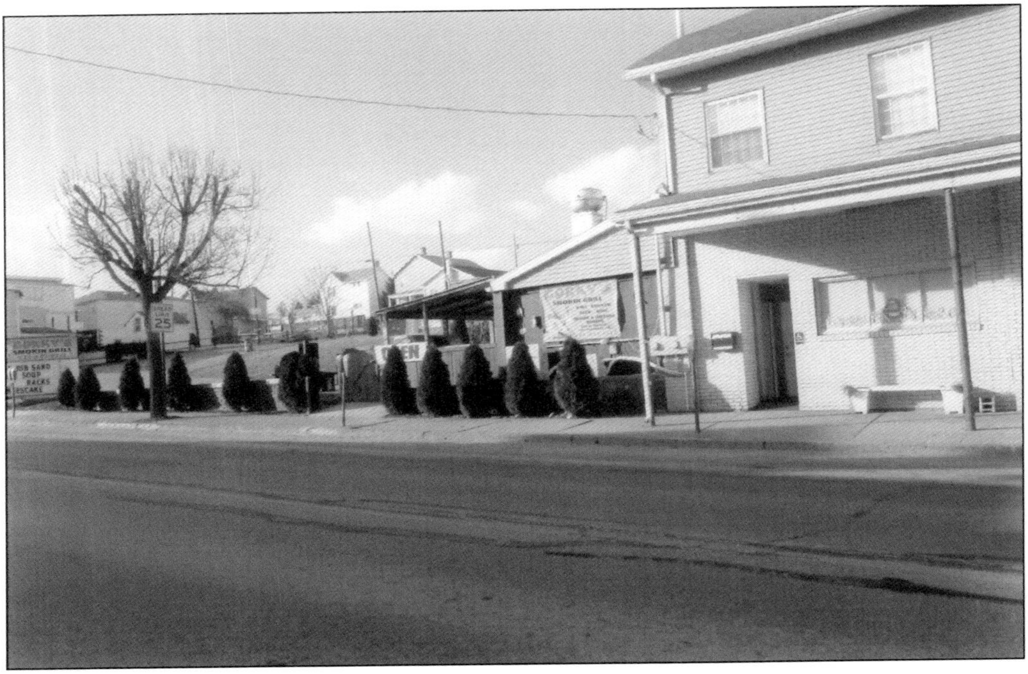

Businesses at the east end of town offer many services. Gorky's Smokin' Grill is known for ribs, fish, and chicken. Demo Depot, formerly Cook's Lumber Company, offers recycled, reclaimed building materials. It is part of the Westmoreland Community Action Program. (Both photographs courtesy of Nancy Sebek.)

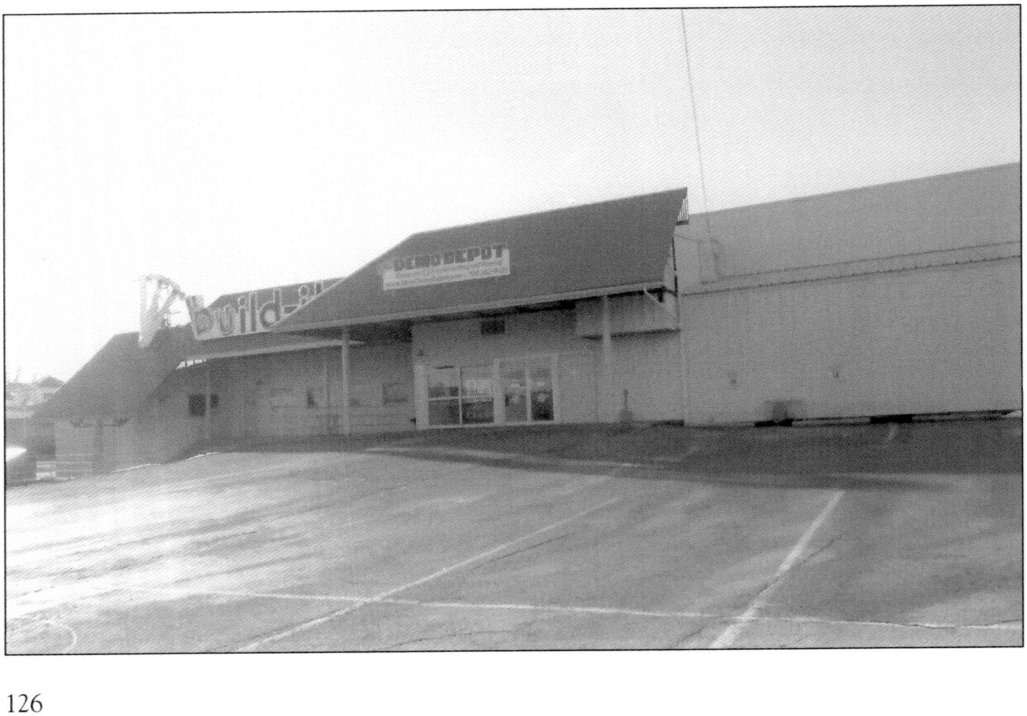

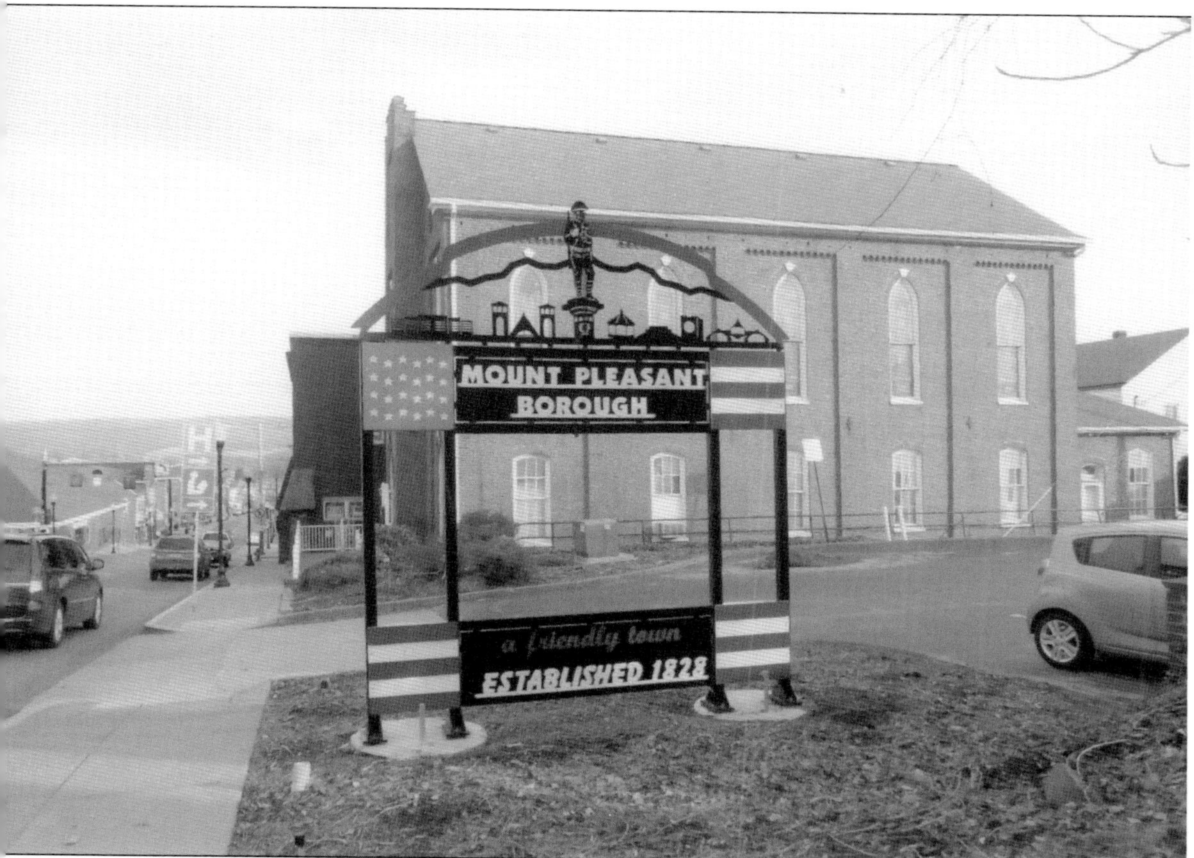

This sign, designed by Colleen Konieczny, is located on the property of the original Frick Memorial Hospital on Main Street. Future plans are to digitalize and illuminate the sign. Even in the 21st century, Mount Pleasant continues its commitment to the preservation and development of its history and artifacts. Established in 1995, the mission of The Mount Pleasant Area Historical Society is to provide a forum for the public to discuss local history, identify and preserve artifacts, and develop historical resources through educational initiatives. The *Crossroad Chronicle*, the society's monthly newsletter, highlights historical figures, memories, and events. (Courtesy of Nancy Sebek.)